GLOBAL FINANCIAL CRISIS AND ITS IMPACT ON DIFFERENT SECTORS

GLOBAL FINANCIAL CRISIS AND ITS IMPACT ON DIFFERENT SECTORS

By

Dr. B. Ramachandra Reddy

Department of Commerce

S.V. University

Tirupati (A.P.)

DISCOVERY PUBLISHING HOUSE PVT. LTD.

NEW DELHI-110 002

Published by:
Tilak Wasan
DISCOVERY PUBLISHING HOUSE PVT. LTD.
4383/4A, Ansari Road, Darya Ganj
New Delhi-110 002 (India)
Phone : +91-11-23279245, 43596064-65
Fax : +91-11-23253475
E-mail : parul.wasan@gmail.com
discoverypublishinghouse@gmail.com
web : www.discoverypublishinggroup.com

***First Edition:* 2012**

ISBN: 978-93-5056-010-5

Global Financial Crisis and Its Impact on Different Sectors

Printed at:
Shree Balaji Art Press
Delhi

Foreword

The United States suffered its first recession during the period between 1797 and 1800. It was primarily caused by the deflating effects of the Bank of England as they crossed the Ocean to American soil. The next recession occurred during 1807 to 1814, called as the Depression of 1807. This depression was primarily caused by the Embargo Act of 1807, signed into effect by then President Thomas Jefferson. This act destroyed a good part of the shipping related industries. Like that several times recession occurred in the years 1819, 1837, 1857, 1929, 1939, 1975 and 1998 due to various reasons. But the recession that started from 2007 in US has been influencing adversely the economic scenario world over.

The economic environment characterized by various imbalances was sparked by the outbreak of the global melt down during 2007–2010. With the collapse of Lehman Brothers on September 15, 2008 and other Wall Street Icons, there was growing economic recession which affected the US, the European Union (EU) and Japan. This was the result of large scale defaults in the US housing market as the banks went on providing risky loans without adequate security and the repaying capacity of the borrower. The principal source of transmission of the crisis has been the real sector, generally referred to as the 'Main Street'. This crisis engulfed the United States in the form of creeping recession resulting in declined US imports from other countries. The fundamental reason for the crisis was largely an unregulated environment which indulged in mortgage lending to sub prime borrowers. Since the borrowers did not have adequate repaying capacity, leads to default and the situation became worse. Once the housing market collapsed, the lender institutions' saw balance-sheets turned into red.

India is not de-linked from the world, and the financial meltdown has certainly impacted on us. In the age of globalization, no country can remains isolated from the fluctuations of world economy. Heavy losses suffered by major International Banks are going to affect all countries of the world. India is facing heat on three grounds: (1) Falling of Share Markets in 2007-09; (2) weakening Rupee against US dollar; and (3) cash crunch experienced by banks lading to liquidity crisis in the market. All these problems are interconnected and they are the out come of global financial crisis.

For the last two years, our stock market was creating new summits which were mainly due to heavy investments by Foreign Institutional Investors (FIIs). Since, the money, which Foreign Institutional Investors realized from selling their stocks, needs to be converted into dollars and the demand for dollars suddenly increased. As long as demands for dollars remain high, the rupee will keep loosing its strength against dollar.

Many of the Indian companies have been entertaining outsourcing deals from the US. There is a decline in the employment market due to the recession in the West. Some companies have laid off their employees and there have been cut in promotions, compensation and perks of the employees. Companies in the private sector and government sector are hesitant to take up new projects and they are continuing the existing projects only. Nearly one crore persons lost their jobs because of Global Financial melt down.

It is observed from surveys that the textile, garment and handicraft industry are worse affected as they lost four million jobs by April 2009. There has also been a decline in the tourist inflow lately. The real estate has also a problem of tight liquidity situations, where the developers are finding it hard to raise finances. IT industries, financial sectors, real estate owners, car industry, investment banking and other industries as well are confronting heavy loss due to the fall down of global economy. Federation of Indian chambers of Commerce and Industry (FICCI) stated that due to global recession, industries such as garment, gems, textiles, chemicals and jewelers had cut down production by 10 to 50 per cent. As a result of global depression there was a steep fall in demand for all consumer goods.

In the broadcasting sector also, it was a case of survival of the fittest as some of the stalwarts of the industry touched the ground. Survival was the key goal during 2008-09 for most media companies. With the financial crisis hitting the world economy hard, it will be difficult for India to maintain its economic growth target of 8 per cent. The Prime Minister's Advisory Council has already estimated that this year our growth is will be less than expected due to the global crisis. If the financial crisis is not resolved soon, then the situation may be much worse.

The present volume is the outcome of National Seminar organised by Prof. B.Ramachandra Reddy, Department of Commerce, Sri Venkateswara University, Tirupati during 26-27th February 2010. The proceedings of this seminar surely help the decision makers to examine the important reasons behind the financial crisis in different sectors and find out feasible and possible measures to come out of the financial crisis. Further, the publication proves a good reference for the researchers, bankers, professionals and policy makers in their pursuits.

PROF. C. SIVARAMI REDDY
Registrar
Yogi Vemana University
Kadapa

Preface

This volume is the product of National Seminar on 'Impact of Global Financial Meltdown on Indian Economy' organised by the Department of Commerce, Sri Venkateswara University, Tirupati during 26-27th February, 2010 funded by UGC and ICSSR. The important objectives of the national seminar were:

(*i*) to examine the origin of global financial crisis;

(*ii*) to analyze the main causes behind the financial crisis;

(*iii*) to evaluate the impact of global financial crisis on Indian economy; and

(*iv*) to assess the extent and magnitude of financial crisis in different sectors of the country.

The Honorable vice-chancellor Prof. N. Prabhakara Rao inaugurated the seminar and delivered the inaugural address. The seminar director Dr B.Ramachandra Reddy presented the theme of the seminar to the delegates. The guests for this function Sri B.V.S.N. Murthy, Zonal Manager, Andhra Bank and Sri T. Viswanatham, Assistant General Manager, SBI main branch, Tirupati delivered thought provoking speech on 'Global Financial Meltdown and Its Impact on Different Sectors of India.' Prof. T. Siddaiah, Principal, SVU College of CM&CS presented the keynote address. Prof. B. Bhagavan Reddy, Head of the department presided over the function. Dr. P.V. Narasaiah proposed vote of thanks.

The department invited several eminent Chartered Accountants, Bankers, Government officials, Research scholars, and Professors from different Universities in South

India. For presentation of papers by the delegates, the two day national seminar has chalked out into three technical sessions. I am grateful to all the participants in the seminar and to the authors whose papers are included in this volume.

In the valedictory function, the Rapporteurs Sri L.Ganesh Murthy, Prof. N.R.V. Ramana Reddy and Dr. B. Yuvaraja Reddy have presented their reports covering the entire proceedings of three technical sessions. Later Prof. K. Rathnaiah, Rector, S.V.University delivered the valedictory address. The Guests Prof. G. Chandra Sekhar Rao and Sri C. Surya Kumar. AGM, State Bank of India spoke and focussed on the various aspects on Global Financial Meltdown. Prof. C. Siva Rami Reddy presided over the function. The seminar director Dr. B. Ramachandra Reddy proposed vote of thanks.

I am deeply indebted to the authorities of UGC, ICSSR and Sri Venkateswara University for their financial support in organising the seminar. I extend my special gratitude to Prof B. Bhagavan Reddy, Head of the Department of Commerce for his continuous support and encouragement in organising the seminar and editing the book. Finally I am highly thankful to Sri Tilak Wasan, Director, Discovery Publishing House Pvt. Ltd., New Delhi who have taken lot of pains to bring out this volume in a more useful manner.

Last but not least I express my heartfelt thanks to my beloved children Geetha, Ramadevi and Venkatesh for their moral support and cooperation.

Prof. B. Ramachandra Reddy

Contents

Foreword

Preface

1. Performance Volatility of Indian Pharmaceutical Industry During Global Financial Meltdown 1

   Dr. M. Syam Babu & Prof. B. Ramachandra Reddy

2. Greed: Reason for Global Financial Crisis 14

   Dr. G. Sudarsana Reddy & Prof. C. Sivarami Reddy

3. Global Recession: A Boon to Indian Medical Tourism 21

   Dr. S. Raghunatha Reddy &
   Dr A. Amrutha Prasad Reddy

4. Global Financial Crisis: Impact on Indian Economy—A Study 31

   Prof. V. Appa Rao

5. Impact of International Financial Crisis : Sources and Solutions 41

   Dr. P. Saritha & Prof. P. Mohan Reddy

6. Effects of Global Financial Collision on Indian Banking 56

   Dr. K. Padmasree, Dr. A. Bharathi Devi &
   Dr. L. Rajani

7. Global Financial Crisis and Its Impact on Indian Corporates : A Sectoral Analysis 65

   M. C. Venkatanath & A. J. Vikram

8. Impact on and Recovery of Indian Stock Market 82

L. Ganesamoorthy

9. Global Financial Meltdown and Its Impact on the Indian Economy 88

M. Rajesh and Dr. NRV. Ramana Reddy

10. Global Meltdown and Its Impact on Indian Economy and the Measures Taken by Govt. of India 101

Dr. R. Rajendra Reddy

11. Impact of Global Financial Crisis on Indian Economy—An Analysis 105

Dr. P. V. Narasaiah & S. Siva Kumar

12. Impact of Global Financial Crisis on Developing Countries 113

E. Lavanya & Dr. K. Nirmala

13. Global Recession—Impact on Indian Financial Markets 124

Dr. L. Rajani & Prof.P.Mohan Reddy & Dr. G. Vijaya Bharati

14. Global Financial Crisis and Its Impact on the Indian Real Estate Sector 138

Dr. A. Amruth Prasad Reddy, Dr. P.V. Varaprabhakar & Prof. C. Sivarami Reddy

15. The Impact of Recession on Indian Financial System and Indian Financial Markets 145

M. Lakshmi Pathi Naidu

16. Impact of Global Recession on Indian Manufacturing Sector 163

P. Nainar Reddy & Dr. D. Raghunatha Reddy

17. The Impact of Recession on Indian Financial System and Indian Financial Markets 174

P. Subramanyam, Prof. B. Ramachandra Reddy & D. Balamuniswamy

18. Impact of Global Financial Crisis in US, China and India 192

Dr. G. Narasimhulu & Dr P. Kothandarami Reddy

19. Global Financial Crisis and Its Impact on Indian Economy 199

Dr. B. Parameswara Reddy & C. Lakshmikantha Reddy

20. The Impact of Global Financial Recession on Indian Banking System 218

B.V. Ananth Ram & Dr. M. Gurumohan Reddy

21. The Global Crisis and Indian Finance 226

*Dr. P. Venugopal, Dr. K. Sudarsan,
C. Uday Kumar Raju & Prof. D. Himachalam*

22. Global Financial Crisis and Its Impact on the Indian IT Sector 237

S. Srinivasa Rao & T. Anil Kumar

23. Global Financial Crisis *vs.* Indian Economy 245

Dr. B. Yuvaraja Reddy & Dr. Y. Mallikarjun Rao

24. Sustainability of Indian Economy Despite Global Financial Meltdown 254

Prof. P.V.Narasaiah

25. India in Global Recession 270

Dr. R. Praveen Kumar Reddy & K. Nirmal Kumar Reddy

26. Impact of Financial Crisis—2009-10 277

Dr. M. Sivasankar

27. Current Financial Crisis in India 288

Dr. S.V. Subba Reddy & Dr. K. Balasubramanyam

28. Impact of Economic Crisis on Housing Finance in India—An Overview 295

*Dr. S.V. Reddy, Dr. B. Sakunthala &
Dr. C. Sukumar Reddy*

29. Global Financial Markets and Economic Crisis: Impact on Indian Economy 300

M. Kumar Raju & A. Reddappa

30. Impact of Global Crisis on the Indian Economy 316

G. Venkatachalam & Prof. P. Mohan Reddy

31. Impact of Financial Crisis on Banking Sector 323

M. Sudhakar Reddy

32. Global Financial Crisis : Its Impact on Indian Economy 334

C. S. Sukumar Reddy & Dr. S. Vijayulu Reddy & M. Sudhakar Reddy

Index 339

CHAPTER

1

Performance Volatility of Indian Pharmaceutical Industry During Global Financial Meltdown

*Dr. M. Syam Babu
**Prof. B. Ramachandra Reddy

Introduction

The Global Economy today seems to be recovering from the most severe crisis since the Great Depression of the 1930s. The economy again surfaced a lot with the subprime mortgage crisis in the US in August 2007 and took the character of a global crisis in September 2008 following the collapse of Lehman Brothers. It is also dubbed as the greatest crisis in the history of financial capitalism because of the way it simultaneously propagated to other countries and collapsed world economic growth rate. The impact of the crisis can be gauged from the sharp upward revisions to the estimates of possible write-downs by banks and other financial institutions from about US$ 500 billion in March 2008 to about US$ 3.5 trillion in October 2009. More than the financial cost, the adverse impact on the real economy has been severe: in 2009, the world GDP is estimated by the IMF to have contracted

* Faculty Associate, FedUni, Hyderabad, A.P.
** Faculty Member, Department of Commerce, Sri Venkateswara University, Tirupti, A.P.

by 0.8 per cent and the world trade volume is estimated to have declined by 12 per cent. India's GDP growth rate was scaled down from 9 per cent to 6.2 per cent. The effect of financial meltdown can be studied at macro level and micro level. This chapter will discuss the impact of financial crisis on Indian pharmaceutical industry and its performance volatility index.

An Overview of Pharmaceutical Industry

Pharmaceutical industry is one of the important industries to build human capital of a nation, which consists complex matrix of processes, operations and organizations involved in the discovery, development and manufacture of various drugs and medications. A nation with a strong pharmaceutical industry has a healthy and strong population which provides a strong human capital. Indian pharmaceutical industry is an excellent example of a highly growth-oriented industry, which is enhancing its value in the process. From being a pure reverse engineering industry focussed on the domestic market, the industry is moving towards basic research-driven, export-oriented global presence, providing wide range of value added quality products and services. Pharmaceutical industry consists commercial business houses, which may focus either on research, manufacturing, marketing and/or distribution of medicine, drugs, and chemicals mostly in the context of healthcare. The roots of pharmaceutical firms can be traced back to 754 B.C. and were known as 'drugstores' in Arabian countries. Arabian pharmacists opened the first known drugstore in 754 BC in Baghdad. In those times, drugstores were famous in mediaeval Islamic world, Europe and North America. After discovering insulin and penicillin in the 1920s and 1930s, the drugstores were converted into major pharmaceutical firms. Mass-manufactured and distributed pharmaceutical firms made entry into Switzerland, Germany, Italy, the UK, the US, Belgium and the Netherlands in those times. Towards the end of 1950s, most of the sophisticated drug manufacturing techniques came into existence as a result of developing systematic scientific approaches, understanding human biology (including DNA). This development made it necessary to enact legislations to test and approve drugs. Prescription and non-prescription drugs became legally distinguished from one another even as the pharmaceutical industry matured.

The global pharmaceutical market reached US$ 778 billion[1] in the year 2009; however, the growth rate moderated from 6.4 per cent in 2007 to 5.10 per cent in 2008. In 2009 the growth rate was scaled down to 4 per cent and it is expected to reach global market to US$ 825 billion in 2010 with 6 per cent growth rate *(Refer Table 1.1 and Fig. 1.1)*. The Pharmaceuticals market had to contend with a number of forces including decline in new product approvals and the global economic recession, marked in particular by a sharp downturn in the world's largest economies—the USA and the EU. However, the U.S. government medical reform and growth in the emerging markets will stimulate the pharmaceutical industry.

Table 1.1 : Global Pharmaceutical Market Size and Growth Rates

Year	2000	2001	2002	2003	2004	2005	2006	2007	2008	2009
Total world market (Current US$)	365	392	428	499	560	605	649	712	748	778
Growth over previous year (Constant US$ Growth)	11.50%	11.80%	9.50%	10.30%	8.00%	7.30%	7.10%	6.40%	5.10%	4%

Source: IMS Health Market Prognosis (includes IMS Audited and Unaudited markets)

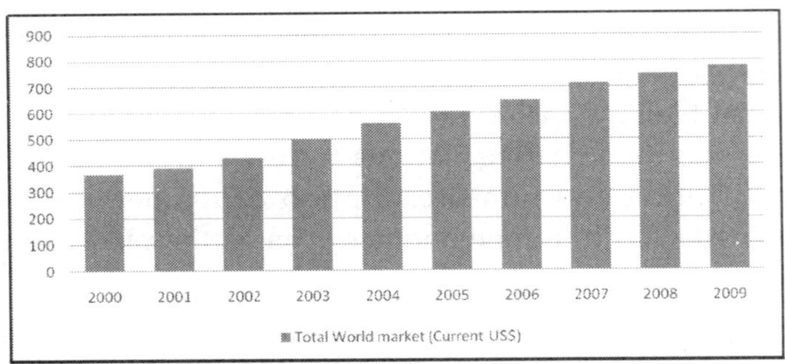

Fig. 1.1. An Overview of Global Pharmaceutical Market

Source: Table 1.1

Industry Segments

Pharmaceutical industry manufactures products that may be broadly classified based on various parameters. The main segments of products of the pharmaceutical industry are formulations (finished dosages) and bulk drugs (Active Pharmaceutical Ingredients).

(*i*) **Bulk Drug:** Bulk drugs are the Active Pharmaceutical Ingredients (APIs) with medicinal properties, which are used for manufacturing formulations. Bulk drugs are Active Pharmaceutical Ingredients (API) or compounds that show specific medicinal properties. Bulk drugs and drug intermediates consist chemicals and solvents; these are the raw materials for the production of drug formulations, which are ultimately sold to the customers. Indian bulk drugs industry registered impressive growth over the past few decades which is very encouraging. India is among the top five bulk drugs producers, producing around 400 different drugs. About 60 per cent of bulk drugs are exported[2] and the balance is sold to domestic formulators.

(*ii*) **Formulation:** Formulations are the end-products of the medicine manufacturing process, and can take the form of tablets, capsules, injectables or syrups, which are ultimately consumed by customers. Formulations constituted nearly 78 per cent (FY2008) of the Indian Pharmaceutical industry's sales, and the remaining accounted for bulk drugs. Out of the formulation sales, about 68 per cent are domestic sales and the rest are exports.

Indian Pharmaceutical Industry

Among the emerging countries, India has the largest Pharmaceutical Industry. It provides essential drugs at affordable prices to its vast population, and also provides employment to millions. Indian Pharmaceutical Industry has attained wide-ranging capabilities in the complex field of drug manufacture and technology. From simple painkillers to sophisticated antibiotics and complex cardiac compounds, almost every type of drug is now made indigenously. Pharmaceutical industry first took root in India in 1930 in Calcutta (Kolkata), West Bengal when the Bengal Chemicals and Pharmaceutical Works was set up in government sector. In India, up to 1960s, multinational companies (MNCs) had a dominant position[3]. These firms imported most of the bulk drugs (the active pharmaceutical ingredients) from their parent companies abroad and sold the end products in the form of tablets and capsules, syrups etc. at prices unaffordable for a majority of the Indian population. This led to a revision of Government of India's (GOI) policy towards this industry. In the early 1960s, the GOI started encouraging the growth of Indian companies that were into manufacturing drugs. With GOI's support and with the Patents Act in 1970, the industry was able to become what it is today[4]. The Patents Act dissipated the dominance of MNCs and the Indian pharmaceutical companies occupied that place. They carved a niche in both the Indian and world markets with their expertise in reverse-engineering and new processes for manufacturing drugs at low costs.

The growth of Indian pharmaceutical Industry may be divided into five phases. The first phase was up to 1970, where foreign companies dominated the market share with very few recognized Indian Companies in existence. The period from 1970-80 comprised the second phase, where drug prices were controlled. The Government of India passed Indian Patent Act, 1970 and domestic pharma companies began to tap the market. The third phase was characterized by pharmaceutical production infrastructure creation, and announcement of export initiatives to domestic pharma companies. The duration of the third phase was from 1980-90. The fourth phase began in 1990 and ended with 2000. During this phase, Indian pharmaceutical companies expanded their businesses in India and outside India very rapidly. In this phase, research orientation production was started. The fifth phase began in the year 2000. Innovation and Research is the chief characteristic of this phase. The Patent Act, 2005 was introduced during this phase, which gave Indian companies the strength to rise to International standards.

At present, the Indian pharmaceutical industry can be broadly segmented to:

(*i*) bulk drugs (APIs) and (*ii*) formulations with very few companies risking investing in primary research aimed at developing and patenting new drugs. The bulk drug business is essentially a commodity business, where as the formulation business is primarily a market driven and brand oriented business. This industry meets about 90 per cent of the country's bulk drug requirement[5].

Growth and Market Size

The Indian Pharmaceutical industry grew from a mere US$0.3 billion turnover in 1980 to about $20 billion[6] of which local market is worth US$11.26 billion and international market is worth US$ 8.74 billion in 2009. It accounts for nearly two per cent of the global market[7] in terms of value and 10 per cent in terms of volume. The Indian Pharmaceutical industry is now ranked 3rd in terms of volume of production and fourteenth in terms of value and 13th in terms of domestic consumption. The country ranks fourth in terms of generic production and seventeenth in terms of export value of bulk actives and dosage forms, one reason for lower value share is the lower cost of drugs in India ranging from 5 per cent to 50 per cent less as compared to developed countries. The industry grew at a CAGR of 13 per cent from 2002 to 2007. Though the Year 2008 ended with the adverse impact of economic recession in global markets, particularly the advanced markets, the Indian pharmaceutical industry is registered a positive growth of 10.20 per cent in 2008. The industry registered 6.78 per cent growth rate in the year 2009 and India's pharmaceuticals market is expected to grow by about 12-13 per cent in 2010 and will grow at a CAGR of 10 per cent in 2011-15. Rising disposable income and rising health consciousness resulted in a positive impact on the pharmaceutical industry. The industry is likely to become one among the top ten in the market in the next decade. It is also playing a crucial social role by distributing quality medicines to society. The industry is poised to usher in a new era showing a tremendous growth in infrastructure development, technology base creation with wide range of production. The industry is self-sufficient and is a low cost producer of high quality bulk drugs and formulations.

Indian Pharmaceutical Industry employs over 42 lakhs people directly and indirectly. It contributes nearly one per cent to the India's GDP[8]. Indian Pharmaceutical Industry meets 40 per cent of the world's bulk drug requirement. The Exports value of bulk actives and dosage makes it to occupy the 17th rank position. Presently, the Indian pharmaceutical industry meets 90 per cent of the country's pharmaceutical needs and imports the remaining 10 per cent drug requirements from other counties. Indian pharma industry exports to more than

Table 1.2 : India's Trade in Pharmaceutical Products

Commodity Name	2003-04	2004-05	2005-06	2006-07	2007-08	2008-09	CAGR (2003-04 to 2007-08) (%)
Exports of Drugs, pharmaceuticals & fine chemicals (Rs. in Crore)	15,213.24	17,857.80	22,115.72	26,895.18	30,760.57	38,433	17.8
Imports of Medicinal & pharmaceutical products (Rs. in Crore)	2,958.04	3,169.35	4,550.87	5,851.64	6,679.87	7,946.37	18.4
Exports Growth Rate (%)	18.61	17.38	23.84	21.61	14.37	24.94	
Imports Growth Rate (%)	3.24	7.14	43.59	28.58	14.15	18.96	

Source: Directorate General of Commercial Intelligence and Statistics (DGCIS) Kolkata

200 countries with a sizeable share in the advanced regulated markets of US and Western Europe. Pharmaceutical industry has shown commendable export performance, the trade balance being positive throughout the years. During the period between 2003-04 and 2008-09, the Compounded Annual Growth Rate (CAGR) of exports was 17.8 per cent *(Refer Table 1.2 and Fig. 1.2)*. According to Ministry of Commerce and Industry, domestic investment in the pharmaceutical sector is estimated at US$ 6.31 billion. The Government of India allowed Foreign Direct Investment upto 100 per cent in pharmaceutical industry. This sector was able to attract FDI worth US$ 1.63 billion (Rs. 72,218.55 million) from April 2000 to December 2009[9].

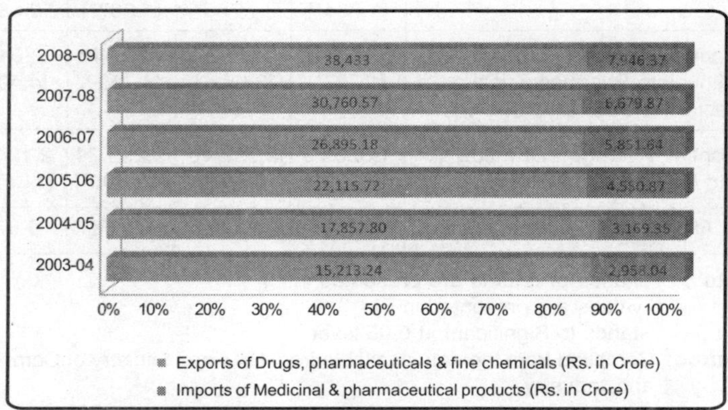

Fig. 1.2 : India's Trade in Pharmaceutical Products

Source: Table 1.2

The Impact of Global Financial Meltdown on Indian Pharmaceutical Industry

As shown in Table 1.2, the impact of global financial crisis on Indian pharmaceutical exports is very less. The domestic sales are also not effected. But the financial meltdown showed a negative effect availability of primary investable funds inform of FDIs and secondary market returns. To present the impact of financial crisis on primary funds and secondary market returns, a 36 months period from January, 2007 to December, 2009 has been taken which is classified into three parts containing 12 months. The performance of various indices during this period is presented in Table 1.3.

Table 1.3 : Performance of Various Indices

Particulars/Period	2007 (12 Months)	2008 (12 Months)	2009 (12 Months)	2007-2009 (36 Months)
Monthly Average return from pharmaceutical stocks at BSE	1.44% (35.96) [0.832*]	–2.65% (122.59) [0.829*]	4.67% (42.43) [2.483*]	1.15% (72.40) [0.813*]
Monthly Average return from Sensex (BSE)	3.45% (40.26) [1.884*]	–5.45% (112.23) [–1.785*]	5.49% (101.81) [1.887*]	1.16% (103.15) [0.688*]
Monthly Average FDI Inflow into Pharmaceutical Sector (In US$ Million)	19.02 [1.767*]	21.98 [2.659*]	20.94 [4.159*]	20.65 [4.403*]
Monthly Average FDI Inflow into India(In US$ Million)	1,326.78 [7.930*]	2,752.40 [6.803*]	2,295.24 [12.490*]	2,124.81 [11.572*]
% Allocation to Pharma sector	1.43%	0.80%	0.91%	0.97%

Note : Variance of returns are presented in ( )
't' values are presented in [ ]
* stands to Significant at 0.05 level

Source: Compiled from the data available from BSE and Ministry of Commerce and Industry.

The calculated beta coefficient of pharmaceutical index is 0.63 which is below one. Less than one beta coefficient elucidate that the volatility in the returns of specific sector are less than the volatility in benchmark returns. It is provided in the table 1.3. The monthly returns from pharmaceutical pack was 1.44 per cent in 2007 where as the monthly sensex return was 3.45 per cent in the same period. In 2008 also the pharmaceutical index gave a negative return of 2.65 per cent where as sensex gave a negative return of 5.45 per cent. It indicates that the pharmaceutical companies cannot give greater returns than market returns in a bull market (refer the returns in 2009) and will not loose more than the market returns in a bear market. The calculated 't' is significant at 5 per cent level of significance. The investment in pharmaceutical stocks is defensive in nature. It is clear from the Table 1.3 that the global financial crisis showed a smaller effect on the secondary market returns along with other sectors but that effect is low. The inflow of FDI into Indian pharmaceutical industry did not affected by the financial crisis. The average monthly inflow of FDIs is more during 2008 compared to 2007 and 2009. It was US$ 21.98 million in 2008 and US$ 19.02 million, US$ 20.94 million in 2007 and 2009 respectively. The inflow of FDI in September, 2007 was only US$ 2.47 million, where as it was US$ 135.16 million in December, 2007. The cumulative FDI inflow upto December, 2007 in pharmaceutical sector was US$ 1,165.26 million, occupied 2.58 per cent of total FDI inflows into India. The cumulative FDI inflow into pharmaceutical industry was increased to US$ 1,428.96 million by December 2008 and to US$ 1,680.29 million by December 2009. It shows a moving upward trend. The financial crisis showed some what positive effect on some segments of pharmaceutical industry. Particularly, the financial crisis motivated the US government to introduce the health care reforms in US. This step boosts the Indian generic segment.

The Performance Volatility Index of Indian Pharmaceutical Industry

Performance Volatility index is a measure of expectations of investors regarding to volatility in rate of return over the near term. In finance terms volatility stands to the level of risk. It is often described as the 'rate and magnitude of changes in returns'. The performance volatility index is a good indicator of market conditions. It gives great advantages in terms of investment, trading and hedging of securities in the sector. It helps to build a risk premium rate, as it depicts the collective consensus of various market factors in the investment in a specific sector.

Calculation Methodology

Performance volatility index is a measure, of the difference between the product of weights multiplied by the difference between the standard derivation of the specific sector returns and the standard derivation of benchmark index. Here the performance volatility index is calculated with the following formula.

Performance Volatility Index = $W_i(\sigma_\partial - \sigma_l) - W_2(\sigma_\pi - \sigma_\Omega)$

Where,

σ_∂ = Standard derivation of benchmark (Sensex) monthly returns

σ_l = Standard deviation of specific (Pharmaceutical) sector monthly returns

σ_π = Standard deviation of monthly increase of total FDI inflow into India

σ_Ω = Standard deviation of monthly increase of FDI inflow into specific sector

W_1 & W_2 = Weights assigned

The factors and the calculated performance volatility index are presented in Table 1.4.

Table 1.4 : Performance Volatility Index

Particulars/ Period	2007 (12 Months)	2008 (12 Months)	2009 (12 Months)	2007-2009 (36 Months)
σ_∂	6.34	10.59	10.09	**10.16**
σ_l	6.00	11.07	6.51	**8.51**
σ_π	1.70	3.13	0.75	**2.23**
σ_Ω	3.61	2.38	1.09	**2.51**
W_1 & W_2	0.5 & 0.5	0.5 & 0.5	0.5 & 0.5	**0.5 & 0.5**
Performance Volatility Index	**1.13**	**–0.61**	**1.96**	**0.96**

Source: Calculated from Appendix

Table 1.4 depicts the performance volatility index for Indian pharmaceutical industry for 36 months (2007-09) is 0.96. It is less than one. The index for 2008 was negative 0.61. It indicates the positive forward look of investors about the Indian pharmaceutical industry. During this period (2008), the FDI inflow was high inspite of the secondary market returns were negative. As the average market returns were more in 2009 than in 2007, the performance volatility index for 2009 is more than the index of 2007. Over all, it can be concluded that the performance index for Indian pharmaceutical industry is less than one which shows the volatility in the returns are less than the volatility in benchmark returns.

Conclusion

The impact of global financial meltdown on Indian pharmaceutical industry was tested with the performance volatility index. This index was at (0.61), which shows the impact of economic recession on pharmaceutical sector was very low. It does not show any effect on primary investable funds (FDI Inflow).

REFERENCES

1. *http://www.sourcejuice.com/1292062/2010/01/04/2009-Review-global-pharmaceutical-industry/*
2. http://www.iloveindia.com/economy-of-india/pharmaceutical-industry.html
3. http://home.iitk.ac.in/~bvphani/PHARMA.pdf
4. http://en.wikipedia.org/wiki/Pharmaceuticals_in_India
5. "*The Indian Pharmaceutical Industry*" ICRA Industry watch series, ICRA Limited, 2002
6. Report on pharmaceutical industry, January 2010 on www.ibef.org
7. *FICCI Report for National Manufacturing Competitiveness Council (NMCC), Competitiveness of the Indian Pharmaceutical Industry in the New Product Regime,* March 2009 (page 2).
8. www.cygnusindia.com
9. FDI inflow data from Ministry of Commerce and Industry

CHAPTER

2

Greed
Reason for Global Financial Crisis

*Dr. G. Sudarsana Reddy
**Prof. C. Sivarami Reddy

Speculators may do no harm as bubbles on a steady stream of enterprise. But the position is serious when the enterprise becomes the bubble in a whirlpool of speculation. —*John Maynard Keynes*

There were financial crisis in the 19th and in the early 20th century. Financial crisis may be associated with banking panics, stock market crashes, currency crisis, and sovereign defaults. The Dutch Tulip Mania, the Wall Street Crash of 1929, the Japanese property bubble of the 1980s, the crash of the dot-com bubble in 2000-01, and now United States housing bubble are the best examples of the crisis. Most of the past crises over the past few decades have had their roots in developing and emerging countries. But, the global financial crisis has had its roots in the US. US housing bubble is quiet different from all other financial crisis during the past 60 years,

---

* Professor of Management, Seshadripuram Institute of Management Studies, Bangalore, Karnataka

** Professor, Department of Commerce, Sri Venkateswara University, Tirupati and Registrar, Yogivemana University, Kadapa, Andhra Pradesh

since it has freezed lending between global banks, the disruption of credit flows in the US and Europe needed to be rescued in 2008. Therefore, the current crisis is not the worst in Asia or Australia, but for the world as a whole and it is the worst financial crisis in the post war period.

How Did It Happen?

The prime reason for the global financial crisis is the sub-prime crisis that began in the US in August 2007. But, the financial crisis was caused by many factors—dramatic change in the ability to create new lines of credit; availability of cheap (sub-prime lending) credit which made it too easy for people to buy houses or make speculative investments; the continuous rise in house prices (hoping further rise and make money in short-run); excessive accommodative monetary policy and tax lending standards in the US during 2002-2006; large rise in mortgage credit to households, particularly loans at low/negligible margin and low initial payments; tight monetary policy containing aggregate demand and output; depressing housing prices, the shift from high inflation to low inflation; default of borrowers, securitization (financial innovation) of low margin non-performing loans—mortgage backed securities, collateral debt securities; the losses were borne by the banks and the financial institutions wiping off capital base. All these combined, have suddenly led to a sharp slowdown in growth momentum in the major advanced economies, especially since the Lehman failure.

Financial Deregulation : Each time a crisis arose, the US Federal Reserve came to the rescue by significantly lowering the federal funds rate, in order to pump liquidity back into the market and avert any further deterioration. After the 1987 stock-market crash, the Gulf War, the 1994 Mexican crisis, the 1997-98 Asian financial crisis, the LTCM debacle of 1998 and the 2000-01 bursting of the internet bubble, the response was always the same. Investors increasingly came to believe that when things went bad, they would be protected by monetary policy in what came to be known as the 'Greenspan put'—low interest rates, high liquidity and the protection of asset prices. Easy monetary policy was seen as an elixir that could cure any market instability that arose. In fact, it added yet more fuel to the fire, in the form of cheap money available for lending.

Availability of Cheap Credit : Low interest rates brought forth a new class of borrowers in the US who were encouraged by mortgage brokers to buy their own home. As a result, a huge amount of capital rushed into the sub-prime mortgage market, where it was directed towards borrowers with weak credit histories. At the same time, the prevailing anti-regulation culture in financial markets fostered a new banking model—the so-called 'originate-and-distribute' model. As a result of availability cheap and easy credit contributed to the US housing bubble. People were able to take loans of various types at cheap rates. This made it too easy for people to buy houses, or make speculative investments. At the same time it crated more money in the system and people wanted to spend that money. People wanted to buy the same that increased demand and caused inflation.

Financial Innovation : As a part of housing and credit boom, the amount of financial agreements called mortgage-backed securities (MBS) and collateralized debt obligations (CDOs) that derived their value from the mortgaged payments and housing prices greatly increased. Ratings agencies provided high credit ratings (AAA) for securities whose underlying loans would normally be regarded as sub-investment grade. Amongst other things, this saw a massive expansion of the securitisation approach to debt financing. This is where a financial organization (say a mortgage lender) 'originates' a loan to a borrower (say a home owner). These loans are then sold to other organisations that package them up with lots of other loans into securities which are 'distributed' to investors all around the world. In other words, this enabled the institutions and investors around the world to invest in the US housing market. People invested in this securities assuming that the underlying real estate asset price will go up and they can make money.

Falling House Prices : House prices declined, major global financial institutions that had borrowed and invested heavily in sub-prime MBS reported significant losses. Falling prices also resulted in homes worth less than the mortgage loan, providing a financial incentive to enter foreclosure. The foreclosure began in late 2006 in US continued to drain wealth from consumers and erodes the financial strength of banking institutions. Defaults and losses on other loan types also increased significantly as the crisis expanded room the housing market to other parts of the economy.

Greed : Global financial crisis is because of the extraordinary greed of mortgage brokers, borrowers (households), equity investors, and financial services community, particularly investment bankers.

Mortgage Brokers : Mainly found in developed economies like US, Western Europe Professionals who are paid a fee to bring together lenders and borrowers sells mortgage loans on behalf of Banks. Mortgage brokers motivated people to take home loan and buy house, since loans are available at cheaper rates and by paying a very nominal down payment or some cases no down payment. Further they told people that housing price will never come down and they further increase. Why did they say this? They are paid a fee, i.e. by the number of mortgages that pass through their hands each month (as, essentially, they were). The more mortgages they can push through, the higher their income. They are required to meet certain guidelines as they do this, but so long as their income depends upon the number of mortgages passing through their hands and not what happens to the mortgages later on—so long as it is a fee-based system—they have every incentive to push the guidelines as hard as they can and to find a way around them whenever possible. If mortgage brokers had done their job and only made loans to people who could pay them back (i.e. with 'reasonable' levels of default), we wouldn't have a financial crisis. So right away, in nearly the first step of the chain, we have to ask what went wrong, why they were willing to take so many questionable loans.

People: With this they can make faster money. People who have own houses also taken loan to buy new house and given old house as mortgage, taken money and gone for speculative investment of investing in real estate. With this type of behaviour, mania for home ownership started.

Banker: Banker who have motivated mortgage broker to bring more business and paid more commission, thinking that they can make more money by landing loans for real estate buying. But they ended up collecting bad loans. People were not able to make payments to bankers, housing prices fallen down, and banks ended up with non-performing loans. Indeed, most regulators around the world have noted approvingly over the years that securitisation allows lenders to alleviate balance-sheet stresses and share some of their risks with third-parties, such as pension funds, who in turn get exposure to typically low volatility 'mortgage-backed securities' that yield higher returns than conventional cash instruments. The very low risk and robust long-term performance of securitised home loans in US has been testament to the merits of this diversification process for consumers, lenders and investors. Therefore, banks issued MBS and CDOs to the public, with fixed interest rate, by securing AAA and BBB bond rating using financial wizardry and 'over Capitalisation'—Banks sold these to other banks, cities and towns, insurance companies, pension funds, every one. Housing mania is over, too many homes and over building homes, housing prices fallen, default, home owners cannot pay mortgage, mortgages worth more than homes. As inflation started creeping up beginning 2004, the US Federal Reserve started to withdraw monetary accommodation. With interest rates beginning to edge up, mortgage payments also started rising. Tight monetary policy contained aggregate demand and output, depressing housing prices. With low/negligible margin financing, there were greater incentives to default by the sub-prime borrowers. Defaults by such borrowers led to losses by financial institutions and investors alike. Although the loans were supposedly securitized and sold to the off balance sheet special institutional vehicles (SIVs), the losses were ultimately borne by the banks and the financial institutions wiping off a significant fraction of their capital. Banks ended up paying interest on MBS and CDOs, and exhausted with liquid funds, since without the revenue from the underlying asset. People started with drawing money from banks, and banks were not able to pay because that the deposit money given as loan, it led to loss of public confidence, and stock prices fallen.

Conclusion

The Global Financial meltdown 2008, mainly resulted from the subprime mortgage crisis of 2007. During boom years, mortgage brokers enticed by the lure of big commissions, talked buyers with poor credit into accepting housing mortgages with little or no down payment and without credit checks. Subprime lending crisis, which began in the United States has become a financial contagion and has led to a restriction on the availability of credit in world financial markets. Hundreds of thousands of borrowers have been forced to default and several major subprime lenders have filed for bankruptcy. Banks and financial institutions often repackaged these debts with other high-risk debts and sold those to world-wide investors creating financial instruments called CDOs or collateralised debt obligations. The serious sub prime mortgage crisis began in June of 2007 when two Bear Stearns hedge funds collapsed. Federal Reserve Bank and European Central Bank dumped $100-billion in liquidity into the system that calmed the market down for a short period. However, the sub prime crisis continued to be solid as long as the housing market continued to escalate and interest rates didn't go up.

In nut shell, the turbulence in the global financial crisis is because of the extraordinary greed of mortgage brokers, borrowers (households), equity investors, and financial services community, particularly investment bankers, who had neglected all standards of financial aptness and morality. Therefore, the 'root' for the financial meltdown is 'Greed'.

REFERENCES

1. Human Greed and Financial Crises, *Business Standard*, 13th February, 2010
2. Greed, the Reason Behind Global Financial Crisis, *The Hindu*, 31st October, 2008
3. Hindus Blame Greed for Current Global Financial Crisis and suggest adopting 'spiritual economics', American Chronical, 7th October, 2008
4. Greed is in the Gene, *The Business Line*, 9th August, 2002.

CHAPTER

3

Global Recession
A Boon to Indian Medical Tourism

*Dr. S. Raghunatha Reddy
**Dr. A. Amrutha Prasad Reddy

Over the last few years, a new trend in the healthcare industry known as Medical Tourism which is gaining popularity among highly industrialized countries like the United States, UK and many other third world countries, where people leave their countries in search for more affordable health options. There are various reasons why the patients travel to other countries for treatment. Many medical tourists from the US are seeking treatment at a quarter or sometimes even a 10th of the cost at home. From Canada, it is often people who are frustrated by long waiting times. From Britain, the patient can't wait for treatment by the National Health Service but also can't afford to see a physician in private practice. And more patients are coming from poorer countries such as Bangladesh where treatment may not be available.

Varying reports containing medical tourism statistics put the number of American patients seeking healthcare abroad

* Associate Professor, Kandula School of Business Management, Kadapa, Andhra Pradesh
** Assistant Professor, Yogi Vemana University, Kadapa, Andhra Pradesh

up from 500,000 in 2006 to 750,000 in 2007.[1] This is a steady increase from the previous year, which medical experts believed as much as 200,000 to half a million Americans travelled out of the country for medical procedures. These figures indicate a significant growth in the Medical Tourism industry, currently a $20 billion market, which can reach $100 billion by 2012.[2] In 2008, it is estimated that approximately 1.3 million Americans travelled abroad to seek healthcare and this figure is doubled in 2010, these estimates indicate a strong potential for medical tourism in the future. The countries which are being actively promoted the medical tourism are Greece, South Africa, Jordan, India, Malaysia, Philippines and Singapore.

Growth in India

Medical tourism of India is opening its feathers to fly high. Equipped with the cutting edge technology, the healthcare sector in India has geared up its speed to be one of the most flourishing industries. The privatization of the healthcare sector has carried with it excellent facilities, bright improvement in infrastructure and world-class treatments. There is a great potential for medical tourism in India from the US and UK, as India becomes a preferred destination for medical tourists from these countries. India's healthcare industry is already growing at 30 per cent annually. The area has shown such growth potential that Indian finance ministers called for India to become a 'Global Health Destination'.

According to a study conducted by the Confederation of Indian Industry (CII) and McKinsey in 2004, some 150,000 foreigners visited India for treatment, with the number rising by 15 per cent a year.[3] The number has increased to around 2,72,000 in 2007.[4] According to The Associated Chambers of Commerce and Industry of India (ASSOCHAM), in 2008, the size of the industry was estimated at ₹ 1,500 crore and it would grow into a ₹ 9,500 crore business by 2015 , with an annual growth rate of 30 per cent. About 1.8 lakh foreigners visited India for treatment in the first eight and half months of 2008-09 and their number would increase by 22 per cent to 25 per cent in the coming years.[5] A nice blend of top-class medical expertise at attractive prices is helping a growing number of Indian corporate hospitals to lure foreign patients, including from developed nations such as UK and US.[6] The Indian Government predicts that India's $17-billion-a-year healthcare industry could grow 13 per cent in each of the next four years, boosted by medical tourism[7]. Globally, medical tourism is said to be $40 billion industry and it is projected that people from Afro-Asian countries spend as much as $20 billion every year on healthcare services outside their countries[8]. The development in medical tourism is due to the cost effectiveness and world class facilities available.

Beneficial Outcome of Global Recession

The US economy has been in recession since December 2007, the impact of which has been felt across the world. Recession is a decrease in the growth of economy of a country. It is a cycle that comes from fear of the future. During this period people stop buying excessively, which decreases the sales and cash outlay. Companies have to lay off people because of lack of business which makes people to spend less, even more. Much before the financial crunch rocked the American economy and the world, a 58-year-old engineer Jill Howard (name changed), from Michigan, had planned to undergo joint replacement surgery in India during Christmas holidays in the year 2008. She planned to visit India because she knew that the costs for the treatment would be much lower here when compared to the US. The global economic meltdown and Mumbai terrorist attacks threatened India's growing tourism industry. However, all this had no effect on Howard's plans for her surgery in India. In fact, now she had all the more reasons to get the surgery done in India as a joint replacement surgery in the US would have cost her a stupendous $50,000 against only $8,000 in India. In the words of Howard "so even if I were to add the airline expenses, travel and stay, it would be cheaper to fly to India for the same treatment,".[9]

Like Howard, several medical industry experts also believe that it could be a better time to fly to India for medical reasons. During the recession, the spending capacity of the people would be less. Those who are suffering and medical intervention is inevitable and urgent, and they are hard pressed to pay from their savings, India is the best option for medical assistance. In fact, many say that the recession was a boon in disguise for the country's medical tourism sector. BK Rao, Chairman, Health Committee, Assocham and Chairman of Gangaram Hospital in New Delhi, says, "The global recession has resulted in rising healthcare costs for foreigners in their own countries. As a result, India has emerged as an attractive alternative for patients seeking surgery."[10] It can expect that the tough economic times would make more people interested in saving money by having their operations in low-cost hospitals in India.

Competitive Advantages of Treatment in India

India became a destiny of Medical Tourism for following reasons:

Cost Effectiveness

India is one of the most attractive medical tourism bargains for someone who is looking for high-end medical procedures or surgery overseas at a low cost. There is a slogan which says, 'First World Class Treatment' at 'Third World Prices'. Significant cost differences exist among US, UK and South Asian countries, and India, The costs in European countries such as Germany and Belgium are less than that of United States, but Europe is still more expensive than India. In fact, the data of AMA shows that India is the least expensive when compared to European as well as other Asian countries.

The American Medical Association (AMA)[11] has conducted a cost comparison study of healthcare in different countries. According to the statistics of AMA, a knee replacement surgery would cost $40,000 in US, $10,000 in Thailand and $13,000 in Singapore; while the same surgery would cost the person $8,500 in India *(see Table 3.1)*.

Table 3.1 : Cost Comparison of Selected Surgeries

Procedure	United States ($)	Thailand ($)	Singa-pore ($)	India ($)	Average Savings when com-pared with the US
Heart bypass	130000	11000	18500	10000	92%
Heart valve replacement	160000	10000	12500	9000	94%
Angioplasty	57000	13000	13000	11000	81%
Hip replacement	43000	12000	12000	9000	79%
Hysterectomy	20000	4500	6000	3000	85%
Knee replacement	40000	10000	13000	8500	79%
Spinal fusion	62000	7000	9000	5500	91%

Source: AMA, June 2007 (www.indiaprofile.com/medical-tourism/cost-comparison.html)

A heart valve replacement surgery would cost the patients $160,000 in the US, $12,500 in Singapore and $10,000 in Thailand. The same procedure in India would cost only $9,000. While a heart bypass would cost $10,000 in India, in US it would cost $130,000 while in Singapore it would cost $18,500 and $11,000 in Thailand. Doctors in Thailand would charge $7,000 for spinal fusion while those in US and Singapore would charge $62,000 and $9,000, respectively. But in India, it costs only $5,500.

Table 3.2 : Cost Comparison of Dental treatment procedures between US and India

Dental procedures	Cost in US ($)*		Cost in India ($)*
	General Dentist	Top End Dentist	Top End Dentist
Smile designing	—	8,000	1000
Metal Free Bridge	—	5,500	500
Dental Implants	—	3,500	800
Porcelain Mental Bridge	1,800	3,000	300
Porcelain Mental Crown	600	1,000	80
Tooth Impaction	500	2,000	100
Root Canal Treatment	600	1,000	100
Tooth Whitening	350	800	110
Tooth Coloured Composite Filling	200	500	25
Tooth Cleaning	100	300	—

Source: www. medicaltourindia.com
*These costs are an average and may not be the actual cost to be incurred.

The table 3.2 depicts that the costs of dental treatment procedures are far less in India when compared with the US. Smile designing is eight times higher in the US than in India. It is $ 8,000 in the US where as it is $ 1,000 in India. Metal Free Bridge is $ 5,500 in US and it is only $ 500 in India. No matter what procedure you undergo, you are sure to save huge amount of healthcare costs. Besides, India is a great place to explore with rich heritage, architecture and culture.

Less/No Waiting Period

Increasingly, waiting for doctors has become the prevailing form of rationing in the West. The waiting period is mild in the US, moderate in Australia and severe in Canada and the

UK. This, in turn, has created millions of frustrated customers who have begun to look elsewhere. India is not only cost effective but the waiting time is almost nil[12]. Especially in the UK where patients have to wait for months together to get medical help.

Table 3.3 : Approximate Waiting Periods in US / UK *(in months)*

Nature of Treatment	Approximate Waiting Periods in US / UK (in months)
Open Heart Surgery	9 – 12
Cranio-facial surgery and skull base	6 – 9
Neuro-surgery with Hypothermia	12 – 15
Complex spine surgery with implants	9 – 12
Simple Spine Surgery	9 – 12
Simple Brain Tumour Biopsy Surgery	6 – 8
Parkinson's Lesion – DBS	9 – 12
Hip Replacement	9 – 12

Source: www. medicaltourindia.com

Table 3.3 displays that for Open Heart Surgery they have to wait 9 to 12 months, for Neuro-surgery with Hypothermia they should wait 12–15 months, whereas in India, the waiting time is almost nil. After all, health cannot be put at stake due to long waiting lists.

Qualified Professionals

India has one of the best pool of qualified professionals in every field of healthcare domain. India is a source market for professionals in the medical field for most of the renowned hospitals around the world. India is producing tens of thousands of skilled physicians and nursing practitioners. Many of these physicians practising in these hospitals and clinics have returned from the U.S. and Europe, leaving behind successful practices. This gives patients more confidence in the healthcare offered by India, generally as they are already used to the expertise and professionalism of Indian medical staff in their own countries.

Services Offered

Every year thousand of visitors are coming to India from around the world just for the medical check up and various type of surgery. Many people from the developed world come to India for the rejuvenation promised by yoga and Ayurvedic massage. One can recuperate in special spas, avail of the fabled Kerala massages and treatments that leave your body nournished and are a part of an Ayurvedic system of alternative healing that is thousands of years old. The corporate hospitals in India offer a comprehensive solution for any and all medical needs, and do this with the highest levels of service, facilities, and professional skills. Indian corporate hospitals are excel in cardiology and cardiothoracic surgery, joint replacement, orthopedic surgery, gastroenterology, ophthalmology, transplants and urology to name a few.

Medical and Infrastructure Facilities

Over the last two decades, the economic boom in India has led to the building of medical and infrastructure facilities. The healthcare sector in India has witnessed an enormous growth in infrastructure in the private and voluntary sector. The private sector, which was very modest in the early stages, has now become a flourishing industry equipped with the most modern state-of-the-art technology at its disposal. India has state of the art hospitals comparable with the US and the UK. In the words of Prasad P.V.R.K.[13], the then Director of Dr. Marri Chenna Reddy Human Resource Development Institute, Hyderabad, "in a corporate hospital, once the door is closed you could feel like you are in a hospital in America". It is estimated that 75-80 per cent of healthcare services and investment in India are now in private sector.

Government Efforts towards Promoting MT

The government is also considering numerous strategies to promote medical and domestic tourism and investment in infrastructure. The government Introduced various policy measures such as the National Health Policy which recognizes the treatment of international patients as an export, which allows private hospitals treating such patients to enjoy benefits such as lower import duties, increase in the rate of depreciation (from 25 per cent to 40 per cent) for life-saving medical equipment, and several other tax sops in order to encourage medical tourism in India. Sujit Banerjee, Secretary, Ministry of Tourism, said: "In 2009 which will be known as 'Visit India Year', we are providing medical tourists a chance to explore options like adventure tourism, spa tourism and rural tourism. The cost for these packages will be borne by the government and hopefully will attract more medical tourists to India."[14]

Conclusion

India's growing economy and global financial crunch are the bright opportunities for the promotion of the medical tourism in India. This is the right time for the government to take advantage of recession to promote medical tourism by highlighting the lower cost of treatment, the world class facilities available and tens of thousands of skilled physicians who have returned from the US and Europe in healthcare sector in the country. Further, the government has to take active role in providing further infrastructure facilities, creating network and connectivity with health, tourism, and other related industries, tie-ups with other countries. The hospitals need to develop efficient logistics system for continuous improvement to meet the requirements of international patients and to attain sustainable competitive advantage.

REFERENCES

1. Fred Hansen, *'A Revolution in Healthcare—Medicine Meets the Market Place'*, *Review*, January 2008, pp. 43-44.
2. *Ibid.*
3. Sankaranarayanan, G., 'Medical Tourism is Becoming a Common Form of Vacationing', *Express: Healthcare Management*, March 1-15, 2005.
4. 'Booming Medical Tourism in India', *A Market Research Report by RNCOS*, India.
5. 'Indian Medical Tourism to Touch ₹ 9,500 Crores by 2015', Economic Times, 6th January 2009.
6. Sankaranarayanan, G., *op.cit.*
7. www.medicaltourism.ca/medicaltourismindia.html
8. S.K. Bichile, *'Is India Prepared for Global Medical Tourism Boom?'*, *Express Healthcare Management*, 28th February, 2005 (www.expresshealthcaremgmt.com).
9. Priyanka Golikeri, *'Recession: A Blessing in Disguise for Medical Tourism'* (www.dnaindia.com/report.asp)
10. Ashwin Ahmad, *'Medical Tourism in India'*, 31st January, 2009 (www.indiafoodandtravelguide.com/medical-tourism-in-india)
11. *Cost Comparison of Medical Treatments: India* vs *The World* (www.tsiindia.com/medicare-india/india-vs-uk.html)
12. Cost Comparison of Medical Treatments: India vs The World, *op. cit.*
13. Ray Marcelo, 'India Fastens Growing Medical Tourism Sector', *The Financial Times*, 2, July 2003.
14. Ashwin Ahmad, *op.cit.*

CHAPTER

4

Global Financial Crisis
Impact on Indian Economy—A Study

*Prof. V. Appa Rao

Introduction

Financial Crisis means a sudden change in the financial stability in the country, clearly to say a situation where some of the huge financial institutions suddenly lose a large part of their assets. Some financial crisis may be due to downturn of banking institutions or due to stock market crashes or huge inflation etc.

The crisis in the real estate, banking, mortgage, credit assets…etc., in the United States had its effect on the other countries across the world. Starting with the collapse of one of the biggest investment bank 'Lehman Brothers' in 2008, it showed its power on the financial and monetary stability of almost all the other countries including India.

The impact on the Indian economy was almost immediate. Credit flows are suddenly dried-up, money market interest rates are increased, and cultivators, migrant workers and home-based workers are also affected. But, the Indian banking system has no direct exposure to any of the mortgage

* Department of Commerce, Osmania University, Hyderabad

and real estate assets or to the failed institutions in the United States. But, the Indian financial market i.e., equity market, credit market, money market, and foreign exchange market went under pressure due to crisis. The impact of the global crisis has been transmitted to the Indian economy through three distinct channels, viz., the financial sector, exports and exchange rates.

Particularly, in India, companies found that their overseas investment is getting reduced, export growth is getting reduced, GDP growth also downgraded from 8 per cent to 7 per cent for the financial year 2009-2010 and there is a decline in output of many industries like; construction, steel, finance and real estate etc.

Against this backdrop, the chapter makes an attempt to: (*i*) analyze the causes of global financial crisis; and (*ii*) study the impact on Indian economy. The present study is based secondary data collected from the Economic Survey-2008, various reports, books and websites.

This chapter is to be presented in National Seminar on 'Impact of Global Financial Melt down on Indian Economy', Organized by Department of commerce, S.V.University, Tirupathi.

Causes of Global Financial Crisis

The collapse of a global housing bubble, which peaked in the U.S. in 2006, caused the values of securities tied to real estate pricing to plummet thereafter, damaging financial institutions globally. Bank solvency, declines in credit availability, and damaged investor confidence had an impact on global stock markets, where securities suffered large losses during late 2008 and early 2009. Economies worldwide slowed during this period as credit tightened and international trade declined. It is argued that credit rating agencies and investors failed to accurately price the risk involved with mortgage-related financial products, and that governments did not adjust their regulatory practices to address 21st century financial markets. The following are the important causes of global financial crisis:

(a) United States Housing Bubble : The immediate cause of the crisis was the bursting of the United States housing bubble which peaked in approximately 2005–2006. High default rates on 'sub prime' and adjustable rate mortgages (ARM), began to increase quickly thereafter. An increase in loan packaging, marketing and incentives such as easy initial terms and a long-term trend of rising housing prices had encouraged borrowers to assume difficult mortgages in the belief they would be able to quickly refinance at more favourable terms. However, once interest rates began to rise and housing prices started to drop moderately in 2006–2007 in many parts of the U.S., refinancing became more difficult. Defaults and foreclosure activity increased dramatically as easy initial terms expired, home prices failed to go up as anticipated, and ARM interest rates reset higher. The combination of easy credit and money inflow contributed to the United States housing bubble.

(b) Easy credit conditions : Lower interest rates encourage borrowing. From 2000 to 2003, the Federal Reserve lowered the federal funds rate target from 6.5 per cent to 1.0 per cent. This was done to soften the effects of the collapse of the dot-com bubble and of the September 2001 terrorist attacks, and to combat the perceived risk of deflation. Additional downward pressure on interest rates was created by the USA's high and rising current account (trade) deficit, which peaked along with the housing bubble in 2006.

(c) Strategic complementarities in financial markets : It is often observed that successful investment requires each investor in a financial market to guess what other investors will do. It has been argued that if people or firms have a sufficiently strong incentive to do the same thing they expect others to do. For example, if investors expect the value of the yen to rise, this may cause its value to rise; if depositors expect a bank to fail this may cause it to fail. Therefore, financial crises are sometimes viewed as a vicious circle in which investors shun some institution or asset because they expect others to do so. Furthermore, in many cases investors have incentives to coordinate their choices. For example, someone who thinks other investors want to buy lots of Japanese yen may expect the yen to rise in value, and therefore has an incentive to buy yen too. Likewise, a depositor in a bank who expects other depositors to withdraw their funds may expect the bank to fail, and therefore has an incentive to withdraw too. Economists call an incentive to mimic the strategies of others *strategic complementarity*.

(d) Leverage : *Leverage* means borrowing to finance investments, is frequently cited as a contributor to financial crisis. When a financial institution (or an individual) only invests its own money, it can, in the very worst case, lose its own money. But when it borrows in order to invest more, it can potentially earn more from its investment, but it can also lose more than all it has. Therefore leverage magnifies the potential returns from investment, but also creates a risk of bankruptcy. Since bankruptcy means that a firm fails to honour all its promised payments to other firms, it may spread financial troubles from one firm to another. The average degree of leverage in the economy often rises prior to a financial crisis.

(e) Asset-liability mismatch : Another factor believed to contribute to financial crises is *asset-liability mismatch*, a situation in which the risks associated with an institution's debts and assets are not appropriately aligned. For example, commercial banks offer deposit accounts which can be withdrawn at any time and they use the proceeds to make long-term loans to businesses and homeowners. The mismatch between the banks' short-term liabilities (its deposits) and its long-term assets (its loans) is seen as one of the reasons bank runs occur (when depositors panic and decide to withdraw their funds more quickly than the bank can get back the proceeds of its loans).

In an international context, many emerging market governments are unable to sell bonds denominated in their own currencies, and therefore sell bonds denominated in US dollars instead. This generates a mismatch between the currency denomination of their liabilities (their bonds) and their assets (their local tax revenues), so that they run a risk of sovereign default due to fluctuations in exchange rates.

(f) Regulatory failures : Governments have attempted to eliminate financial crises by regulating the financial sector. One major goal of regulation is transparency: making institutions' financial situations publicly known by requiring regular reporting under standardized accounting procedures. Another goal of regulation is making sure institutions have sufficient assets to meet their contractual obligations, through reserve requirements, capital requirements, and other limits on leverage.

Some financial crises have been blamed on insufficient regulation, and have led to changes in regulation in order to avoid a repeat. For example, the Managing Director of the IMF, Dominique Strauss-Kahn, has blamed the financial crisis of 2008 on 'regulatory failure to guard against excessive risk-taking in the financial system, especially in the US'.

(g) Frauds : Fraud has played a role in the collapse of some financial institutions, when companies have attracted depositors with misleading claims about their investment strategies, or have embezzled the resulting income. Fraud in mortgage financing has also been cited as one possible causes of the sub prime mortgage crisis-2008.

(h) Contagion : *Contagion* refers to the idea that financial crises may spread from one institution to another, as when a bank run spreads from a few banks to many others, or from one country to another, as when currency crises, sovereign defaults, or stock market crashes spread across countries. When the failure of one particular financial institution threatens the stability of many other institutions, this is called *systemic risk.*

Global Financial Crisis—Its impact on Indian Economy

The impact of the global financial crisis has been transferred to the Indian economy through different channels. Particularly, the global financial crisis is affected on financial sector, exports, exchange rates, cultivators, migrant employees and home-based women workers.

(*i*) **Financial sector:** The financial sector including the banking sector, equity markets, external borrowings and remittances has not remained intact though, the Indian banking sector was not significantly exposed to the sub-prime crisis. Only one of the larger banks, ICICI, was partly affected but managed to prevent a crisis because of its strong balance sheet and timely action by the government, which virtually guaranteed its deposits. The equity markets have seen a near 60 per cent decline in the index and a wiping off of about USD 1.3 trillion in market capitalization since January 2008 when the Sensex had peaked at about 21,000. This is primarily due to the withdrawal of about USD 12 billion from the market by foreign portfolio investors between September and December 2008. The foreign investors withdrew these funds in order to strengthen the balance sheet of their parent companies. Commercial credit, both for trade finance and medium-term advances from foreign banks has virtually dried-up. This has had to be replaced with credit lines from domestic banks but at higher interest costs and has caused the Rupee to depreciate raising the cost of existing foreign loans. Lastly, the remittances from overseas Indians have reportedly fallen as oil producing economies in the Gulf and West Asia begin to suffer from decline in oil prices.

(*ii*) **Indian Exports:** It is observed that there is a steep decline in demand for India's exports in its major markets. The first sector to be hit was the gems and jeweler which felt the impact in November itself and where more than 300,000 workers have lost their jobs. The negative impact has since covered other export-oriented sectors garments and textiles, leather, handicrafts, and auto components. The 21 per cent decline in exports in February 2009 is the steepest fall in exports for the last two decades. While exports of both goods and services, still account for only about 22 per cent of the Indian GDP, their multiplier effect for economic activity is quite large as the import content is not as high as for example in the case of Chinese exports.

(*iii*) Exchange rates: It is also noticed that the exchange rate as the Rupee has come under pressure with the outflow of portfolio investments, higher foreign exchange demand by Indian entrepreneurs seeking to replace external commercial borrowing by domestic financing, and the consequent decline in foreign exchange reserves. This is likely to continue because current account will remain in deficit and the capital account, which has been in deficit in the second and third quarters of 2008-09, will not generate the needed surplus to cover the current account deficit. This will imply further drawing down of foreign exchange reserves and continued downward pressure on the exchange rate. The nearly 25 per cent depreciation in the Rupee's exchange rate has partially nullified the benefits from the decline in global oil and gas prices and increased the cost of commercial borrowings. The weaker Rupee should encourage our exporters and it is possible that with imports declining as sharply as exports, the country's trade deficit may actually improve in the short-run and the external sector balance may remain stable and not pose any major policy issue.

(*iv*) Cultivators: The impact of the crisis on agriculture is much more severe than has been recognized.

Cultivators in India have already been through more than a decade of agrarian crisis, which persisted even through the period of rising international crop prices. The problems of farming in India are both deep and varied. They include weather problems such as less reliable monsoons, more frequent droughts or floods, soil degeneration, lack of institutional credit and insurance leading to excessive reliance on private moneylenders, problems in accessing reliable and reasonably priced input, difficulties in marketing and high volatility of crop prices. Indian farmers tend to respond quickly and extensively to price signals by shifting to more high-priced crops. This caused large and often undesirable shifts in cropping pattern. As a result of the shift away from traditional staple grains to cash crops, there was much greater use of a range of purchased inputs, including new varieties of seed and related inputs marketed by major multinational companies. Small cultivators, who took on debt (often from informal credit sources at very high rates of interest) in order to pay for these cash inputs, then found themselves in real difficulty if crops failed or output prices remained low. Volatility of output prices remains a huge problem for farmers. Particularly, the cultivators who opted for commercial crops when their prices were at their peak now face a completely different environment with very different costs and prices that could easily make the cultivation process financially unviable.

(*v*) **Migrant employees:** It is observed that there has already been a sharp fall in employment in the export-oriented sectors like textiles and garments and gems and jewelers, and even in industries catering more to the domestic market like metal products, automobiles and construction. Many newly unemployed are migrant workers, often short-term migrants with casual contracts whose very existence tends to be ignored by our official statistics. The economic boom of the past decade relied heavily on such workers: Not just in the sectors mentioned above but in labour-intensive services, such as cleaning, maintenance, private security, driving and related services. These were not simply informal activities; many of them catered to the requirements of the expanding corporate sector, and in effect subsidized it by providing a cheap and flexible external labour force. Such workers are now forced either to stay in insecure conditions in the urban areas, or go back to their places of origin—villages or smaller towns.

(*vi*) **Home-based workers:** The recent evidences shows that the export-based industries like, garments face high competitive pressure due to crisis, and they pass this pressure on to home-based women workers by reducing the effective rates for piece-rate work.

Conclusion

Hence, it can be concluded that the timing of the external shock from the global financial crisis has been rather unfortunate and its impact is reflected in the exports, banking sector, exchange rates, equity markets, commercial borrowings, cultivators, migrant workers and home-based workers. Particularly, the India's GDP growth was falling to 6.7 per cent in 2009 which is less than the expected growth rate of 8 per cent. This negative impact has been, to some extent, controlled by the quick policy-decisions taken by the Reserve Bank of India and the Central Government.

REFERENCES

1. *'Economic Survey'*, Oxford University Press, Government of India, New Delhi, 2007-2008.
2. Ruddra Dutt, Sundaram and Ashwini Mahajan *'Indian Economy'*, S. Chand Publications, New Delhi, 2009.

3. Rakesh Mohan, Deputy Governor, Reserve Bank of India, *Remarks prepared for IMF-FSF High-Level Meeting on the Recent Financial Turmoil and Policy Responses* at Washington D.C. October 9, 2008
4. Websites visited:
   (*i*) http://www.citehr.com/135362-global-financial-crisis-impact-indian economy.
   (*ii*) http://www.scribd.com/doc/17428029/Global-Financial-Crisis-and-its-Impact-on-the-Indian-Economy.

CHAPTER

5

Impact of International Financial Crisis
Sources and Solutions

*Dr. P. Saritha
**Prof. P. Mohan Reddy

Introduction

An economic and financial crisis has engulfed the world. The financial crisis that hit the global economy since the summer of 2007 is without precedent in post-war economic history. Although its size and extent are exceptional, the crisis has many features in common with similar financial-stress driven recession episodes in the past. The crisis was preceded by long period of rapid credit growth, low risk premiums, abundant availability of liquidity, strong leveraging, soaring asset prices and the development of bubbles in the real estate sector. Over-stretched leveraging positions rendered financial institutions extremely vulnerable to corrections in asset markets. Banks have collapsed, stock prices have slumped and there has been an unprecedented decline in economic activity. The crisis began in 2007, in the wake of financial and

* Assistant Professor, Department of Business Administration, Yogi Vemana University, Kadapa-3, Andhra Pradesh.

** Professor, Department of Commerce, Sri Venkateswara University, Tirupati-517502, Andhra Pradesh.

real estate speculation in the United States, but it came after a long period of international financial instability, trade imbalances and several local or regional crises. By late 2008, the crisis had spread to many countries. Governments responded with massive emergency measures, but the crisis continued to spread and large numbers of workers have been laid off all over the world. Many see the crisis as an opportunity for renewed regulation and democratic restructuring of the global economy. But solutions are complicated by the depth of the crisis, by the lack of strong global institutions, and by overlapping crises in the environment, natural resources and global trade. A financial crisis refers to a loss of confidence in a country's currency or other financial assets causing international investors to withdraw their funds from the country. Financial crisis is applied broadly to a variety of situations in which some financial institutions or assets suddenly lose a large part of their value. In the 19th and early 20th centuries, many financial crises were associated with banking panics and many recessions coincided with these panics. Other situations that are often called financial crises include stock market crashes and the bursting of other financial bubbles, currency crises, and sovereign defaults.

The 'Global Financial Crisis' of 2008, also called as global financial meltdown, global financial turmoil mainly resulted from the subprime mortgage crisis of 2007. Subprime lending crisis, which began in the United States has become a financial contagion and has led to a restriction on the availability of credit in world financial markets. Hundreds of thousands of borrowers have been forced to default and several major subprime lenders have filed for bankruptcy. The term financial crisis is applied broadly to a variety of situations in which some financial institutions or assets suddenly lose a large part of their value. In the 19th and early 20th centuries, many financial crises were associated with banking panics and many recessions coincided with these panics. Other situations that are often called financial crises include stock market crashes and the bursting of other financial bubbles, currency crises, and sovereign defaults. Many economists have offered theories about how financial crises develop and how they could be prevented. There is little consensus, however, and financial crises are still a regular occurrence around the world.

International Financial Crisis and Wealthy Countries

The developing world, the rise in food prices as well as the knock-on effects from the financial instability and uncertainty in industrialized nations are having a compounding effect. High fuel costs, soaring commodity prices together with fears of global recession are worrying many developing country analysts. Summarizing a United Nations Conference on Trade and Development report, the *Third World Network* notes the impacts the crisis could have around the world, especially on developing countries that are dependent on commodities for import or export. Uncertainty and instability in international financial, currency and commodity markets, coupled with doubts about the direction of monetary policy in some major developed countries are contributing to a gloomy outlook for the world economy and could present considerable risks for the developing world.

US and the Financial Crisis

The current financial crises in the U.S. have originated in the indiscriminate lending of housing loans in that country's sub-prime mortgage market. Among the clients were the investors with poor credit histories or insufficient financial resources. Sub-prime lending has resulted in high levels of defaults. The banks were laying huge bets with each other over loans and assets. Complex transactions were designed to move risk and disguise the sliding value of assets. As the investors are risk averse, they realized the situation, losses occurred, and the market as a whole plummeted. This led to a deep credit crunch in the U.S., the effect of which was felt across the globe. Investor confidence has eroded. Initially the companies affected were those directly involved in home construction and mortgage lending such as Northern Rock and Countrywide Financial. Financial institutions which had engaged in the securitization of mortgages such as Bear Stearns then fell prey. On July 11, 2008, the largest mortgage lender in the US collapsed. IndyMac Bank's assets were seized by federal regulators after the mortgage lender succumbed.

Thereafter, US government saved mortgage lenders Fannie Mac and Freddie Mac, by placing the two companies into federal conservatorship on September 7, 2008. It then began to affect the general availability of credit to non-housing related businesses and to larger financial institutions not directly connected with mortgage lending. Exposure to these mortgage-backed securities, or to the credit derivatives used to insure them against failure, threatened an increasing number of major FIs. Beginning with bankruptcy of Lehman Brothers on Sunday, September 14, 2008, the financial crisis entered an acute phase marked by failures of prominent American and European banks and efforts by the American and European governments to rescue distressed financial institutions. Even before this global financial crisis took hold, some commentators were writing that the US was in decline, evidenced by its challenges in Iraq and Afghanistan, and its declining image in Europe, Asia and elsewhere. Many blame the greed of Wall Street for causing the problem in the first place because it is in the US that the most influential banks, institutions and ideologues that pushed for the policies that caused the problems are found. The crisis became so severe that after the failure and buyouts of major institutions. America is having an economic meltdown. This is the largest since the depression. The sub-prime mortgage lending rate, though, was not the only risk factor involved.

Lehman's collapse marked at the very least a powerful symbol of a new low in confidence, and the reverberations continued. America's financial system failed in its two crucial responsibilities: managing risk and allocating capital. It was all done in the name of innovation, and any regulatory initiative was fought away with claims that it would suppress that innovation. They were innovating, all right, but not in ways that made the economy stronger.

Europe and the Financial Crisis

Europe, a number of major financial institutions failed. Others needed rescuing. In Iceland, where the economy was very dependent on the finance sector, economic problems have hit them hard. The banking system virtually collapsed and the government had to borrow from the IMF and other neighbours to try and rescue the economy. In the end, public dissatisfaction at the way the government was handling the crisis meant the Iceland government fell. A number of European countries have attempted different measures. For example, some nations have stepped in to nationalize or in some way attempt to provide assurance for people. This may include guaranteeing 100 per cent of people's savings or helping broker deals between large banks to ensure there isn't a failure.

The EU is also considering spending increases and tax cuts said to be worth •200bn over two years. The plan is supposed to help restore consumer and business confidence, shore up employment, getting the banks lending again, and promoting green technologies. Russia'a economy is contracting sharply with many more feared to slide into poverty. One of Russia's key exports, oil, was a reason for a recent boom, but falling prices have had a big impact and investors are withdrawing from the country.

Asia and the Financial Crisis

Countries in Asia are increasingly worried about what is happening in the West. Many believed Asia was sufficiently decoupled from the Western financial systems. Asia has not had a subprime mortgage crisis like many nations in the West have, for example. Many Asian nations have witnessed rapid growth and wealth creation in recent years. This lead to enormous investment in Western countries. In addition, there was increased foreign investment in Asia, mostly from the West. However, this crisis has shown that in an increasingly inter-connected world means there are always knock-on effects and as a result, Asia has had more exposure to problems stemming from the West.

Many Asian countries have seen their stock markets suffer and currency values going on a downward trend. Asian products and services are also global, and a slowdown in wealthy countries means increased chances of a slowdown in Asia and the risk of job losses and associated problems such as social unrest.

India and *China* are the among the world's fastest growing nations and after Japan, are the largest economies in Asia. From 2007 to 2008 India's economy grew by a whopping 9 per cent. Much of it is fuelled by its domestic market. However, even that has not been enough to shield it from the effect of the global financial crisis, and it is expected that in data will show that by March 2009 that India's growth will have slowed quickly to 7.1 per cent. Although this is a very impressive growth figure even in good times, the speed at which it has dropped.

China, similarly has also experienced a sharp slowdown and its growth is expected to slow down to 8 per cent (still a good growth figure in normal conditions). However, China also has a growing crisis of unrest over job losses. Both have poured billions into recovery packages.

With China concerned about its economy, it has been trying to encourage its companies to invest more overseas, hoping it will reduce the upward pressure on its currency, the Yuan. China has also raised concerns about the world relying on mostly one foreign currency reserve, and called for the dollar to be replaced by a world reserve currency run by the IMF.

Japan, which has suffered its own crisis in the 1990s also faces trouble now. While their banks seem more secure compared to their Western counterparts, it is very dependent on exports. Japan is so exposed that in January alone, Japan's industrial production fell by 10 per cent, the biggest monthly drop since their records began. Japan's output for the first 3 months of 2009 plunged at its quickest pace since records began in 1955, mostly due to falling exports. A rise in industrial output in April was expected, but was positively more than initially estimated. However, with high unemployment and general lack of confidence, optimism for recovery has been dampened. Towards the end of October 2008, a major meeting between the EU and a number of Asian nations resulted in a joint statement pledging a coordinated response to the global financial crisis. However, as *Inter Press Service* (IPS) reported, this coordinated response is dependent on the entry of Asia's emerging economies into global policy-setting institutions. Asian nations are mulling over the creation of an alternative Asia foreign exchange fund, but market shocks are making some Asian countries nervous and it is not clear if all will be able to commit.

Africa and the Financial Crisis

Perhaps ironically, Africa's generally weak integration with the rest of the global economy may mean that many African countries will not be affected from the crisis, at least not initially, as suggested by *Reuters* in September 2008. The wealthier ones who do have some exposure to the rest of the world, however, may face some problems. In recent years, there has been more interest in Africa from Asian countries such as China. As the financial crisis is hitting the Western nations the hardest, Africa may yet enjoy increased trade for a while. These earlier hopes for Africa, above, may be short lived, unfortunately. In May 2009, the International Monetary Fund (IMF) warned that Africa's economic growth will plummet because of the world economic downturn, predicting growth in sub-Saharan Africa will slow to 1.5 per cent in 2009, below the rate of population growth.

African countries could face increasing pressure for debt repayment, however. As the crisis gets deeper and the international institutions and western banks that have lent money to Africa need to shore up their reserves more, one way could be to demand debt repayment. This could cause further cuts in social services such as health and education, which have already been reduced due to crises and policies from previous eras. Much of the debts owed by African nations are odious, or unjust debts, as detailed further below, which would make any more aggressive demands of repayment all the more worrisome. Some African countries have already started to cut their health and HIV budgets due to the economic crisis. Their health budgets and resources have been constrained for many years already, so this crisis makes a bad situation worse.

Latin America and the Financial Crisis

Much of Latin America depends on trade with the United States. As such Latin America will also feel the effect of the US financial crisis and slower growth in Latin America is expected. Due to its proximity to the US and its close relationship via the NAFTA and other agreements, Mexico is expected to have one of the lowest growth rates for the region next year at 1.9 per cent, compared to a downgraded forecast of 3 per cent for the rest of the region. A number of countries in the region have come together in the form of the Latin American Pacific Arc and are hoping to improve trade and investment with Asia. Diversifying in this way might be good for the region and help provide some stability against future crises. For the moment, the integration is going ahead, despite concerns about the financial crisis.

SOURCES/CAUSES AND CONSEQUENCES OF FINANCIAL CRISES

Following a period of economic boom, a financial bubble, global in scope, has now burst. A collapse of the US sub-prime mortgage market and the reversal of the housing boom in other industrialized economies have had a ripple effect around the world. Furthermore, other weaknesses in the global financial system have surfaced. Some financial products and instruments have become so complex and twisted, that as things start to unravel, trust in the whole system started to fail.

Strategic Complementarities in Financial Markets

It is often observed that successful investment requires each investor in a financial market to guess what other investors will do. Furthermore, in many cases investors have incentives to coordinate their choices. For example, someone who thinks other investors want to buy lots of Japanese yen may expect the yen to rise in value, and therefore has an incentive to buy yen too. Economists call an incentive to mimic the strategies of others *strategic complementarity*. It has been argued that if people or firms have a sufficiently strong incentive to do the same thing they expect others to do, then *self-fulfilling prophecies* may occur. For example, if investors expect the value of the yen to rise, this may cause its value to rise; if depositors expect a bank to fail this may cause it to fail. Therefore, financial crises are sometimes viewed as a vicious circle in which investors shun some institution or asset because they expect others to do so.

Leverage

Leverage, which means borrowing to finance investments, is frequently cited as a contributor to financial crises. When a financial institution (or an individual) only invests its own money, it can, in the very worst case, lose its own money.

But when it borrows in order to invest more, it can potentially earn more from its investment, but it can also lose more than all it has. Therefore leverage magnifies the potential returns from investment, but also creates a risk of bankruptcy. Since bankruptcy means that a firm fails to honor all its promised payments to other firms, it may spread financial troubles from one firm to another. The average degree of leverage in the economy often rises prior to a financial crisis. For example, borrowing to finance investment in the stock market ('margin buying') became increasingly common prior to the Wall Street Crash of 1929.

Asset-Liability Mismatch

Another factor believed to contribute to financial crises is *Asset-Liability mismatch,* a situation in which the risks associated with an institution's debts and assets are not appropriately aligned. For example, commercial banks offer deposit accounts which can be withdrawn at any time and they use the proceeds to make long-term loans to businesses and homeowners. The mismatch between the banks' short-term liabilities (its deposits) and its long-term assets (its loans) is seen as one of the reasons bank runs occur (when depositors panic and decide to withdraw their funds more quickly than the bank can get back the proceeds of its loans).

Uncertainty and Herd Behaviour

Many analyses of financial crises emphasize the role of investment mistakes caused by lack of knowledge or the imperfections of human reasoning. Behavioural finance studies errors in economic and quantitative reasoning. Psychologist Torbjorn K A Eliazonhas also analyzed failures of economic reasoning in his concept of 'œcopathy'. Historians, notably Charles P. Kindleberger, have pointed out that crises often follow soon after major financial or technical innovations that present investors with new types of financial opportunities, which he called 'displacements' of investors' expectations.

Early examples include the South Sea Bubble and Mississippi Bubble of 1720, which occurred when the notion of investment in shares of company stock was itself new and unfamiliar and the Crash of 1929, which followed the introduction of new electrical and transportation technologies. More recently, many financial crises followed changes in the investment environment brought about by financial deregulation, and the crash of the dot com bubble in 2001 arguably began with 'irrational exuberance' about Internet technology.

Unfamiliarity with recent technical and financial innovations may help explain how investors sometimes grossly overestimate asset values. Also, if the first investors in a new class of assets (for example, stock in 'dot com' companies) profit from rising asset values as other investors learn about the innovation (in our example, as others learn about the potential of the Internet), then still more others may follow their example, driving the price even higher as they rush to buy in hopes of similar profits. If such 'herd behaviour' causes prices to spiral up far above the true value of the assets, a crash may become inevitable. If for any reason the price briefly falls, so that investors realize that further gains are not assured, then the spiral may go into reverse, with price decreases causing a rush of sales, reinforcing the decrease in prices.

Regulatory Failures

Governments have attempted to eliminate or mitigate financial crises by regulating the financial sector. One major goal of regulation is transparency: making institutions' financial situations publicly known by requiring regular reporting under standardized accounting procedures. Another goal of regulation is making sure institutions have sufficient assets to meet their contractual obligations, through reserve requirements, capital requirements, and other limits on leverage. Some financial crises have been blamed on insufficient regulation, and have led to changes in regulation in order to avoid a repeat.

Fraud

Fraud has played a role in the collapse of some financial institutions, when companies have attracted depositors with misleading claims about their investment strategies, or have embezzled the resulting income. Fraud in mortgage financing has also been cited as one possible cause of the 2008 sub prime mortgage crisis; government officials stated on Sept. 23, 2008 that the FBI was looking into possible fraud by mortgage financing companies Fannie Mae and Freddie Mac, Lehman Brothers, and insurer American International Group.

Contagion

Contagion refers to the idea that financial crises may spread from one institution to another, as when a bank run spreads from a few banks to many others, or from one country to another, as when currency crises, sovereign defaults, or stock market crashes spread across countries. When the failure of one particular financial institution threatens the stability of many other institutions, this is called *systemic risk*. One widely-cited example of contagion was the spread of the Thai crisis in 1997 to other countries like South Korea. However, economists often debate whether observing crises in many countries around the same time is truly caused by contagion from one market to another, or whether it is instead caused by similar underlying problems that would have affected each country individually even in the absence of international linkages.

Recessionary Effects

There are many theories why a financial crisis could have a recessionary effect on the rest of the economy. These theoretical ideas include the 'financial accelerator', 'flight to quality' and 'flight to liquidity', and the Kiyotaki-Moore model. Some 'third generation' models of currency crises explore how currency crises and banking crises together can cause recessions. The global financial crisis, brewing for a while, really started to show its effects in the middle of 2007 and into 2008. Around the world stock markets have fallen, large financial institutions have collapsed or been bought out, and governments in even the wealthiest nations have had to come up with rescue packages to bail out their financial systems. On the one hand many people are concerned that those responsible for the financial problems are the ones being bailed out, while on the other hand, a global financial meltdown will affect the livelihoods of almost everyone in an increasingly inter-connected world. The problem could have been avoided, if ideologues supporting the current economics models weren't so vocal, influential and inconsiderate of others' viewpoints and concerns.

SOLUTIONS FOR FINANCIAL CRISIS

Most economic regions are now facing financial crisis, or are in it. This includes the US, the Euro zone and many others. At such times governments attempt to stimulate the economy. Standard macro-economic policy includes policies to:

Increase Borrowing

Borrowing at a time of recession seems risky, but the idea is that this should be complimented with paying back during times of growth.

Reduce Interest Rates

Likewise, reducing interest rates sounds like there would be less incentive for people to save money, when banks need to build up their capital reserves. However, as the real economy starts to feel the pinch, reduced interest rates are an attempt to encourage people to take part in the economy.

Reduce Taxes

Tax reduction is something that most people favour and yet during times of economic downturn it would seem that a reduction in tax would result in reduced government revenues just when they need it and then spending on health, education, etc, would be at risk. However, because higher taxes during downturns mean more hardship for more people, increased borrowing is supposed to offset the reduction in taxes, hopefully affording people a better chance to weather the economic storm.

Spend on Public Works Such as Infrastructure

Finally it is at this time that public infrastructure work, which can potentially employ many, many people, is palatable. Often, under free market ideals, government involvement in such activities is supposed to be minimal. Even the other forms of 'interference' are usually frowned upon. However, most states realize that markets are not always able to function on their own; pragmatic and sensible adoption of market systems means governments can guide development and progress as required.

SUMMING UP

Capital mobility was high and rising during the classical gold standard prior to 1914. An international capital market with its centre in London flourished during this first period of globalisation. By 1929, the international capital market had not returned to the pre-war levels. The Great Depression in the 1930s contributed to a decline in cross-border capital flows as countries took measures to reduce capital outflows to protect their foreign reserves. Following the 1931, currency crisis, Germany and Hungary for example banned capital outflows and imposed controls on payments for imports. As a result the international capital market collapsed during the Great Depression. This was one channel through which the depression spread across the world. During the present crisis there has hardly been any government intervention to arrest the flow of capital across borders. However, the contraction of demand and output has brought about a sharp decline in international capital flows. Private portfolio investment capital is actually projected to flow out of emerging and developing countries already in 2009. Once the recovery from the present crisis sets in, cross-border capital flows are likely to expand again. However, it remains to be seen if the present crisis will have any long-term effects on international financial integration.

REFERENCES

1. http://www2.standardandpoors.com/spf/pdf/index/CSHomePrice
2. http://www.federalreserve.gov/boarddocs/speeches/2005/20050414/default.htm.
3. National Review—Mastrobattista
4. http://www.economist.com/world/unitedstates/displaystory.cfm
5. 'BBC—Stimulus Package 2009'. BBC News. 2009-02-14.
6. http://www.economist.com/opinion/displaystory.cfm

CHAPTER

Effects of Global Financial Collision on Indian Banking

*Dr. K. Padmasree
**Dr. A. Bharathi Devi
***Dr. L. Rajani

The year 2008 has created chaos particularly in the world of finance because of the present financial crisis. It may be due to general causes like investor reflexes, free market system, excessive leveraging, asset-liability mismatch, uncertainity and herd behaviour, regulatory failures, fraud, contagion or specific causes like securitization process, flawed credit rating mechanism, complex innovative products, liquidity risk, changing role of banks, appalling corporate governance etc.

The collapse of the Lehman Brothers in mid September 2008 had aggrevated the situation. The situation slowly spreaded among the countries of the world like a contagion because of the consequence of greater integration of nations. Being a part of the globalised economy, India is not an exception to this present contagion. It has discouraged the

* Associate Professor and Head, Dept. of Commerce, Yogi Vemana University, Kadapa-516 003, Andhra Pradesh

** Assistant Professor, Department of Economics, ANU PG Centre, Ongole Campus, Ongole-523 001, Andhra Pradesh

*** Academic Consultant Dept. of Commerce, Yogi Vemana University Kadapa-516 003, Andhra Pradesh

inflow of Foreign Institutional Investors(FIIs) to India and nearly 11 billion dollors of FII were pulled out from the Indian equity market, crashed down the Indian stock markets to a record low level.

The present economic meltdown has by and large adversely affected majority of the Industires, particularly sectors dealing with exports, real estates, iron and steel etc. According to Mr. C. Rangarajan, (Chairman of Economic Advisory Council to the Prime Minister) India, has escaped from direct impact of recession because the banks were not exposed to toxic assets.

A study by Brand finance PLC in association with the Bankers Magazine revealed that thirteen public sector banks namely Punjab National Bank, Bank of India, Canara Bank, Bank of Baroda, Union Bank of India, Indian Overseas Bank, Indian Bank, Oriental Bank of Commerce, Syndicate Bank, and State Bank of Hyderabad, State Bank of Patiyala, State Bank of Bikaner & Jaipur found place out of 19 Indian banks found place in the top 500 global financial brands of 2009 year. This number is tripled against the six Indian banks which found place in the list in the year 2007. Indian banks do not have any direct exposure to sub-prime mortgages. .

In US and Europe the housing market collapsed first and then dragged down banking system. They together have dragged down the real economy. But in India, it is the real economy that got impacted first on account of exports, discouraging inflow of funds Foreign Institutions Institutors (FIIs) (FIIs pulled out $11 billions from Indian equity market), drying up of overseas finance from many firms. Hence the Indian Banks were affected indirectly by the slowing down of the economy.

The direct impact of the crisis on the Indian Banking system was insignificant because Indian banks do not have big exposure to the sub prime market, our unique approach to the issue of banking ownership and regulation, our reliance on home grown solutions, and sticking to the prudential banking norms, regular flow of information sharing arrangement among the strong regulators, unflawed credit rating agencies, role played by the RBI governors in implementing right policies at right rimes have made our banking system more resilience to the present global financial crisis.

Hence it can be noted clearly that the Indian Banks are well placed to weather the impact of global financial crisis. There are good reasons for such optimism. The present chapter intends to study such reasons, and to indentify the lessons for resilient banking system on crisis prevention management and recommendations in the light of the present crisis

The Major objective of the present study is:

To study the effects of global financial collision on Indian banking by taking the parameters like, Capital Adequacy Ratio, Non-performing Assets, and Off-Balance Sheet Items were taken.

Methodology

The data have been collected from secondary source comprising RBI Bulletin, IBA Bulletin, Statistical tables, Annual reports of RBI, for the period from 2004-05 to 2008-09. The collected data has been classified and analysed in a systematic manner. For analysis various statistical tools like percentages and comparative analysis were employed. The parameters like, Capital Adequacy Ratio, Non-performing Assets, and Off-Balance Sheet Items were taken to study the objectives of the present study. Indian Commercial Banks comprising Scheduled Commercial Banks, Public sector Banks, Private Sector Banks and Foreign Banks were taken to study the impact of global financial crisis on Indian Banking Sector.

Capital Adequacy Ratio

Basel II adopted a broad bush approach of requiring banks to maintain 8 per cent of loan as capital requirement because of the tough stance taken by the RBI. In India the Central Bank kept Capital Adequacy norms well above the levels prescribed by Basel II. As per this requirements, banks in India have to maintain a capital adequacy ratio of 9 per cent as against 8 per cent Basel II norms. From the Table 6.1 it is crystal clear that the CRAR of all the banks though decreased from 2004-05 to 2005-06 thereafter increased from 2005-06 to 2008-09 except in Public Sector Banks. It is indeed gratifying to see from the Table that the CRAR of scheduled commercial has gone up by 0.73 per cent points over the previous year from 12.28 per cent. By and large CRAR of all the banks are more than 3 per cent than required norm of 9 per cent. Private sector banks and foreign banks are better than their Public Sector banks in terms of CRAR. From the Table 6.1 it clearly indicates that Indian Banks have enough internal strength to weather out the crisis. Now It is the time for the Indian banks to shift from Capital adequacy to efficient capital Management and Balance Sheet Management for proper utilization of the capital. The banks in India, are not involved in risky business as was prevalent elsewhere in the world. This may be because of sticking to the basic banking business which has safeguarded Indian banks from falling prey to the credit crisis.

Table 6.1 : Capital Adequacy of Scheduled Commercial Banks

Name of the Bank	2004-05	2005-06	2006-07	2007-08	2008-09
Scheduled Commercial Banks	12.80	12.32	12.28	13.01	13.2
Public Sector Banks	12.90	12.17	12.36	12.51	12.3
Private Sector Banks	12.50	11.69	12.08	14.08	14.3
Foreign Banks	14.00	13.02	12.39	13.08	15.1

Source: Report on Trend and Progress of Banking in India 2004-05 to 2008-09.

Non-performing Assets

Gross NPAs and NET NPAs of Commercial banks were consistently came down by 1.22 per cent in Scheduled. Commercial banks from 2004-05 to 2008-09, decreased by 1.53 per cent in Public Sector Banks from 2.73 per cent to 1.2 per cent decreased by 0.75 per cent in Private Sector Banks from 2.05 per cent to 1.3 per cent during 2004-05 to 2008-09 but where as in the Foreign Banks Gross NPAs to Total Advances decreased by 0.61 per cent during 2004-05 to 2007-08 and there after increased by 0.72 per cent over the year from 2007-08 to 2008-09, and an increase by 0.07 per cent from 2004-05 to 2008-09. But the overall position of Indian Banks except public sector banks in reducing NPAs is appreciable even during these times of global recession.

Table 6.2 : Gross Non-performing Assets to Total Advances

Name of the Bank	2004-05	2005-06	2006-07	2007-08	2008-09
Scheduled Commercial Banks	2.52	1.83	1.46	1.30	1.3
Public Sector Banks	2.73	2.05	1.60	1.34	1.2
Private Sector Banks	2.05	1.37	1.24	1.38	1.3
Foreign Banks	1.43	0.97	0.82	0.78	1.5

Source: Report on Trend and Progress of Banking in India 2004-05 to 2008-09.

Table 6.3 : Net Non-performing Assets to Total Advances

Name of the Bank	2004-05	2005-06	2006-07	2007-08	2008-09
Scheduled Commercial Banks	0.92	0.67	0.58	0.57	0.6
Public Sector Banks	0.95	0.72	0.62	0.59	0.6
Private Sector Banks	0.98	0.55	0.54	0.60	0.7
Foreign Banks	0.42	0.41	0.34	0.34	0.7

Source: Report on Trend and Progress of Banking in India 2004-05 to 2008-09.

The position of Net NPAs to Total advances were also decreased by 0.32 per cent, 0.35 per cent, 0.28 per cent from the years 2004-05 to 2008-09, in Scheduled Commercial Banks, Public sector Banks and Private Sector Banks. Whereas in Foreign Banks the Net NPAs to Total Advances increased by 0.28 per cent during the above period it may be due to increase in gross NPAs in this sector.

Off Balance Sheet Items (OBS)

These are the obligations that are contingent liabilities of a bank which do not appear on its balance sheets. In general these items include direct credit substitutes in which a bank substitutes its own credit for a third party including stand by letters of credit, irrecoverable letters of credit that guarantees repayment of commercial papers of tax exempt securities, risk. participations in bankers acceptance, sale and repurchase agreements and assets also with recourse against the seller, interest rate swaps, interest rate options and currency options and so on.

Table 6.4 shows the Off-balance sheet items in Indian Banking system and figures in brackets indicate their percentage to total liabilities. The Ratio of OBS exposure to Total Liabilities increased from 120.25 per cent to 333.47 per cent during the year from 2004-05 to 2007-08 and thereafter decreased drastically by 129.87 per cent from 2007-08 to 2008-09 in Scheduled Commercial Banks.

But whereas in Public sector banks they increased by 12.15 per cent from 38.55 per cent to 50.7 per cent, by 35.15 per cent from 169.15 per cent to 204.3 per cent , by 5.47 per cent from 44.93 per cent to 50.4 per cent and by 534.77 per cent from 1035.33 per cent to 1570.1 per cent in public, private and foreign banks respectively. But we can notice a great decline of OBS percentage to total liabilities from 2007-08 to 2008-09 by 129.87 per cent, 10.75 per cent, 97.49 per cent, 6.72 per cent and

Table 6.4 : Off Balance Sheet Items

Name of the Bank	2004-05	2005-06	2006-07	2007-08	2008-09
Scheduled Commercial Banks	2832508.03 (120.25)	4249541.72 (152.43)	7431714.10 (214.58)	14427369.59 (333.47)	10671961 (203.6)
Public Sector Banks	683896.89 (38.55)	842206.98 (41.09)	1051277.50 (43.09)	1857172.53 (61.45)	1909422 (50.7)
Private Sector Banks	498007.85 (169.15)	790142.13 (187.39)	1258139.07 (215.12)	2250147.68 (301.79)	1625037 (204.3)
Private Sector Banks OLD	59967.26 (44.93)	63024.24 (42.09)	71953.69 ((44.81)	111137.00 (57.12)	116834 (50.4)
Foreign Banks	1590636.03 (1035.33)	2554164.92 (1267.04)	5050343.85 (1816.56)	10208912.24 (2803.88)	7020667 (1570.1)

Source: Report on Trend and Progress of Banking in India 2004-05 to 2008-09.
Figures in parentheses are % of Off-Balance sheet to Total Liabilities.

1233.78 per cent in Scheduled commercial banks, public sector banks private sector and foreign banks respectively. The Biggest exposures of Off-balance sheet items are among Foreign Banks (15701.1%) New Private Sector Banks (204.3%) at the end of March 2009.

Being a part of the global financial system Indian Banking Sector cannot remain isolated from the rest of the financial world. Indian Banks should have a broad based strategy to face the new range of challenges and to convert every challenge into an opportunity by taking into consideration a few following points.

The following suggestions are made with ostensible intention of strengthening the banking system and making the government policies acumen for facing such crisis more boldly in future.

Though the Indian banks are well equipped with the capital Adequacy Ratios, now its the time to shift from Capital adequacy to Efficient Capital Management and Balance Sheet Management for proper utilization of the capital. It is not only necessary for the Indian Banks to try to achieve global benchmarks in diverse areas, but also must review their performance in an on-going basis in attaining the highest ratios.

Best Corporate Governance Practices

Indian banks have to ensure highest ethical standards in the process of conducting business to increase the value of all its stake-holders. Basel Committee recommendations like prescribing and enforcing clear lines of responsibility and accountability, qualified directors on the board, effectively using the finding of audit and ensuring the compensation policies should be in consistent with banks ethical values and conducting of operations in a transparent manner should be strictly adhered.

Transparency

To evaluate the position and performance of the banks different users are intended to know the liquidity, solvency, risk position and profitability of the banks. Hence Indian banks should strictly follow the Generally Accepted Accounting Principles and Standards in preparation of their balance sheets. The banks should not only provide the adequate details in their financial statements but also should provide commentary and notes on the financial statement for clarity and understanding. Further more, Accounting Standards should also clearly specify how to account for losses and profits arising out of derivative transactions which is a great concern in recent days.

Best Practices

For developing and strengthening domestic financial architecture and for facilitating smooth integration with global financial markets, and to become stronger, sounder and enduring performances of our banking system, implementation of internationally accepted best banking practices, standards, codes and other global bench marks are very essential.

REFERENCES

1. Ammannaya, K.K. (2009), "Indian Banking—Stronger and Sounder Performance Through Best Practices", *Southern Economist*, Feb 15, 2009, pp. 9-12.
2. Basic Statistics of Commercial Banks, 2004-2009.
3. Chandra Sekhar CP (2009), "How Sound is Indian Banking"? *Economic and Political Weekly*, Vol. XLIV, No. 19, May 9, pp. 8-9.
4. Prabha Ranjan Gopal,et.al., (2009) "Global Financial Crisis—Issues and Challenges", *Banking Finance*, June, pp. 6-14.
5. Ravi Kant, (2009), "Global Financial Shocks, Resilence of Indian Banks", *The Indian Banker*, Vol. IV, No. 9, September, pp. 30-34.
6. RBI Statistical Tables Relating to Banks in India, RBI, Mumbai, 2004-2009.

CHAPTER

7

Global Financial Crisis and Its Impact on Indian Corporates
A Sectoral Analysis

*M.C. Venkatanath
**A.J. Vikram

We felt that the slow down would not have a great impact on our growth rate. We were wrong.

–Ashok H Advani, Editor, Business India

Introduction

Amidst all round consensus about Indian economy emerging from its recent slowdown, there is also some recognition that the road to recovery could be long and steep. It would be fair to say that nobody expected or foresaw the global economic crises. As far as our companies are concerned, there were significantly reduced profits and many were even pushed into losses. Most companies learnt the hard way to cut costs and wasteful practices and drive efficiencies. Export-oriented companies were the worst hit and will take longer to recover till world markets pick-up. But on the whole, companies will continue to grow.

* M.Com, B.L., FCA, DISA, Research Scholar, Dept. of Commerce, Sri Venkateswara University, Tirupati
** M. Com, FCA, Tirupati, Andhra Pradesh

Global credit and trade crunches may cause Indian economy to recover slowly. The world bank expects 6.1 per cent contraction in world trade volume and fall in world trade value because of declining commodity prices. US and EU region account for 55 per cent of Indian exports. The downturn had started with cancellation of retail orders in mid 2008. These regions were principal importers of merchandise exports. Even 2010-11 could turn out to be quite challenging for the export sector.

The worst of financial crisis unfolded between the last quarter of 2008 and early 2009.

The ADB study shows the overall dip of US $79.9 billion in Asia's global exports of merchandise goods in 2009.India is projected to suffer as the exports of merchandise is expected to decline by US$3.4 billion. The recent forecast of IMF and WTO have stated that world trade will contract by as much as 9-11 per cent in 2009.

For quarter ended Sept. 2009, new projects declined by 68 per cent and the number of stalled projects has doubled. Overall the period of shock has been eighteen months.

Effect on Sectoral Performance

Data have shown that the US economy is recovering slowly, but is still weak particularly in the areas of employment. It will be difficult for the US economy recovering to gather steam without a pick-up in consumer spending as it accounts for two thirds of US economy. There has been a deluge of liquidity in the global financial system as governments and central banks around the world have injected trillions of dollars in the past one year or so to pull the world out of a most severe recession. But on 20th November 2009, the European Central Bank took its first step toward unwinding stimulus measures after the global credit crisis last year. A weak dollar has been at the centre of rally across the global markets this year. Fears that policy makers may consider measures to curb excessive capital inflows had spooked.

Indian Corporates did not Disappoint

Corporate performance in the Quarter three of Financial year 2009-10 (Oct.-Dec. 2009) has been the strongest after the financial meltdown in October 2008 (Q3 of FY2008-09 being the worst). After the four quarters of decline in profit growth Sensex earnings grew in double digits in December 2009. Growth numbers are exaggerated as it is achieved on a relatively small base last year. The year ago quarter was a washout and most companies saw their earnings take a dive because of severe contraction in demand. Inventory losses due to crash in commodity prices, foreign exchange losses due to weak rupee also aggravated the corporate performance. Though the growth returned to normalcy the picture appears rosy only due to comparison with an exceptionally bad quarter. Sectors that came back on track do not inspire confidence in future growth owing to the fact that there would not be positive effect on other sectors:

Growth Sectors

- Automobiles—Passenger cars and two wheelers
- Consumer Goods
- Pharma
- Cement
- Metals
- Software services

Sectors that Showed Negative Growth

- Banking
- Automobiles—Commercial Vehicles
- Real Estate
- Telecom

Companies that stood out in the past two years are worthy of appreciation considering they were up against the worst recessions the world has everfaced.

1. Automobiles : Post its re-birth in 1991, the automobile industry in India was delicensed and allowed 100 per cent foreign direct investment. By 2003 the India's car and two wheeler companies really took off. Unprecedented growth followed as middle classs consumers fulfilled their dream of owning a car at affordable EMIs. By end 2006 the production had hit 10 million mark. The industry grew at 17 per cent in 2006. 18 per cent growth in sales of passenger vehicles was a three-fold compared to the year 2005. The onset of 2007 saw a drastic change in industry fortunes for the worse. The April – September 2007 auto sales were down by 5.91 per cent (compared to April-Sept. 2006).

In Oct. 2007 too, sales declined by 5 per cent this continued for much of 2008. This slide stayed its course for much of 2008 only getting accentuated due to tight credit conditions following the failure of Lehman brothers. In October 2008 overall production fell by 12.32 per cent (Compared with Oct. 2007). Commercial vehicle segment showed negative growth at 2.97 per cent during April-Oct. 2008 compared with Apr-Oct. 07. In FY 2008-09 commercial vehicle sales declined 21.69 per cent compared with FY 2007-2008. Entire Industry was grappling with credit crunch and demand drying up. By December 2008 the government stepped in with its first stimulus package. The measure took their time playing out. While production for Jan. 2009 was lower by 11.92 per cent over January 2008, lower prices and huge discounts ensured that January 2009, with most companies reporting volume growth ahead of expectations although on a lower base. Analysts believed that the government stimulus had stated showing effect.

Recovery

However, auto sales volumes were upbeat in the Quarter ended Dec 2009. Partly due to low base effect and partly due to recovery, Low interest rates, financial availability. Total sales volume grew b 37 per cent backed by growth across all segments in Dec. 2009 quarter compared to Dec. 2008 quarter. The robustness is expected to flow into March 2010 quarter partly due to continuing low base effect. 2009 was a sad script for global auto industry with reduced spending and hardening loans. The performance in the quarter ended Dec. 2008 was disastrous. There is general improvement in economy with decline in interest rates and increased credit availability.

2. Aviation : The nation grew and so did the domestic aviation sector post liberalization from 3 million passengers in 1993 to 44.5 million in 2009. Much before slow down cast its shadow on the global economy, the domestic aviation sector had started rotting and right from the top. The causes of the low performance—Illogical fleet, Geographical expansion, Miscalculated Mergers, Fractured Infrastructure and Over staffing. This has culminated in capacities over running logical demand. Aggregate losses for three years upto FY 2008-09 ₹ 190 billion. Expected losses for FY 2009-10 ₹ 70 billion (*Source:* Centre for Asia Pacific Aviation). Big three players – Air India, Jet Airways, Kingfisher—accounted for losses of almost 230 billion rupees for 3 years ending FY 2009. Loss for current FY 2010 is 65 – 70 billion. The big three accounted for 59.4 per cent of the Market share.

Globally, the sector is witnessing a rise in traffic although yields continue to remain under pressure. There has been increase in volumes. However, the damage inflicted by 2009 will time beyond 2010 to repair. The bad news is the profit making days are more than just a year away for the sector. The good news is that 2010 will see a definite improvement with narrower losses. With revival in air traffic being witnessed in the second half of 2009, the sector will experience a better 2010. High debt and fuel price fluctuation remain two big concerns for 2010. Indian private airlines are expected to make a combined profit of $250-300 million during the coming financial year. Currently, the Indian aviators have a combined debt in excess of $ 10 billion and they would need urgent capital raising of up to $ 12 billion over the next 2-3 years to finance aircraft deliveries with a need to increase equity by $1.2 billion over the next 3-6 months. An operating model which was non-exisent in the Indian market until six years back accounted for almost 70 per cent of domestic capacity within the next two-three quarters. This is due to decision taken by carriers to reconfigure the majority of their domestic aircraft to operate all economy, no frills service. There is a limited market for full service travel, particularly business class. Full service may in future be restricted to just a handful of services and may even disappear entirely. Big players are already operating about 70 per cent of the capacity in the budget model. The transition to lower cost operations should allow the big carriers to develop a more competitive cost structure essential for survival.

3. Hospitality and Hotels : The global recession has brought the highlife business to a halt. As corporations strain under global slowdown, expensive travel was the first on the list of corporate benefits to get the axe. Overseas trips have been cut short and substituted by conference calls and luxurious stays in five star hotels have been replaced by meetings over ordinary coffee.

Discounts and lower rates are not helping either. Even as late as September 2009, foreign travel has not picked up. Global recession, Swine-flu fears and the Mumbai terror attack have kept the cash away from the hotels across the country. The hotel industry and airlines are among the first hit by the economic downturn and are among the slowest to recover. Current occupancy levels are a far cry from the peak levels of 2006-07. Among the big hotel groups, occupancy rate dropped by 9 per cent for the first half of FY 2009-10 from previous year. The terror attack caused the biggest drop in revenues per available room to 20 per cent in Mumbai for FY 2009. One year on the industry seems to be still weighed down by the impact of that horrifying attack. International business tourist traffic at the end of the first half of this fiscal year is down 7 per cent from a year ago. The average occupancy rate stood at 57 per cent at the end of September, down 11 per cent from a year ago and far lower than 70 to 75 per cent seen in 2006-07. Many hotels decided to cut averate room rates which slumped by 21 per cent this year as compared to a year earlier. The first half of FY 2010 continued to see declining demand as companies cut back on travel. This period saw quite steep declines in average rates as companies renegotiated their corporate rates aggressively and hotels focussed on retaining key corporate accounts and maintaining occupancy levels. Room rates in Bangalore, North Mumbai, Delhi and Pune sank the most (24 – 31 per cent). In the past three years, hotels had been charging rates that were 50 – 75 per cent higher than average global rates. This earlier differential of 50-75 per cent has now come down to 20-25 per cent. Industry is undergoing a tough phase during FY 2010 and the demand growth can be expected from FY 2011. Occupancies and Rates will remain under pressure over the next 1-2 years. IT is expected that the average occupancies will decline to 62 per cent in FY2010 and average rates decline 6 per cent in FY 2010. The earnings growth remains negative for the current financial year. Aggregate revenues and earnings declined by 22 per cent and 96 per cent respectively for the for the three largest hotel chains.

4. Real Estate : After five years of robust growth, till 2008 which catapulted seven Indian real estate promoters to the Forbes list of the worlds 100 most wealthy Indians, it remains to be seen if the industry has learnt its lessons well. Real estate sector contributes 5 per cent to the country's GDP. A buoyant economy and bubbling financial services and IT services industry proved to be a great boost for the real estate industry. Post listing of DLF in July 2007, there was a buzz around listed real estate stocks. Much of the housing boom can be attributed to the strong growth in IT/ITES sector. The strong housing loan growth of 32 per cent CAGR during FY 2003-07, that is the time when the employee base of top three Indian IT companies grew by 44 per cent annually followed by moderate growth in FY 2007-08, caused the real estate boom. Over FY 2005-07 around 20 real estate companies estimated to have raised a little more than US$4 billion from public. Construction activity was in full swing, to meet the strong demand. This lead to a mad rush for acquiring land banks. While developers were claouring for land, prices shot up by 100 – 150 per cent over FY 2005-07.

When the financial crisis hit the world markets, late 2008, investors and speculators were the first to ditch the realtors. Pay cuts and job losses became order of the day for IT and financial services employees. As funding sources dried up, private equity investors turned wary, sales stagnated, construction costs jumped and high interest rates hampered demand. Commercial property constructions came to a stand still as demand for office space hit an all time low, with volumes a 10th of that of previous year.

SEZ euphoria also died down completely given the severe impact on the IT and Engineering sector. The situation had become worrisome by the middle of 2008. Two fiscal stimulus packages were announced in October 2008 and January 2009 which included measures for real estate sector. Following government instructions, the public sector banks extended special interest rates for housing loans. A 4 per cent duty cut on steel and cement products also reduced raw material costs. Relaxation of NPA norms saw leading developers successfully refinance/reschedule a substantial amount of Short-term debt into Long-term. Residential Inventory continues to be major challenge for leading developers. Real estate players registered a sharp fall in revenues and profits since September 2008. No significant recovery in volumes was noticed in Bangalore, Chennai, Hyderabad and Kolkata except in Mumbai and National Capital Region. Despite such measures most realtors ended up with bloated balance sheets for the FY 2008-09. In many cases sales were almost equal to receivables and companies faced a severe cash crunch. The real estate industry was forced to look at budget homes/affordable housing for survival. By early 2009 developers made a bee line to launch below 25 lakh projects across all cities. Central Government announced that housing loans under 20 lakh would be considered as priority sector lending. This brought a reversal in the attitude of property developers. Earlier, the developers were only interested in high end, luxury segment. But recession saw the advent of a whole new segment of affordable housing in residential property. Between October 2008 - July 2009 450 projects were launched in 5 lakh – 30 lakh bracket. The turnaround in the equity markets from March 2009 saved the day for the industry. Realty firms have managed to get on to the road to recovery but experts remain skeptical.

5. Information Technology : The sector had impressive annual growth rates and healthy balance sheets and holding the promise of a bright future. Then the credit crises struck and plunged the global economy into one of its worst recessions in decades. Almost over night, the fortunes of the Indian tech industry took a bit hit. With the industry deriving more than half of its revenues from the US and more than one third of its revenues from the beleaguered global financial services sector, the bets were off on growth. Valuations tumbled to new lows in the early part of 2009. There is no denial that 2009 has been the most challenging for global IT. According to most estimates the IT spending declined by 6-8 per cent. Even though the outlook for the global economy does not look bright, Indian IT companies managed to report 3-4 per cent quarter on quarter revenue growth in the September 2009 Quarter. Many tech companies managed the downturn much better than the last time, an indication of the maturity of the business models. Unlike the previous slowdown, when a likely lack of maturity had caused vendors to offer cost savings to clients primarily through price cuts, the response this time has been far more extensive including improving the offshore mix (moving more work to India) and increasing the contribution from fixed price projects. Cost cuts were not the only way companies adopted to survive the downturn, many of them also took measures to become more efficient operationally. Indian IT vendors have not hesitated from taking tough decisions, slashing salaries and getting rid of unproductive employees while keeping a tight control on the number of new hires. Most companies have reported resilient margins in a tough environment. The revenue growth has dropped from the peaks to negative post recession. Growth had stalled to a scenario of flat to marginal growth. Pricing pressure was huge. Most clients got pricing discounts from 5-15 per cent. Margin on new contracts in 2009 was any where from –5 per cent to 0 per cent. In October 2008 customers were in a state of shock , the budgeting cycle was on a month to month basis. IT would be premature to say that the companies would be back to pre downturn levels soon. IT budgets will be largely flat in 2010 with a global growth of 1.3% over 2009. That's a significant improvement considering that they declined by 8.1 per cent in 2009 over 2008.

6. Media : According to KPMG, the Media industry which until the early part of 2008, had been roaring ahead, with TV industry grew at an annual rate of 14 per cent from 2006 to 2008. The print industry also showed a similar pace of growing during the same period. During this boom time the media industry was overflowing with cash to spend, with practically every TV company rushing to add a new channel to its existing portfolios. There were close to 400 channels being beamed into Indian homes. Before the global economic melt down of 2008, most media companies were focusing only on the top line, leaving profitability to suffer. There are mainly two major revenue sources for the print industry, circulation and ad revenue and traditionally ad revenue is always higher. Advertisement is the major revenue driver contributing 65 per cent of total revenue. In the second half of 2008 print media took a battering as inventory levels of advertisements dropped. Bigger spenders such as the banking and financial services, real estate and automobile sectors, which contributed almost 40-50 per cent of the total ads booked in the various media simply disappeared. Most newspapers were left with a yawning gap in their ad revenues. With more than 60,000 newspapers published in 22 languages.

During the slowdown print companies with an all india presence got hit more badly compared with companies that have only a regional presence and publish in local languages. The soaring price of news print (accounting for 50 per cent of the total cost) for most of 2008 and dropping ad revenues has hit the print media. In 2008, both domestic and international news print prices were trading at peak levels, going to ₹ 43,500 per metric tonne in June from ₹ 30,000 in January, while international news print prices soared to $960 MT by November from and 600 a year ago. Prices were mainly driven by the soaring price of crude which sizzled their way of $147 a barrel by July 2008. High news print prices took a heavy toll on the profitability of most newspaper publishers. National players which are highly dependent on imported news print, suffered a huge dent in margings during FY 2009 while companies that rely on domestic newsprint were comparatively less affected. Across the board, operating margins declined by an average 51 per cent in FY 2009.

In the broadcasting sector also, it was a case of survival of the fittest. While the stalwarts of the industry touched the ground, the ones with more business sense remained afloat and did well too. Most analysts attribute their decline to too much aggression when it comes to new property launches. Survival was the key goal during 2008-09 for most media companies.

7. Cement : The world's second largest production of cement with a production capacity of 230 million tones per annum is at the crossroads. It was a rip roaring trip up to FY 2007-08, with demand rising by 10 per cent CAGR and limited availability of fresh capacity which kept average capacity utilization rates at 95 per cent. Over the same period, cement prices increased at around 13 per cent CAGR. After a period of relative inertia from FY 01 to FY 05, the cement producers charged ahead with plans to boost capacity most of which are to be implemented between FY 07 to FY 10. Capacity of 38 million tones was added in FY 2008 alone. Towards the end of 2008, the excess capacity expansion is expected to dog the industry in the medium term with capacity utilization rates potentially dropping below 80 per cent levels. After clocking a robust 21 per cent growth in top line in FY 2007, revenue growth halved to 10 per cent in FY 2008 following a slow down in real estate, which accounts for 65 per cent of cement demand. Analysts estimated that nearly 40 per cent of additional capacity of 40 million tones was put on hold following the crisis. More than falling demand, cement companies were squeezed on the raw materials and fuel, which shot up almost 25 per cent in FY 2008 from 20 per cent in FY 2007. While most big players went ahead with their capacity expansions, it was the smaller regional players who were on a weak footing. In cement industry, the down turn came after the best ever prices and therefore, the highest ever operating profit/tonne. The capex was funded primarily through internal accruals/sale of assets. The cut in central excise by 4 per cent in December 2008, the 60 per cent fall in the international coal prices from July peaks, and 70 per cent fall in the crude prices relavant for packaging cost and cut in diesel prices significantly reduced cost pressures. The cost of sales has come down by ₹ 461 per tonne in December 2008 quarter i.e., a reduction of ₹ 23 per bag over previous quarter. ₹ 200 per tonne was on account of a duty cut and the balance from the reduction in the cost of production. The benefit of cost savings was overshadowed by capacity additions. The last quarter of 2009 saw cement prices falling significantly in the south as increased capacity came on steam. Capacity in the south till October 2009 has expanded by nearly 26 per cent resulting in utilization rates dipping below 72 per cent from 86 per cent a year ago.

8. Banks : Indian banking sector did not witness any dramatic fall-out because of global financial crisis, helped in part by the conservative policies from the central bank, introduced in 2005-06 to tame rapid credit expansion. RBI came to the rescue much before things got out of hand. Not only did it provide monetary stimuli to the banking system by way of cuts in the repo rate, CRR and SLR it also relaxed some prudential regulations on restructured accounts as a one time measure. As a result the banks did not gasp for liquidity as did those in the west, and by the end of FY 2009 the country's top banks had restructured assets worth ₹ 36,266 crore, putting them in financially good shape. Banks had to take swift action in detecting weaknesses and putting in place restructured packages to benefit from the modified asset classification. Those that did restructure some portion of their loans deferred the interest income on these loans. Most of these loans were provided to real estate companies or export led sectors such as textiles. Together, both sectors accounted for 5-9 per cent of the total loans given out by banks. Public sector banks also had to make provisions for the loss on interest caused by the waiver of farm loans by the government, the cost of which mounted from ₹ 1.42 lakh crore in FY 2008 to ₹ 2.36 lakh crore in FY 2009.

On the deposits side, public sector banks turned into overnight winners. Looking at the private sector banks in the developed world, distrust in such institutions hit a high during the crisis. Worried about never getting their money back, people preferred the safe arms of public sector banks, comforted by the fact that the government would not allow depositors of these banks to be left in the lurch should anything go disastrously wrong with their operations. So deposit levels at public sector banks jumped during the period. Meanwhile private sector banks concentrated on streamlining their processes through technology initiatives such as more ATMs, Online banking services etc.

Despite severe liquidity pressure and poor credit appetite from retail and corporate borrowers, Indian banks managed to grow their advances and deposits by 24 per cent and 22 per cent respectively in FY 2009 from a year ago. The lower cost of funds also improved margins.

Growth for Indian banks essentially came from a sharp expansion in term deposits and agricultural and large corporate credit. However, higher delinquency levels in retail credit and debt restructuring took a toll. By the end of FY 2009, gross net performing assets of Indian banks had climbed to 2.4 per cent of the of the advances from 1 per cent a year ago.

During the period of the credit crisis, while a few banks like ICICI Bank switched on the consolidation button and chose to reduce their balance sheet size, others decided to continue expanding their franchise and assets. But for nearly 70 per cent of the banks, advances in the first half of FY 2010 have expanded by less than 10 per cent. At ICICI Bank loans fell by 13 per cent, while Kotak Bank witnessed a 12 per cent fall.

Public sector banks out did their private sector counter-parts in terms of growth and franchise expansion in the last fiscal year. Right now, most banks seem to be showing a preference for mortgages and auto finance. There has been renewed interest in Current accounts and savings accounts levels to keep the cost of funds low.

Without a doubt, the credit crunch of 2008 set in motion the next phase of the credit cycle. In the 12 months to October 2009 credit demand decelerated significantly to a 12 year low of 9.7 per cent. That compares with a nearly 30 per cent growth in credit in the previous year.

After the credit crisis lenders have become far more discerning in lending to small and medium enterprises, which is considered a relatively unsafe segment.

The area of concern is jump in restructured assets. By the end of September 2009, banks had restructure about ₹ 1,11,000 crore, accounting for nearly 5 per cent of advances. Adding restructured assets to the overall gross NPA ratio of

2.4 per cent (as of March 2009) the stress for banks on this score rises to about 7 per cent of advances.

9. Infrastructure : During the boom period up to March 2008, the sector saw a massive expansion and, consequently, there was a flood of new companies raising capital from the primary markets. Of the 96 listed infrastructure companies (Power, Construction, Engineering and Capital goods) almost half of them (45) tapped the primary market between 2004 and 2008. With copious foreign inflows and private investments continuing to climb, the order books of infrastructure firms were stuffed to their limits. The euphoria was running so high that some companies were quoting at 60 times their earnings in early 2008 compare with the average multiple of 16 times for the sector since 2002. The financial crisis played spoilsport.

From the middle of 2008, rapidly deteriorating financial markets made it difficult for companies to raise fresh capital. While the order books were still robust, the problem was obtaining working capital. Shaken by the financial crisis, banks were refusing to lend, no matter how credit worthy a company was. Average Non-food bank credit growth, which peaked in the December 2008 quarter to 27 per cent, dropped to 20 per cent by March 2009; the average prime lending rate of major bank shot up to 13-17 per cent as well. In the last quarter of FY 2009 the industry was still in a state of shock. There was anxiety and apprehension about the extent of the crisis. Consequently, orders got delayed, cash flows were getting difficult.

It was no surprise when, for the first time in six years, the growth rate of gross fixed capital formation dropped to 8.8 per cent in FY 2009 from 12.9 per cent in FY 2008. Around the same time, the average valuation of infrastructure stocks came crashing down to 10 times. Even though a strong order book helped the 69 companies in the infrastructure pack clock a 30 per cent top line growth on average in FY 2009, interest and commodity costs did affect the profitability. The higher cost of steel and cement led to operating profit expanding by just 11 per cent . The credit squeeze resulted in interest costs as a proportion of sales rising to 4 per cent, with the capital intensive power segment bearing the biggest load. As a result, the aggregate net profit growth for the sector came crashing down to 4.5 per cent after clocking a healthy average of 43 per cent during FY 2008. The traumatic second half of FY 2009 had smothered confidence levels and the ability of companies to bid for projects. The state of inertia resulted in bank credit growth tumbling to 10.6 per cent until November 2009.

Reflecting the challenging environment, net sales grew a sluggish 12 per cent in the first half of the current fiscal for the sector. The only ray of light came from lower input prices and interest cost savings, allowing higher growth in operating and net profit.

10. Pharma : The $ 16 billion Indian market is considered to be one of the fastest growing pharma markets in the world. It is the tenth largest pharma market in the world and expected to be worth $ 50 billion by 2015. Contract Research and Manufacturing Services (CRAMS) has really caught on in the past few years. Several multinational giants of original drugs are facing tremendous pressure to keep on innovating. But coming up with that breakthrough drug that promises to be block buster is getting tougher and costlier with each passing day. In the face of a drying product pipeline, original drug makers have little choice but to team up with cost effective Indian companies in a bid to protect their bottom lines. Indian companies offer far lower manufacturing costs and a plentiful supply of skilled labour, so no wonder it has become the favoured destination for outsourcing drug research and manufacturing processes.

The economic slow down did take a toll on the CRAMS business in 2009. CRAMS oriented companies struggled for business as large and mid sized global pharma companies slashed inventory levels and downsized operations. Demand from several research companies also slumped as many of them tightened their R & D budgets. All this led to poor performance by Indian CRAMS companies. While combined revenues grew by a modest 9 per cent, profits plunged by 34 per cent on a trailing twelve month basis. Globallly, the $51 billion pharma outsourcing industry grew by more than 10 per cent during 2006-09. Indian CRAMS companies grew by an average of more than 60 per cent in the same period. In the near future their growth rate is expected to average a little more than 25 per cent.

CHAPTER

8

Impact on and Recovery of Indian Stock Market

*L. Ganesamoorthy

Introduction

Stock market plays an important role in Indian economy. People have started to invest in stock market in recent decades. It attracts many people because of its high growth and high return with high risk. There are many reasons for the rapid growth of Indian stock markets, among them the liberalization policy is the important cause. Developing country such as India suffered due to lack of capital. Due to globalization developed countries were able to bring their investment into India. They are bringing their capital into India because of lower return in their countries. After Foreign Institutional Investment were allowed to flow into Indian stock market, it saw enormous growth. Even though there are certain benefits due to globalization, there are some drawbacks also. The above statement has been proved since September 2008, from which period onwards its impact was clear in the Indian stock market. In this chapter it is attempted to bring out some facts of global financial crisis: its impact on and recovery of Indian stock market.

* Lecturer in Commerce, Annamalai University, Annamalainagar, Tamilnadu.

Indian Stock Market-growth Pattern

In India stock markets began to gain momentum from the second half of 19th century. Its development was not so good till 1990s. After 1990s it got gradual development because of liberalization policies of India. Number of stock exchanges also increased growth. There were 7 recognised stock exchanges in the year 1961 it was 8 in 1971, 9 in 1980 and 14 in 1985, 20 in the year 1991. Six new stock exchanges had been started after 1985. Presently there are 23 recognised stock exchanges in India including Over the Counter Exchange of India(OTCEI).

The growth pattern of stock market in India can be understood by the indices of Sensex and Nifty. At the end of 1997 the index of Sensex was 3658.98 at the same period Nifty was 1079.40. The same were 9397.93 and 2836.55 respectively at the end of 2005. These indices were 20286.99 and 6138.60 at the end of 2007. These facts help us to understand the growth pattern of Indian stock market in recent years. There are many reasons for the growth of Indian stock market, among them the foreign institutional investment into the Indian stock market is also one of the main reasons. Net investment of Foreign Institutional Investors (FII) was ₹ 8574 crore in 1996-97, and ₹ 45881 crore in the year 2004-05. But the same was 66179 crores in 2007-08. So, according to the FIIs the Indian stock markets also were getting growth.

Indian stock markets grasped the benefits of globalization and also it could not escape from the global financial crisis. Indian stock market was affected more due to global financial crisis than any other sector.

Global Financial Crisis

In September 2008 a big and severe financial crisis affected the entire economies of the world. This was the first crisis in 21st century. USA is the origin for the financial crisis and also the country affected more than any other country in the world. It led to failure of large financial institutions in the country. India was also affected by the financial crisis but not much as other countries in the world. Because of the strong fundamentals of our financial system we could prevent ourselves from the adverse impact of world the financial crisis. The impact of the financial crisis was very severe in the stock market of India than any other sector. Stock markets were affected more than any other sector because of contains high foreign investment.

Impact on and Recovery of Stock Market

The growth of Indian stock market was rapid in recent decades especially in the last decade. But it was affected due to the big financial crisis of the world. To analyse the impact of global financial crisis on Indian stock market the index of Sensex has been take for the period of three years on monthly basis. The impact of global financial crisis in the Indian capital market and its recovery can be analysed with help of the movement of Sensex. The following table gives details of Sensex index at the end of every month from January 2007 to December 2009.

From the Table 8.1 the trend of Sensex over the period of three years namely 2007, 2008 and 2009 can be seen. The global financial crisis accrued in the month of September 2008 but its impact begins before few months the table 8.1 illustrates it. The growth of Sensex in the year 2007 were positive except few months and also the decline was very meager. The growth of Sensex was rapid in the year 2007 in this year it grown by 6500 points. But in the year 2008 except three months all other months have negative growth especially after September it got severe decline. In September over August it declined by 11.70 per cent in the next month around 24 per cent over September. In the year 2008 the index of Sensex declined by over 10000 points.

Table 8.1 : Trend and change percentage of Sensex

Year/ Month	2007		2008		2009	
	Sensex	% change over previous month	Sensex	% change over previous month	Sensex	% change over previous month
January	14,090.92	—	17,648.71	—	9,424.24	—
February	12,938.09	– 8.18	17,578.72	– 0.4	8,891.61	– 5.66
March	13,072.10	1.04	15,644.44	– 11.00	9,708.50	9.19
April	13,872.37	6.12	17,287.31	10.50	11,403.25	17.46
May	14,544.46	4.84	16,415.57	– 5.04	14,625.25	28.26
June	14,650.51	7.29	13,461.60	– 18.00	14,493.84	– 0.90
July	15,550.99	6.14	14,355.75	6.64	15,670.31	8.12
August	15,318.60	– 1.49	14,564.53	1.46	15,666.64	– 0.03
September	17,291.10	12.88	12,860.43	– 11.70	17,126.84	9.32
October	19,837.99	14.72	9,788.06	– 23.89	15,896.28	– 7.18
November	19,363.19	– 2.39	9,092.72	– 7.11	16,926.22	6.48
December	20,286.99	4.77	9,647.31	6.10	17,464.81	3.77
Year over year change	6500.08		- 10639.68		7817.50	

Source: www.bseindia.com

In the year 2009 the index of Sensex started growing gradually. In the year 2009 it was grown by 7817 points. Even though it has negative growth in the month of February over January it was seeing positive growth in latter months. Except in the months of February, June, August and October other months were getting growth. Among the four months June and August got less than 1 per cent decline. Hence in the year 2009 the stock market of India started to recover from the severe impact of global financial crisis. The impact of global financial crisis on Indian stock market and its recovery from the crisis can be understood by analyzing the above data by using Compound Annual Growth Rate(CAGR). The calculated CAGR for the year 2007 is 4.16 per cent but in the year 2008 in which the financial crisis happened is in negative that is –4.77 per cent. The movement of Sensex started to get its growth again in the year 2009 in which year the CAGR is 6.23 per cent.

The above table 8.1 has been presented as chart for easy understanding.

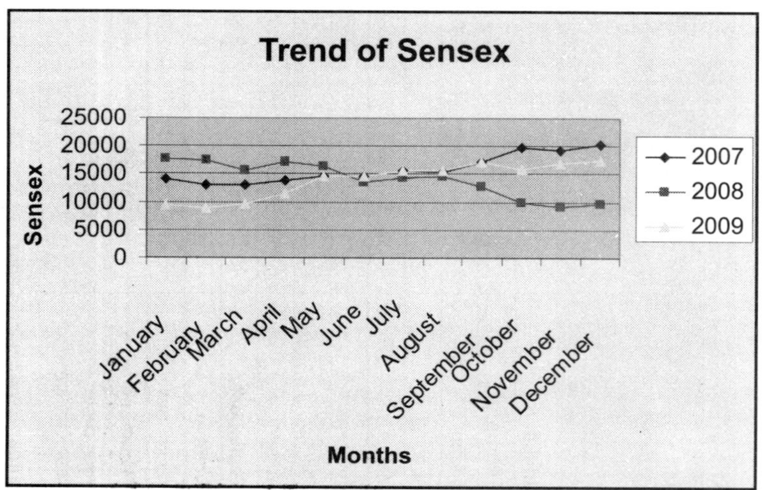

Conclusion

There are certain benefits from globalization. Even though there are certain benefits there are certain drawbacks also. Developing countries like India grasps many benefits by globalization. But they may be affected at the time of global financial crisis which was happened in the year 2008. They could prevent themselves from the impacts in the future periods. Fundamentals of our economy and the financial sector are strong compared to other countries and hence we could avoid the crisis in certain sectors to some extent. We have affected a lot in stock market, hence new effective policies and regulations should be framed in case of foreign investments in the stock market.

CHAPTER

9

Global Financial Meltdown and Its Impact on the Indian Economy

*M. Rajesh
**Dr. N.R.V. Ramana Reddy

Background of the Global Financial Crisis; What is it all about?

It all began with the one and all American dream, that every American should have a home. Regardless of who you are and what you do, if you are an American, you should have something called a home. Real Estate business was in a boom, and financial agents thought that there wasn't a better time to give away loans. The household sector was given a boost with increased monetary supply by commercial financial companies, and people were given loans regardless of the credit rating they received. It was never expected that the boom in the Real Estate business would come to such an abrupt end, and the prices would reach all time low.

The US economy being a capitalist driven economy didn't bother to indulge itself in the policies pursued by the

* Assistant Professor, Department of Business Administration, Annamacharya P.G. College of Computer Studies, Andhra Pradesh
** Principal, Annamacharya P.G. College of Management Studies, Rajampet, Kadapa Distinct, Andhra Pradesh

prominent financial giants. Gradually these financial giants in this business started feeling the heat as 'sub-prime' clients started defaulting in their repayment of loans. The properties which were mortgaged by the clients weren't even covering the principal amount of the loan, leave alone the interest commitments. The credit offered to the people in indiscriminate fashion, achieving short-term goals and ignoring warnings from leading economists about long-term sustainability of the policy, backfired completely and companies like Lehmann Brothers, Merill Lynch, Freddie Mac and Fannie Mae's 'bad assets' reached magnanimous proportions. An acute credit shortage was experienced in the economy, and simultaneous negative effects started occurring. The credit crunch meant that borrowing interest rates shot up in the market, companies slowed down their investment policies, production declined, lay-offs increased, consumption decreased and the whole economy followed the downward spiral. The unemployment rate in the US reached an all time high of 6.1 per cent and industrial growth saw its largest decline in the past three years and fell to 1.1 per cent. The US governments realized the gravity of the situation, and started using monetary as well as fiscal policies to check the diminishing economy. Fiscal policy boost in the way that, an amount of around US$ 1 trillion was pumped into the economy to increase the liquidity scenario. The financial companies which filed for bankruptcy were nationalized, or there non-performing assets were accounted for by the government. The Federal Bank of US also lowered the monetary policy rates, like Statutory Liquidity Ratio (SLR), relating to the amount of money required to be deposited by commercial banks to the Federal bank, so as to have some check on the sky high interest rates. These policies which were targeted to cushion the huge credit shortage scenario has taken somewhat affect and the situation has stabilized a bit. But, as leading economists say, it is too early to comment on whether the trough of the graph has reached or not, or it is still the 'tip of the iceberg' scenario. This fear is out there still because there is uncertainty over how many more 'sub-prime' creditors are still there in the economy, and how many more companies will get affected by the fallacious policy, which was followed by short-sighted profit oriented companies.

Effects of Economic Recession on Aggregate Demand-Aggregate Supply Curve Scenario

Here, after economic recession, the equilibrium (pt. O) shifts from y_0 to y_1. Supply decreases considerably and prices of goods and commodities increases drastically (pt. A). After the government decides to give monetary thrust to the economy through the apex bank, money supply in the household sector increases. This leads to an increase in demand but the supply curve remains the same (pt. B). After sometime, which is after the inside and outside lags of the measures are over, the investment by the Industry sector increases which leads to an increase in supply curve and hence prices reduces to a stable p_2 and output also increases to y_2 (pt. C). Thus we see the effects of the economic recession on the Short Run Aggregate Supply Curve and the Aggregate Demand Curve.

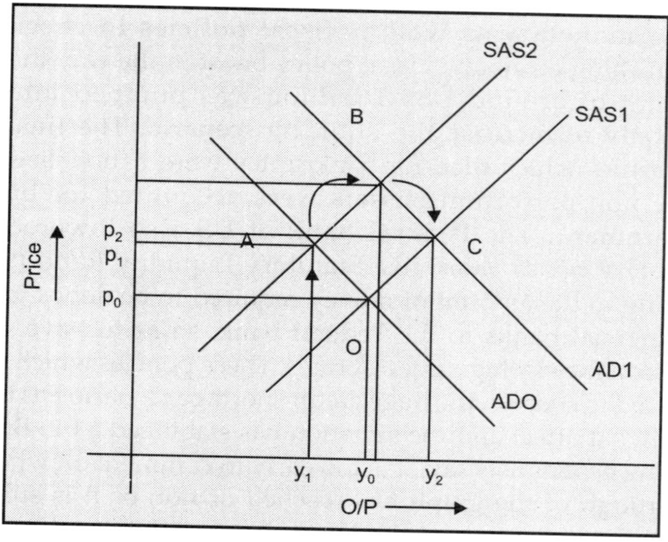

Impact on Indian Economy

The industries most affected by weakening demand were airlines, hotels, real estate. Besides this, Indian exports suffered a setback and there was a setback in the production of export-oriented sectors. The government advised the sectors of weakening demand to reduce prices. It provided some relief by cutting down excise duties, but such simplistic solutions were doomed to failure. Weakening demand led to producers cutting production. To reduce the impact of the crisis, firms reduced their workforce, to reduce costs. This led to increase in unemployment but the total impact on the economy was not very large. Industrial production and manufacturing output declined to 5 per cent in the last quarter of 2008-09. Consequently, a vicious cycle of weak demand and falling output developed in the Indian economy.

A weakening of demand in the US affected our IT and Business Process Outsourcing (BPO) sector and the loss of opportunities for young persons seeking employment at lucrative salaries abroad. India's famous IT sector, which earned about $ 50 billion as annual revenue, is expected to fall by 50 per cent of its total revenues. This would reduce the cushion to set off the deficit in balance of trade and thus enlarge our balance of payments deficit. It has now been estimated that sluggish demand for exports would result in a loss of 10 million jobs in the export sector alone.

Packages Announced by Government of India to Lift Economy Out of Recession

The Government announced a package of ₹ 35,000 crores in the first instance on December 7, 2008. The main areas to benefit were the following:

(*a*) Housing : A refinance facility of ₹ 4000 crores was provided to the National Housing Bank. Following this, public sector banks announced to provide small home loans seekers loans at reduced rates to step up demand in retail housing sector.

(*i*) Loans up to ₹ 5 lakhs: Maximum interest rate fixed at 8.5 per cent.

(*ii*) Loans from ₹ 5-20 lakhs: Maximum interest rate at 9.25 per cent.

(*iii*) No processing charges to be levied on borrowers.

(*iv*) No penalty to be charged in case of pre-payment.

(*v*) Free life insurance cover for the entire outstanding amount.

This means a borrower can get a loan up to 90 per cent of the value of the house. The government hopes to disburse ₹ 15,000 to 20,000 crores under the new package.

The housing package is the core of the government's new fiscal policy. It will give a fillip to other sectors such as steel, cement, brick kilns etc. Besides, the small and medium industries (SMEs) too get a boost by manufacturing all kinds of fittings and furnishings.

The success of the housing package will, however, depend on the State governments efforts to free up surplus land so that land prices come down and the cost of housing becomes reasonable.

(*b*) Textiles : Due to declining orders from the world's largest market the United States, the textile sector has been seriously affected. An allocation of ₹ 1400 crores has been made to clear the entire backlog in the Technology Upgradation Fund (TUF) scheme.

The Apparel Export Promotion Council (AEPC) Chairman, however, said: "It is a disappointing package. The allocation of ₹ 1,400 crores has been pending for many years and thus, it is the payment of arrears only. There is nothing new in it. It would have been much better if more concrete measures have been taken to reverse the downturn in the exports of readymade garments and avoid further job losses in the textile sector."

***(c)* Infrastructure :** The government has been proclaiming that infrastructure is the engine of growth. To boost the infrastructure, the India Infrastructure Finance Company Ltd. (IIFCL) has been authorised to raise ₹ 14,000 crores through tax-free bonds. These funds will be used to finance infrastructure, more especially highways and ports. It may be mentioned that 'refinance' refers to the replacement of an existing debt obligation with a debt obligation bearing better terms, meaning thereby at lower rates or a changed repayment schedule. The IIFCL will be permitted to raise further resources by the issue of such bonds so that a public-private partnership (PPP) programme of ₹ 1,00,000 crores in the highway sector is promoted.

***(d)* Exports :** Exports which accounted for 22 per cent of the GDP are expected to fall by 12 per cent. The government's fiscal package provides an interest rate subsidy of 2 per cent on exports for the labour–intensive sectors such as textiles, handicrafts, leather, gems and jewellery, but the Federation of Indian Export Organization (FIEO) felt the measures are not enough as they will not make the exports price-competitive and, therefore, will not boost exports. G.K. Pillai, the Commerce Secretary, has estimated a loss of 1.5 million jobs in the export sector alone during 2008-09 on account of the $15 billion decline in the expected exports.

***(d)* Small and Medium Enterprises (SMEs) :** The government has announced a guarantee cover of 50 per cent for loans between ₹ 50 lakhs to ₹ 1 crore for SMEs. The lockin period for loans covered under the existing schemes will be reduced from 24 months to 18 months to encourage banks to cover more loans under the scheme. Besides, the government will instruct state-owned companies to ensure prompt payment of bills of SMEs so that they do not suffer on account of delay in the payment of their bills.

In short, the fiscal package is aimed at boosting growth in exports, real estate, auto, textiles and small and medium enterprises. The aim is to encourage growth and boost employment which have been threatened by the recession in the world economy, more especially in the United States.

Just within a month, the government announced another package to bail out the Indian economy. Dr. Montek Singh Ahluwalia said: "We should expect, from all global projections that the next year (2009) is going to be a very difficult year for the global economy."

The purpose of the new package announced on January 1, 2009 was to minimise the pain. With this end in view, the new package included the following measures:

1. To boost investment and spending to revive growth, the RBI cut the repo rate, which it charges on short-term loans to banks from 6.5 per cent to 5.5 per cent and also reduced the Cash Reserve Ratio (CRR)—the share of deposits which has to be kept with the RBI from 5.5 per cent to 5 per cent;
2. To revive exports which have resulted in a contraction of industrial output, drawback benefits have been enhanced for some exporters. Export-Import Bank also gets ₹ 5000 crores as credit from the RBI.
3. To help the realty sector, realty companies have been allowed to borrow from overseas to develop 'integrated townships'.
4. To boost infrastructure, the India Infrastructure Finance Company Ltd. (IIFCL) has been allowed to raise ₹ 30,000 crores from tax-free bonds. Besides, Non-Banking Finance Companies (NBFCs) need no government approval to borrow from overseas for infrastructure projects. This will sustain the growth momentum on infrastructure.
5. To make more funds available, ceiling on foreign institutional investments (FIIs) in corporate bonds has been increased to $ 15 billion from $ 6 billion. The purpose is to seek much bigger FII investment.

6. To stimulate the Commercial Vehicles (CVs) sector, depreciation benefit on commercial vehicles has been increased from 15 per cent to 50 per cent on purchases. Besides, the States will get one-time funding from the Centre to buy buses for urban transport. In addition, public sector banks would provide finance firms funds for commercial vehicles. It is hoped that Tata Motors and Ashok Leyland's sales would revive.

On February 24, 2009, the government announced a slashing down of excise duty from 10 per cent to 8 per cent a reduction by 2 per cent. Since 90 per cent of the manufactured goods attract 10 per cent excise duty, this measure is designed to reduce the prices of colour TV sets, washing machines, refrigerators, soap, detergents, colas, cars and commercial vehicles. Cement prices are likely to drop ₹ 4-5 per bag of 50 kg while steel prices may cost ₹ 500-600 per tonne less. In addition to this, the government decided to cut service tax form 12 per cent to 10 per cent a reduction by 2 per cent. As a consequence, phone bills, airline tickets, credit card charges, tour packages etc. would cost less. A 2 per cent reduction in service tax will directly touch the lives of over 500 million persons by reducing monthly expenses. The entire stimulus package of ₹ 30,000 crores to boost demand in the economy and thus reduce the impact of recession.

Commerce and Industry Minister Kamal Nath announced a small relief package of ₹ 325 crores for leather, textiles, gems and jewellery on February 26, 2009.

Assessment of the Impact of the Fiscal Package

There is no doubt that the government is motivated with good intentions and is thus aiming to spend a huge amount of ₹ 1,00,000 crores for developing infrastructure in roads, ports etc. which pose a serious handicap to growth. Besides, the aim of other measures is to boost exports and help sectors like textiles and small and medium industries which are labour-intensive and generate more employment.

But the success of the fiscal package will depend on the quality and speed of implementation so that delays in implementation may not aggravate the economic recession to move into the dangerous zone of depression.

One of the major stumbling blocks which may neutralise the positive effects of large expenditure on infrastructure is corruption. In case corruption is not simultaneously curbed to reasonably low levels, it may delay and reduce the much-desired effect in enlarging infrastructure. It may result in the Indian infrastructure network being geared into a temporary employment generation programme with much smaller impact on the economy as against the intended objectives.

For reducing corruption, two things need to be ensured—transparency and avoidance of arbitrariness. By cutting arbitrariness in decision-making, corruption can be curbed to a great extent. Transparency instills confidence in the government.

Secondly, there is a need to orient the fiscal package towards inclusive growth so that the weaker sections benefit. This would require special emphasis, for instance, on rural infrastructure—rural roads and housing, instead of only highways and urban housing. Similarly, a much larger expenditure on primary and secondary education, health and sanitation can also result in a more inclusive growth process.

Thirdly, the chances of our exports increasing are very limited unless the G-3 economies, namely, the US, EU and Japan, are able to bring about a positive shift in their growth in the near future for which the predictions at present are not very optimistic. The World Bank has projected the world output to grow at 0.9 per cent in 2009 as against 2.5 per cent in 2008. If these predictions come out to be true, there is a fear of the recession in 2008 turning into a depression in 2009. But the Indian economy is predicted to grow at about 7 per cent in 2008 and about 6 per cent in 2009. Since the G-3 economies of the US, EU and Japan are affected seriously by the present recession, the chances of Indian exports increasing in these countries appear to be very dim. The natural conclusion is that the Indian economy should concentrate on developing the domestic market. Thus, inward looking policies should be preferred as against the outward looking approach of integrating the Indian economy to the world economy is followed during the last decade. It is heartening that the Prime Minister intends to insulate the Indian economy from the world economy.

Fourthly, although there is a demand for a much larger Fiscal Package to bail out the Indian economy, there are serious limitations faced by the government because it has to fight terrorism on the one hand and financial meltdown on the other. The government has to undertake a huge expenditure at the Central as well as State levels to enhance security. It is difficult to precisely estimate this expenditure at this stage since it entails larger recruitment of police and paramilitary forces along with equipping them with the most uptodate weapons. But there is a massive increase in expenditure to combat terrorism, along with a fiscal package to boost the Indian economy; there is also likely to be shortfall in tax revenues. Consequently, the Budget deficit is bound to increase. The government will not be able to reduce the fiscal deficit to 2.5 per cent of GDP, it may increase to three to 3.5 per cent during 2008-09. But this is inevitable and the target of reducing it according to the schedule prescribed by the Fiscal Responsibility and Budget Management Act, has to be postponed. But the Finance Minister has not agreed to the abolition of the FRBM Act since it would be imprudent to relax or abrogate the FRBM. To quote Dr Ishar Ahluwalia: "The FRBM is like a chastity belt, but don't loosen it without a better alternative."

It may, however, be mentioned that the quasi fiscal deficit (the deficit left out of the Budget) is presently estimated as 6 per cent of the GDP. A comprehensive view of the fiscal deficit (as shown in the Budget and kept outside the Budget) would be in the range of nine to 9.5 per cent of the GDP, though it may now be lower due to a very sharp decline in international crude oil prices from $140 per barrel to about $ 40 per barrel at present. This is a welcome relief. If the government is also able to push the fertiliser prices to lower levels which is possible in the changed circumstances, eventually the total fiscal deficit (shown as well as kept outside the Budget) may come down to 6.5 per cent to 7 per cent of the GDP. This is quite large but it is inevitable in the present situation.

Conclusion

As against the US package of $ 800 billion to bail out the US economy and the Chinese package to $ 580 billion to salvage its economy, the Indian fiscal package of ₹ 35,000 crores ($ 7.3 billion approximately) is a small measure to boost the Indian economy. It is due to this reason that the chieftains of industry want a much bigger package to bail out the Indian economy, as against the minuscule announced by the government.

But the plan to spend more on housing is commendable if it can be implemented in a short time and an effective manner. The government should have transparency and avoid arbitrariness in the implementation so that corruption can be kept within reasonable limits.

The government has been provided relief with the sharp fall in the international price of crude oil and this should be taken advantage of in reducing expenditure to subsidise oil imports. Additional employment generation by helping SMEs will be a step towards inclusive growth since they are labour intensive.

The intention to create infrastructure by expanding highways and ports and to spend ₹ 1,00,000 crores through the IIFCL is commendable. However, it may be more prudent to expand rural roads and rural housing so as to promote more inclusive growth. This would require proper planning which may take more time and does not provide immediate benefit.

Now that the three packages have been announced, it is high time that the policy-makers in the Ministry of Finance, Commerce, Industry and Rural Development should get together to ensure that the planned expenditure—budgeted and provided in the two stimulus packages-is quickly translated into productive capacities so as to create the much-needed multiplier effect on private investment.

It is easier to provide funds, but it is more difficult to ensure their speedy and proper utilisation. In infrastructure, we suffer from inordinate delays and these results in cost overruns which the nation has to bear. The huge amount of funds placed with the India Infrastructure Finance Company Ltd (IIFCL) would require identification of new projects or expansion of the existing projects. This is not an easy task because the IIFCL is only a funding agency and implementation has to be carried out by other entities, may be the State governments, public sector undertakings or private sector corporations. To upgrade the level of infrastructure spending by a factor of two requires gigantic efforts of co-ordination between different agencies for speedy implementation. The government should, therefore, concentrate its efforts to remove hurdles in the path of implementation.

The package has also provided finances to the non-banking finance companies (NBFCs), but there is serious lack of skill with the NBFCs on project appraisals and to ascertain the credit-worthiness of the borrowers and the accompanying project risks. There has to a national campaign for training the NBFCs in project appraisals.

Similarly, the State governments must improve the share of their implementation and co-operate with the Central Government to improve various infrastructure projects in their domain or in collaboration with the Centre.

It needs to be emphasised that implementation holds the key to bail out the Indian economy from the economic crisis.

Pranab Mukherjee Union Finance Minister has also suggested that to reduce the pain of recession, employers should cut wages all along the line to reduce costs, rather than retrenching workers and thus add to job losses. To quote: "Jobs must be protected even if it means some reduction in compensation at various levels." This is a useful tool to fight recession and it has also been tried in several countries. This suggestion should be implemented until such time that the economy gets revived.

REFERENCES

1. Indian Economy: Wikipedia. (n.d.). Retrieved 12 18, 2008, from Wikipedia website: http://en.wikipedia.org/wiki/Indian_economy
2. Speeches: RBI. (n.d.). Retrieved 12 18, 2008, from RBI Website: http://rbidocs.rbi.org.in/rdocs/Speeches/PDFs/87784.pdf
3. Files: Worldbank. (n.d.). Retrieved 12 18, 2008, from Worldbank website:

http://crisistalk.worldbank.org/files/Oct_31_JustinLin_KDI_remarks.pdf

http://www.commodityonline.com/hottopics/US-Recession.html

http://www.fibre2fashion.com/industry-article/9/877/impact-of-recession-in-americaneconomy-on-india1.asp

http://www.indiadaily.com/editorial/09-12f-04.asp

http://www.economywatch.com/world_economy/usa/indo-usa-trade-relation.html

http://www.thehindubusinessline.com/2008/12/31/stories/2008123151300500.htm

http://profit.ndtv.com/2008/11/01005242/IndoUS-trade-relations-What.html

http://www.thestandard.com/news/2008/03/20/five-reasons-why-recession-good-time-startcompany

http://forum.lowyat.net/topic/610764

Print Media

The Economic Times

The Hindu

The Times of India

CHAPTER

10

Global Meltdown and Its Impact on Indian Economy and the Measures Taken by Govt. of India

*Dr. R. Rajendra Reddy

With the collapse of Lehman Brothers and other Wall Street Cons, there was growing recession which affected the US, the Eeropean Union and Japan. As a consequence, US demand for imports from other countries indicated a decline.

Although at one time it was thought that the economic recession of US will not affect the Indian economy, at a later stage it was found that gradually it affects the investments in India through Foreign Direct Investment. The Industries affected by the economic recession were textiles, airlines and real estate. Due to the downfall of Indian exports, production in export-oriented industries suffered a setback. Because of this, firms reduced their labour force so as to reduce costs. The vicious circle of less demand and less production developed in the Indian economy.

A less demand in US affected our IT and BPO sector and lakhs of youth who are seeking employment abroad forgo their opportunities. IT sector in India, which earned about

* Reader in Commerce, Govt. Degree College, Palamaner

$ 50 billion as annual revenue expected to fall by 50 per cent. This would enlarge our balance of payments deficit. It has been estimated that the economic recession would result in a loss of 10 million jobs in the export sector alone.

Measures taken by the Govt. of India

To overcome the problem of economic recession, various measures were taken by the Government of India. The Government announced a package of ₹ 35000 crores in December. 2008. The main features of the said package and the main areas to benefit were the following:

(*a*) **Housing :** A refinance facility of ₹ 4000 crores was provided to the National Housing Bank and the Public sector banks announced to provide home loans at reduced rates to step up demand in retail housing sector. Because of the package the borrowers can take loans upto ₹ 5 lakhs at the rate of 8.5 per cent and also they can get a loan up to 90 per cent of the value of the house.

Due to the liberal loons to housing sector, it will give a boon to other sectors such as steel, cement, brick industry etc. Further, the small and medium industries also get boost by manufacturing all kinds of fittings and furnishings.

(*b*) **Textiles :** Due to economic recession in United States and other European Union countries, the textile sector has been seriously affected. The Government of India has allotted ₹ 1400 crores to clear the entire backlog. But the Chairman of Apparel Export Promotion Council expressed his dissatisfaction about the package.

(*c*) **Infrastructure:** There is a saying that infrastructure is the engine of growth. To improve the infrastructural facilities, the Infrastructure Finance Company Ltd. has been allowed to raise ₹ 14,000 crores by issuing tax-free bonds to the public. By raising funds it was proposed to utilize the said funds to finance infrastructure, particularly highways and ports.

(*d*) **Exports :** Due to economic recession, it is being expected that exports are expected to fall by 12 per cent. Through the package, the government provides an interest rate subsidy of two per cent on exports for the labour intensive sectors, such as, textiles, leather, jewellery etc.

(*e*) **Small and Medium Enterprises :** The government has a guarantee cover of 50 per cent of loans between ₹ 50 lakhs to ₹ 1 Crore for Small and Medium Enterprises.

The above fiscal package is aimed at boosting growth in exports, textiles, small and medium enterprises, real estate etc. The aim is to encourage growth and also to improve employment opportunities in the country.

Second Package Announced by Govt. of India

The Government of India announced another package to overcome the problem of economic recession. This was announced on 1st January 2009 mainly with the objective of minimize the pain. The measures which are included in the package are explained below :

1. To revive growth and to improve the investment, the RBI reduced the repo rate from 6.5 per cent to 5.5 per cent and also reduced Cash Reserve Rate from 5.5 to 5.0 per cent.
2. The Reserve Bank of India sanctioned the credit to EXIM Bank an amount of ₹ 5000 crores mainly to revive exports.
3. Realty companies are allowed to borrow from other countries to develop townships.
4. Indian Infrastructure Finance Company Ltd. has been allowed to raise ₹ 39,000 crores through tax-free bands to sustain growth momentum on infrastructure.

5. To boost up the commercial vehicles sector, allowing rate of depreciation has been increased from 15 to 50 per cent on new purchases.

Other Measures taken by the Government

1. Reducing the rate of excise duty from 10 per cent to 8 per cent. This was done with the object of reducing the prices of Colour TVs, Washing Machines, Refrigerators, Motor Vehicles etc. Further, it was expected that cement prices will be dropped by ₹ 4 – 5 per bag and steel also may cost ₹ 500 – 600 less per tonne.
2. Government decide to reduce service tax from 12 to 10 per cent. As a result, telephone bills, airline charges etc. would cost less.
3. On February 26th 2009, the Government announced a small relief package of ₹ 325 crores for the benefit of leather and textile industries.

CHAPTER

11

Impact of Global Financial Crisis on Indian Economy

An Analysis

*Dr. P.V. Narasaiah
**S. Siva Kumar

Introduction

The open up of the Indian economy gates to the world partially in 1991 leads to the danger of changes in world economy effect over the Indian economy. The Indian economy is now a relatively open economy, except that the capital account is not fully open. The current account, as measured by the sum of current receipts and current payments, amounted to about 53 per cent of GDP in 2007-08, up from about 19 per cent of GDP in 1991. Similarly, on the capital account, the sum of gross capital inflows and outflows increased from 12 per cent of GDP in 1990-91 to around 64 per cent in 2007-08. Due to this openness, the changes in international markets are bound to affect the Indian economy. In addition, the impact of the crisis in financial markets of the advanced economies over the Indian financial markets need to be assessed.

The financial market crisis has led to the collapse of major financial institutions and is now beginning to impact the real

* Ph.D. Professor
** M. Com., Research Scholar

economy in the advanced economies in the world. As this crisis is unfolding, credit markets appear to be drying up in the advanced economies. With the substantive increase in financial globalisation, how much will these developments affect India? In the starting period of the financial crisis it was thought that this crisis would not affect the Indian economy, later it was identified that the flow of Foreign Direct Investments got reduced and this affected investments in the Indian economy. It was; therefore, felt that the Indian economy will grow at about seven per cent in 2008-09 and at six per cent in 2009-10. A redeeming feature of the current crisis is that its magnitude is much lesser than that of the Great Depression of the 1930s when unemployment rate in the United States exceeded 25 per cent. Currently, it stands at 6.5 per cent and is predicted to remain around eight per cent in 2009.

Against this backdrop the present chapter seeks to review the causes for global financial crisis and its impact an Indian economy from different angles. Also, the chapter throws light on the challenges that emerge from the global financial crisis.

CAUSES FOR GLOBAL FINANCIAL CRISIS

The following are the major causes for global financial crisis. The primary cause of the current financial crisis can be attributed to the sub-prime mortgage sector in the United States of America. At a fundamental level, however, the crisis could be attributed to the persistence of large global imbalances, which, in turn, were the outcome of long periods of excessively loose monetary policy in the major advanced economies during the early part of this decade.

Global imbalances have been manifested through a substantial increase in the current account deficit of the US mirrored by the substantial surplus in Asia, particularly in China, and in oil exporting countries in the Middle East and

Russia These imbalances in the current account are often seen as the consequence of the relative inflexibility of the currency regimes in China and some other emerging market economies. According to Portes (2009), global macro-economic imbalances were the major underlying cause of the crisis. These saving-investment imbalances and consequent huge cross-border financial flows put great stress on the financial intermediation process. The global imbalances interacted with the flaws in financial markets and instruments to generate the specific features of the crisis. Such a view, however, offers only a partial analysis of the recent global economic environment. The role of monetary policy in the major advanced economies, particularly that in the United States, over the same time period needs to be analysed for a more balanced analysis.

IMPACT OF GLOBAL FINANCIAL CRISIS ON INDIAN ECONOMY—AN ASSESSMENT

The initial impact of the sub-prime crisis on the Indian economy was rather muted. Indeed, following the cuts in the US Federal rate in August 2007, there was a massive jump in net capital inflows into the country. The Reserve Bank had to sterilise the liquidity impact of large foreign exchange purchases through a series of increases in the cash reserve ratio and issuances under the Market Stabilisation Scheme.

With persistent inflationary pressures emanating both from strong domestic demand and elevated global commodity prices, policy rates were also raised. Monetary policy continued with pre-emptive tightening measures up to August 2008.

The direct effect of the sub-prime crisis on Indian banks was almost negligible because of limited exposure to complex derivatives and other prudential policies put in place by the Reserve Bank. The relatively lower presence of foreign banks in the Indian banking sector also minimized the direct impact on the domestic economy. The larger presence of foreign banks can increase the vulnerability of the domestic economy to foreign shocks, as happened in Eastern European and Baltic countries. In view of significant liquidity and capital shocks to the parent foreign bank, it can be forced to scale down its operations in the domestic economy, even as the fundamentals of the domestic economy remain robust. Thus, domestic bank credit supply can shrink during crisis episodes. For instance, in response to the stock and real estate market collapse of early 1990s, Japanese banks pulled back from foreign markets – including the United States—in order to reduce liabilities on their balance sheets and thereby meet capital adequacy ratio requirements. Econometric evidence shows a statistically significant relationship between international bank lending to developing countries and changes in global liquidity conditions, as measured by spreads of interbank interest rates over overnight index swap (OIS) rates and U.S. Treasury bill rates. A 10 basis-point increase in the spread between the London Interbank Offered Rate (LIBOR) and the OIS sustained for a quarter, for example, is predicted to lead to a decline of up to 3 per cent in international bank lending to developing countries (World Bank, 2008).

Even though no direct impact of the Lehman failure on the domestic financial sector in view of the limited exposure of the Indian banks. However, following the Lehman failure, there was a sudden change in the external environment. Further, there was a sell-off in domestic equity markets by portfolio investors reflecting deleveraging. Consequently, there were large capital outflows by portfolio investors during September-October 2008, with concomitant pressures in the foreign exchange market. While foreign direct investment flows exhibited resilience, access to external commercial borrowings and trade credits was rendered somewhat difficult. On the whole, net capital inflows during 2008-09 were substantially lower than in 2007-08 and there was a depletion of reserves.

The contraction of capital flows and the sell-off in the domestic market adversely affected both external and domestic financing for the corporate sector. The sharp slowdown in demand in the major advanced economies is also having an adverse impact on our exports and industrial performance. On the positive side, the significant correction in international oil and other commodity prices has alleviated inflationary pressures as measured by wholesale price index. However, various measures of consumer prices remain at elevated levels on the back of continuing high inflation in food prices.

Fiscal Impact

Government finances, which had exhibited a noteworthy correction starting 2002-03, came under renewed pressure in 2008-09 on account of higher expenditure outgoes due to:

(*i*) higher international crude oil prices (up to September 2008) and the incomplete pass-through to domestic prices;

(*ii*) higher fertiliser prices and associated increase in fertiliser prices;

(*iii*) the Sixth Pay Commission award; and

(*iv*) debt waiver scheme.

The fiscal stimulus packages involving additional expenditures and tax cuts have put further stress on the fiscal. Reflecting these factors, the Central Government's fiscal deficit more than doubled from 2.7 per cent of GDP in 2007-08 to 6.0 per cent in 2008-09, reaching again the levels seen around the end of the 1990s. The revenue deficit at 4.4 per cent of GDP will be at its previous peak touched during 2001-02 and 2002-03. Net market borrowings during 2008-09 almost trebled from the budgeted ₹ 1,13,000 crore to ₹ 3,29,649 in the revised estimates (actual borrowings were ₹ 2,98,536 crore as per RBI records) and are budgeted at ₹ 3,08,647 crore (gross borrowings at ₹ 3,98,552 crore) in 2009-10.

Impact on the Real Economy

Reflecting the slowdown in external demand, and the consequences of reversal of capital flows, growth in industrial production decelerated to 2.8 per cent in 2008-09 (April-February) from 8.8 per cent in the corresponding period of 2007-08. On the other hand, services sector activity has held up relatively well in 2008-09 so far (April-December) with growth of 9.7 per cent (10.5 per cent in the corresponding period of 2007-08). Services sector activity was buoyed up by acceleration in 'community, social and personal services' on the back of higher government expenditure. Overall, real GDP growth has slowed to 6.9 per cent in the first three quarters of 2008-09 from 9.0 per cent in the corresponding period of 2007-08. On the expenditure side, growth of private final consumption expenditure decelerated to 6.6 per cent from 8.3 per cent. On the other hand, reflecting the fiscal stimuli and other expenditure measures, growth in government final consumption expenditure accelerated to 13.3 per cent from 2.7 per cent.

GLOBAL FINANCIAL CRISIS—EMERGING CHALLENGES

The crisis has shown that irrespective of the degree of globalization of a country and the soundness of domestic politicies, it can be impacted by a crisis in any other economy due to the interlinkages in the global economy.

The policy objectives of central banks would have to be broader than price stability as conventional defined. The lesson for central banks that emerged from the crisis is that financial stability can be jeopardised even if there is price stability and macro-economic stability. While there is more of an agreement to recognise financial stability as an objective, there is less of an agreement about the instrumentalities for achieving this objective.

There is a need for fiscal consolidation to generate the fiscal space for macro management. But the massive fiscal support, though appropriate as a crisis response, has raised questions about debt sustainability. This is reflected in increase in sovereign CDS (credit default swap) spreads even for advanced countries which has implications for macro-financial stability. It is, therefore, important that fiscal buffers are established in good times to provide the necessary fiscal space for countercyclical fiscal measures in bad times.

Financial institutions would have to be less leveraged and better regulated. All systemically important financial institutions, markets and instruments should be subject an appropriate degree of regulation and oversight depending on their relative importance for overall financial stability. At the same, it needs to be recognised that regulation in itself can act to magnify cycles which should be minimized.

The international financial architecture needs to be strengthened to address the challenges of the global economy of the 21st century.

Conclusion

To conclude, the ongoing global financial crisis can be largely attributed to extended periods of excessively weak monetary policy in the US over the period 2002-04. Very low interest rates during this period encouraged an aggressive search for yield and a substantial compression of risk-premium globally. Abundant liquidity in the advanced economies generated by the weak monetary policy found its way in the form of large capital flows to the emerging market economies. All these factors boosted asset and commodity prices, including oil, across the spectrum providing a boost to consumption and investment. Global imbalances were a manifestation of such an accommodative monetary policy and the concomitant boost in aggregate demand in the US outstripping domestic aggregate supply in the US. This period coincided with careless lending standards, inappropriate use of derivatives, credit ratings and financial engineering, and excessive leverage. As inflation began to edge up reaching the highest levels since the 1970s, this necessitated monetary policy tightening. The housing prices started to witness some correction. Lax lending standards, excessive leverage and weaknesses of banks' risk models/stress testing were exposed and bank losses mounted wiping off capital of major financial institutions.

As the current crisis shows, the problems in finance and financial regulation need to be addressed at a national as well as global level to ensure that the benefits of financial developments become more widespread and enduring in nature. Thus, what needed is not more regulation net sharper regulation of the financial system to ensure sustained financial development with stability.

REFERENCES

1. Bernanke, Ben (2009), 'The Crisis and the Policy Response', Stamp Lecture at London School of Economics.
2. Committee on the Global Financial System (2009), Report of the Working Group on Capital Flows to Emerging Market Economies (Chairman: Rakesh Mohan).
3. Group of Thirty (2009), 'Financial Reform: A Framework for Financial Stability' (Chairman: Paul A. Volcker), Washington D.C.
4. Geneva Report (2009), 'The Fundamental Principles of Financial Regulation', Markus Brunnermeier, Andrew Crocket, Charles Goodhart, Avinash D. Persaud and Hyun Shin.
5. Reserve Bank of India (2009), 'India's Financial Sector: An Assessment' Committee on Financial Sector Assessment.

NEWSPAPER

1. *The Business Standard*
2. *The Economic Times*
3. *The Times of India*
4. *Business line*

Websites

www.indianmba.com

www.investopedia.org

www.wikipedia.org

CHAPTER

12

Impact of Global Financial Crisis on Developing Countries

*E. Lavanya
**Dr. K. Nirmala

1. Prelude

In 2008, a series of bank and insurance company failures triggered a financial crisis that effectively halted global credit markets and required unprecedented government intervention. Fannie Mae (FNM) and Freddie Mac (FRE) were both taken over by the government. Lehman Brothers declared bankruptcy on September 14th after failing to find a buyer. Bank of America agreed to purchase Merrill Lynch (MER), and American International Group (AIG) was saved by an $85 billion capital injection by the federal government .shortly after, on September 25th, J P Morgan chase (JPM) agreed to purchase the asset of Washington Mutual (WM) in what was the biggest bank failure in history. In fact, by September 17, 2008, more public corporations had filed for bankruptcy in the U.S. than in all of 2007. These failures caused a crisis of

* Research Scholar, Dept. of Commerce, S.V. University, Tirupati-517 502, Andhra Pradesh.
** Lecturer, Canara Bank School of Business Management, Bangalore University, Bangalore, Karnataka.

confidence that made banks reluctant to lend money amongst themselves, or for that matter, to anyone.

The crisis has its roots in real estate and the sub-prime lending crisis. Commercial and residential properties saw their values increase precipitously in a real estate boom that began in the 1990s and increased uninterrupted for nearly a decade. Increases in housing prices coincided with a period of government deregulation that not only allowed unqualified buyers to take out mortgages' but also helped blend the lines between traditional investment banks and mortgage lenders. Real estate loans were spread throughout the financial system in the form of CDOs and other complex derivatives in order to disperse risk; however, when home values failed to rise and home owners failed to keep up with their payments, banks were focussed to acknowledge huge write downs and write offs on these products. These write downs found several institutions at the brink of insolvency with many being forced to raise capital or go bankrupt.

2. Causes for Financial Crisis

(a) Sub prime Lending : The concept of subprime lending (providing loans to borrowers with low credit ratings or poor loan repayment histories) has been around for as long as lending has been around. Fannie Mae and Freddie Mac led mortgage industry in the 1990's promoting home ownership amongst lower income borrowers. However they acquired only conforming loans (they just lowered the standard for confirming loans).the commercial mortgage industry adapted to this change by making more and more sub-prime loans. For decades banks engaged in a practice called 'redlining' or not loaning to anyone in a 'low-income' neighbourhood. Many believed this unfairly discouraged home ownership for low income citizens. The passage and subsequent revision of the Community Reinvestment Act (CRA) (which required banks to offer credit to their entire market area—not just the affluent parts) was instrumental in prompting bank lending reform.

The purpose of the act was to disallow the practice of 'redlining' or denying loans to individuals who lived in certain neighbourhoods (usually low income, minority neighbourhoods).

(b) Deregulation in the Banking Industry : In 1999, the Gramm-Leach-Bliley act repealed the Glass-Steagall act of 1933, which was previously enforced the separation of investment and commercial banking activities. For example, under Glass-Steagall, a bank could not offer investment services and originate loans. Repealing Glass-Steagall allowed banks to get into the lending business. Banks could work with mortgage loan origination companies to write loans to people without proper collateral and then sell the loans to investors. The loans were pooled together to mortgage-backed securities and collateralized debt obligations. Banks like Citi group lobbied for the repeal of the Glass-Steagal Act for two decades. The groups spent more than $200 million in 1998 alone lobbying to this end.

(c) Credit Ratings Agencies Mis-Rate Mortgage Securities: The 2008 financial crisis has exposed flaws in both the credit rating procedures and the incentives model for credit rating agencies. Credit rating agencies assign ratings to bonds and other debt instruments (such as the pooled subprime loans that were at the root of mortgage-backed securities).credit rating agencies like Moody's and Standard and Poor's evaluate the like hood that the debt will be paid back and assign a letter ranking on a scale of AAA to B, CC, etc .anything below BBB is considered speculative while a AAA rating is the highest credit rating available.

3. The Impact of the Financial Crisis on Developing Countries

The debate in rich countries about the impact of the global financial crisis has largely ignored its impact on developing countries. But it is vital that policy makers from both north and south understand how this crisis may impact developing countries and the implications for development policy.The report identifies six main pathways of impact,which are given below:

(a) Exports : Export growth is already slowing markedly in several developing countries.In Bangladesh, orders for readymade garments from Europe and the US dropped 7 per cent in September. Year on years exports from the Philippines to the US are down by 15 per cent. In Kenya the cut flower industry is suffering as European customers are hit by the crisis.

(b) Foreign Investment : Both portfolio and direct foreign investment have dropped dramatically in several countries as investors shy away from markets that are perceived to be risker. The Ethiopian Electric Power Corporation has indicated that is investment plans will be severely affected due to crisis.

(c) Exchange Rate: The sudden withdrawl of foreign capital from several developing countries has caused dramatic falls in their exchange rate. Companies and government with substantial foreign currency denominated debts may contact or even collapse as a result. The Rand lost 35 per cent of its value between mid-September and mid-October the Philippines Peso was down 12.3 per cent over the year. The Indian rupee hit a record low to the dollar.

(d) Interest Rates : As foreign investors withdraw, risk premium and interest rates have risen for developing countries on global capital markets. Philippine sovereign bond spreads and credit default swap spreads widened as of the end of September, the latter to 283.1 basis.

(e) Remittance : A key concern for some countries (e.g. Philippines, Ethiopia)is the decline in remittances from workers in recession affected rich countries. Orders for Mbuzi Ya Jamii (goat for the family) are down sharply at online stores that allow Kenyans abroad to pay for products and services for their families back home.

(f) Foreign Aid : Many countries expect that aid from rich countries will decline as governments reassess their fiscal priorities during a downturn. This could have particularly negative consequences for Africa. Private foundations are already scaling down their budget allocations, while contributions from Kenya, Ghana and Ethiopia all believe that there will be a decline in official aid.

4. Responses to Financial Crisis

(i) Emergency and Short-term Responses : The US Federal Reserve and central banks around the world have taken steps to expand money supplies to avoid the risk of a deflationary spiral, in which lower wages and higher unemployment lead to a self-reinforcing decline in global consumption .in addition, governments have enacted large fiscal stimulus packages, by borrowing and spending to offset the reduction in private sector demand caused by the crisis. The US executed two stimulus packages, totaling nearly $1 trillion during 2008 and 2009.

This credit freeze brought the global financial system to the brink of collapse. The response of the US Federal Reserve, the European central bank, and other central banks was immediate and dramatic. During the last quarter of 2008, these central banks purchased us $2.5 trillion of government debt and troubled private assets from banks. This was the largest liquidity injection into the credit market, and the largest monetary policy action, in world history. The government of European nations and the USA also raised the capital of their national banking systems by $1.5 trillion, by purchasing newly issued preferred stock in their major banks.

Governments have also bailed out a variety of firms as discussed above, incurring large financial obligations. To date, various U.S. government agencies have committed or spent trillions of dollars in loans, asset purchases, guarantees and direct spending.

(ii) Regulatory Proposals and Long-term Responses: United States president Barak Obama and key advisers introduced a series of regulatory proposals in June 2009. The proposals address consumer protection, executive pay, bank financial cushions or capital requirements, expanded regulation of the shadow banking system and derivatives, and enhanced authority for the Federal Reserve to safely wind-down systemically important institutions, among others. In January 2010, Obama proposed additional regulations limiting the ability of banks to engage in proprietary trading.

5. Impact of India

The crisis is no longer confined to the developed world. The heat is being felt by the developing world, including India. The impact on India can be both direct and indirect. The direct impact comes from exposure to the 'toxic' or 'distressed' assets by Indian banks and other financial institutions. This is expected to be minimal. Indian banks, in general, have very little exposure to the asset markets of the developed world. Indian banks have very few branches abroad. The indirect impact will be through trade and capital flows. With the fall of international commodity prices such as crude oil, the import bill will come down sharply from earlier estimates.

On the other hand, export growth will be adversely affected by the recession in the developed world. It will have an impact both on merchandise exports and service exports. Taking exports and imports together, the current account deficit will moderate and may in the range of 2 per cent of GDP in the current year. The declaration in export growth may sharply affect some segments of the economy, which are export-oriented. Given the nature of the crisis, it is only to be expected that capital inflows in to the country will dry up. Foreign institutional investors (FII) have already disinvested and taken out close to $10 billion. This has had the most serious impact on the stock market.

Stock prices had fallen by 60 per cent during global financial crisis from the peak they had reached 10 months ago before financial crisis. Apart from the lose to stock holders, this will have the most serious impact on the primary market. Inability to raise fresh funds will affect investment and capital formation in the corporate sector. Conversion of positive flows on portfolio capital can also lead to a fall in the value of the rupee.

Disinvestment by FIIs will put additional pressure on dollar demand. The availability of dollars is affected by the difficulties faced by Indian firms in raising funds abroad. This, in turn, will put pressure on the domestic financial system for additional credit. Though the initial impact of the financial crisis has been limited to the stock market and the foreign exchange market, it is spreading to the rest of the financial system, and all of these are bound to affect the real sector. Some slowdown in real growth is inevitable.

The first priority should be to ensure that the financial system is liquid and is able to meet the legitimate credit needs of different segments of the economy. As external sources of funds dry up, the pressure on the domestic banking system will increase. The Reserve Bank of India's decisions to reduce CRR and Repo rates are in the right direction and taken on time. As the reserves come down, this will also suck out liquidity. It is, therefore, important for the RBI to keep a watch on liquidity and take such actions as reduction in CRR and Repo rates to enlarge the availability of liquidity.

The RBI's ability to keep other institutions such as mutual funds and non-banking finance companies (NBFC's) directly limited right now. It can only help them indirectly by reducing the pressure of the corporates on them for redemption through the enlargement of liquidity of the banking system. The pressure of the corporates will come down only if banks use the additional liquidity made available to them to them to provide the needed credit to corporate.

It has been argued that along with the measures to support the financial system, we must increase public spending. There can be no dispute with the contention that public spending should remain at a high level in a situation like the present one. With the supplementary grants approved recently by parliament, it is almost apparent that the fiscal deficit of the center in the current year may touch 4 per cent of GDP, at least 1 per cent above the fiscal responsibility and budget management (FRBM) target. While it can be argued that the fiscal deficit target should be an average over the cycle, we need to remember that even in boom years we have not been able to hold the deficit at the target level. The level of public spending currently envisaged is appropriate and should be adequate to meet the situation.

What is needed at present is to focus on the financial system and enable it to fulfill adequately its functions in terms of the provision of credit to productive sectors. The domestic credit system must also fill the gap created by the drying up of external sources. We ought to be thinking of a scheme to provide additional funds for long-term capital requirements, since the ability to raise funds from the capital market is bleak. There will be some tendency for the rupee to depreciate, which cannot be avoided. In relation to the exchange rate, the monetary authority should use the reserves to prevent extreme volatility in the market.

6. Indian Economy : Effects of the US Financial Crisis in India

It is often said that when the US sneezes the rest of the world catches a cold. This three-part series look at how India, China and Russia have been affected by the US financial crisis. Before we get in to detail about how much this US problem is spreading globally, we should understand the severity of it and the possible consequences in the US.

Some have compared the situation in the US with the Great Depression of 1929, but this situation is far from a depression-in fact it's not even a recession. In the Great Depression, there was no work and there was widespread poverty. People struggled through the winter with no heating and no food. We are not seeing such extensive suffering in the US.

In the US, August 2008 unemployment figures were at 6.1 per cent according to the US Bureau of Labour Statistics. In Great Depression, unemployment was higher than 25 per cent. The Commerce Department reported that GDP growth was at 2.8 per cent, hardly indicative of a recession, although this was revised down from the 3.3 per cent figure it projected.

Even before the controversial rescue plan was shot down, Indian markets took a dive. The stock market sank to an 18-month low and the rupee a 5-year low. The stock market dropped 5.3 per cent to 12,595.75 during the time of recession.

7. Measures taken by the Reserve Bank in Response to the Global Financial Market Developments

- CRR cut by 250 points to 6.5 per cent, effective fortnight beginning October 11, 2008.
- Repo rate cut by 100 basis points to 8.0 per cent
- As a temporary measure, banks permitted to avail of additional liquidity support under the LAF to the extent of up to 1 per cent of their NDTL.
- The mechanism of a Special Market Operations (SMO) for public sector oil marketing companies instituted in June-July 2008 taking in to account the extraordinary situation then prevailing in the money and forex markets will be instituted when oil bonds become available.
- Under the Agriculture Debt Waiver and Debt Relief Scheme, Government had agreed to provide to commercial banks, RRB's and co-operative credit institutions a sum of ₹ 25,000 crore as the first

installment. At the request of the Government, RBI agreed to provide the sum to the lending institutions immediately.

- Interest rates on FCNR (B) deposits and NRE(R)A deposits were increased by 100 basis points each to Libor/Euribor/Swap rates plus 25 basis points respectively.
- Banks allowed to borrow funds from their overseas branches and correspondent banks up to a limit of 50 per cent of their unimpaired Tier 1 capital as at the close of the previous quarter or USD 10 million, whichever is higher, as against the existing limit of 25 per cent.
- Special 14 days repo to be conducted every day up to a cumulative amount of ₹ 20,000 crore with a view to enabling banks to meet the liquidity requirements of Mutual Funds.
- Purely as a temporary measure, banks allowed to avail of additional liquidity support exclusively for the purpose of meeting liquidity requirements of Mutual Funds. To the extent of up to 0.5 per cent of their NDTL.
- Under the existing guidelines, banks and FIs are not permitted to grant loans against certificate of deposits (CDs). Furthermore; they are also not permitted to buy-back their own CDs before maturity. It was decided to relax these restrictions for a period of 15 days effective October 14, 2008, only in respect of CDs held by mutual funds.
- For fine-tuning the management of bank reserves on the last day of the maintenance period, a second LAF (SLAF) on reporting Fridays, was introduced with effect from August 1, 2008. It was decided to conduct the SLAF on a daily basis till further notice.

REFERENCES

1. Henry, Peter Blair (2007), "Capital Account Liberalization: Theory, Evidence, and Speculation", *Journal of Economic Literature*, Vol. XLV, December.
2. International Monetary Fund (2008a), "Global Financial Stability Report", October (2008b), *'World Economic Outlook',* October.
3. Mohan, Rakesh (2006), "Coping With Liquidity Management In India: A Practitioner's View, *Reserve Bank Of India Bulletin, April* (2007a). "Development of Financial Markets In India", *RBI Bulletin, June* (2007b),"India's Financial Sector Reforms : Fostering Growth While Containing Risk", *RBI Bulletin, December.*
4. Prasad Eswar. S, Raghuram. G, Rajan and Aravind Subramanian (2007),"Foreign Capital and Economic Growth", *Brookings Papers* on Economic Activity.
5. Reserve Bank Of India (2008), Annual Policy Statement for the Year 2008-09, April, World Bank (2008), *"Global Development Finance 2008",* June.

CHAPTER

13

Global Recession
Impact on Indian Financial Markets

*Dr. L. Rajani
**Prof. P. Mohan Reddy
***Dr. G. Vijaya Bharati

Introduction

Today the world is in a financial mess. Everyone is talking about financial crisis all over the world. But nothing lasts for long. Everyday we can't expect our economy to be in boom. The economy tends to move in various phases i.e. from expansion to peak and then peak to recession and along the way of 'Phase to recovery' and once again to peak. This is because of two human emotions. Greed during expansion as the cause and sufferance during recession as the result.

The term *financial crisis* is applied broadly to a variety of situations in which some financial institutions or assets suddenly lose a large part of their value. In the 19th and early 20th centuries, many financial crises were associated with banking panics and many recessions coincided with these panics. Other situations that are often called financial crises

* Academic Consultant, Dept. of Commerce, Y.V. University, Kadapa, Andhra Pradesh
** Professor, Dept. of Commerce, S.V. University, Tirupati, Andhra Pradesh
*** Assistant Professor, Dept. of Commerce, Y.V. University, Kadapa, Andhra Pradesh

include stock market crashes and the bursting of other financial bubbles, currency crises and sovereign defaults. The current financial crisis is the worst of its kind since the great depression of 1930s. It becomes prominently visible in September 2008 with the failure of several large US-based financial firms. The global financial meltdown has spelt disaster for the world economy in general and for the US and the European economies in particular. But surprisingly when world's developed economies are suffering, there the developing countries like India and China are still spending money in many projects.

The economic slowdown of the advanced countries which started around mid-2007, as a result of sub-prime crisis in USA, led to the spread of economic crisis across the globe. Many hegemonic financial institutions like Lehman Brothers or Washington Mutual or General Motors collapsed and several became bankrupt in this crisis. According to the current available assessment of the IMF, the global economy is projected to contract by 1.4 per cent in 2009. Even as recently as six months ago, there was a view that the fallout of the crisis will remain confined only to the financial sector of advanced economies and at the most there would be a shallow effect on emerging economies like India. These expectations, as it now turns out, have been belied. The contagion has traversed from the financial to the real sector; and it now looks like the recession will be deeper and the recovery longer than earlier anticipated. Many economists are now predicting that this *'Great Recession'* of 2008-09 will be the worst global recession since the 1930s.

Recession

A recession is a decline in a country's gross domestic product (GDP) growth for two or more consecutive quarters of a year. A recession is also preceded by several quarters of slowing down. An economy, which grows over a period of time, tends to slow down the growth as a part of the normal economic cycle. An economy typically expands for 6-10 years and tends to go into a recession for about six months to 2 years. A recession normally takes place when consumers lose confidence in the growth of the economy and spend less. This leads to a decreased demand for goods and services, which in turn leads to a decrease in production, lay-offs and a sharp rise in unemployment. Investors spend less, as they fear stocks values will fall and thus stock markets fall on negative sentiment. Risk aversion, deleveraging and frozen money markets and reduced investor interest adversely affect capital and financial flows, import-export and overall GDP of an economy. This is exactly what happened in US and as a result of contagion effect spread all over the world due to high integration in the global economy. India is facing the position of recession as globalization showing its negative scenario.

Impact of the Crisis of India

While the overall policy approach has been able to mitigate the potential impact of the turmoil on domestic financial markets and the economy, with the increasing integration of the Indian economy and its financial markets with rest of the world, there is recognition that the country does face some downside risks from these international developments.

In India, the adverse effects have so far been mainly in the equity markets because of reversal of portfolio equity flows, and the concomitant effects on the domestic forex market and liquidity conditions. The macro effects have so far been muted due to the overall strength of domestic demand, the healthy balance sheets of the Indian corporate sector, and the predominant domestic financing of investment. Total net capital flows fell from US$17.3 billion in April-June 2007 to US$13.2 billion in April-June 2008. Nonetheless, capital flows are expected to be more than sufficient to cover the current account deficit this year as well. While Foreign Direct Investment (FDI) inflows have continued to exhibit accelerated growth (US$ 16.7 billion during April-August 2008 as compared with US$ 8.5 billion in the corresponding period of 2007), portfolio investments by foreign institutional investors (FIIs) witnessed a net outflow of about US$ 6.4 billion in April- September 2008 as compared with a net inflow of US$ 15.5 billion in the corresponding period last year. Similarly, external commercial borrowings of the corporate sector declined from US$ 7.0 billion in April-June 2007 to US$ 1.6 billion in April-June 2008, partially in response to policy measures in the face of excess flows in 2007-08, but also due to the current turmoil in advanced economies. With the existence of a merchandise trade deficit of 7.7 per cent of GDP in 2007-08, and a current account deficit of 1.5 per cent, and change in perceptions with respect to capital flows, there has been significant pressure on the Indian exchange rate in recent months. Whereas the real exchange rate appreciated from an index of 104.9 (base 1993-94=100) (US$1 = ₹ 46.12) in September 2006 to 115.0 (US$ 1 = ₹ 40.34) in September 2007, it has now depreciated to a level of 101.5 (US $ 1 = ₹ 48.74) as on October 8, 2008. With the volatility in portfolio flows having been large during 2007 and 2008, the impact of global financial turmoil has been felt particularly in the equity market.

The BSE Sensex (1978-79=100) increased significantly from a level of 13,072 as at end-March 2007 to its peak of 20,873 on January 8, 2008 in the presence of heavy portfolio flows responding to the high growth performance of the Indian corporate sector. With portfolio flows reversing in 2008, partly because of the international market turmoil, the Sensex has now dropped to a level of 11,328 on October 8, 2008, in line with similar large declines in other major stock markets.

Reasons of Impact Crisis in India

- Indian financial sector particularly our banks have no direct exposure to tainted assets and its off-balance sheet activities have been limited. The credit derivatives market is in an embryonic stage and there are restrictions on investments by residents in such products issued abroad.

- India's growth process has been largely domestic demand driven and its reliance on foreign savings has remained around 1.5 per cent in recent period.
- India's comfortable foreign exchange reserves provide confidence in our ability to manage our balance of payments notwithstanding lower export demand and dampened capital flows.
- Headline inflation, as measured by the wholesale price index (WPI), has declined sharply. Consumer price inflation too has begun to moderate.
- Rural demand continues to be robust due to mandated agricultural lending and social safety-net programmes.
- India's merchandise exports are around 15 per cent of GDP, which is relatively modest.

Impact on the Indian Banking System

One of the key features of the current financial turmoil has been the lack of perceived contagion being felt by banking systems in EMEs, particularly in Asia. The Indian banking system also has not experienced any contagion, similar to its peers in the rest of Asia. A detailed study undertaken by the RBI in September 2007 on the impact of the subprime episode on the Indian banks had revealed that none of the Indian banks or the foreign banks, with whom the discussions had been held, had any direct exposure to the sub-prime markets in the USA or other markets. However, a few Indian banks had invested in the collateralised debt obligations (CDOs) / bonds which had a few underlying entities with sub-prime exposures. Thus, no direct impact on account of *direct exposure* to the sub-prime market was in evidence.

Out of 77 reporting banks, 14 reported exposures to Lehman Brothers and its related entities either in India or abroad. An analysis of the information reported by these banks revealed that majority of the exposures reported by the banks pertained to subsidiaries of Lehman Bros Holdings

Inc. which are not covered by the bankruptcy proceedings. Overall, these banks' exposure especially to Lehman Brothers Holding Inc. which has filed for bankruptcy is not significant and banks are reported to have made adequate provisions. In the aftermath of the turmoil caused by bankruptcy, the Reserve Bank has announced a series of measures to facilitate orderly operation of financial markets and to ensure financial stability which predominantly includes extension of additional liquidity support to banks.

I. Stock Market

The economy and the stock market are closely related. The stock markets reflect the buoyancy of the economy. Due to the impact of global economic recession, Indian stock market crashed from the high of 20000 to a low of around 8000 points. Corporate performance of most of the companies remained subdued, and the impact of moderation in demand was visible in the substantial deceleration during the current fiscal year. Corporate profitability also exhibited negative growth in the last three successive quarters of the year. Indian stock market has tumbled down mainly because of 'the substitution effect of:

- Drying up of overseas financing for Indian banks and Indian corporates;
- Constraints in raising funds in a bearish domestic capital market; and
- Decline in the internal accruals of the corporates.

Thus, the combined effect of the reversal of portfolio equity flows, the reduced availability of international capital both debt and equity and the perceived increase in the price of equity with lower equity valuations has led to the bearish influence on stock market.

II. Forex Market

In India, the current economic crisis was largely insulated by the reversal of foreign institutional investment (FII), external commercial borrowings (ECB) and trade credit. Its spillovers became visible in September-October 2008 with overseas investors pulling out a record US $ 13.3 billion and fall in the nominal value of the rupee from ₹ 40.36 per US $ in March 2008 to ₹ 51.23 per US $ in March 2009, reflecting at 21.2 per cent depreciation during the fiscal 2008-09. The annual average exchange rate during 2008-09 worked out to ₹ 45.99 per US dollar compared to ₹ 40.26 per US $ in 2007-08 which is the biggest annual loss for the rupee since 1991 crisis. Moreover, there is reduction in the capital account receipts in 2008-09 with total net capital flows falling from USD 17.3 billion in April-June 2007 to USD 13.2 billion in April-June 2008. Hence, sharp fluctuation in the overnight forex rates and the depreciation of the rupee reflects the combined impact of the global credit crunch and the deleveraging process underway in Indian forex market.

III. Money Market

The money market consists of credit market, debt market and government securities market. All these markets are in some or other way related to the soundness of banking system as they are regulated by the Reserve Bank of India. According to the Report submitted by the Committee for Financial Sector Assessment (CFSA), set up jointly by the Government and the RBI, our financial system is essentially sound and resilient, and that systemic stability is by and large robust and there are no significant vulnerabilities in the banking system. Yet, NPAs of banks may indeed rise due to slowdown as Reserve Bank has pointed out. But given the strength of the banks' balance sheets, that rise is not likely to pose any systemic risks, as it might in many advanced countries. Nevertheless, the call money rate went over 20 per cent immediately after the Lehman Brothers' collapse and banks' borrowing from the RBI under daily liquidity adjustment facility overshot ₹ 50,000 crore on several occasions during September-October 2008 under tight liquidity situation.

IV. Slowing GDP

In the past 5 years, the economy has grown at an average rate of 8-9 per cent. Services which contribute more than half of GDP have grown fastest along with manufacturing which has also done well. But this impressive run of GDP ended in the first quarter of 2008 and is gradually reduced. Even before the global confidence dived, the economy was slowing. According to the revised estimates released by the CSO (May 29, 2009) for the overall growth of GDP at factor cost at

	2003-04	2004-05	2005-06	2006-07	2007-08	2008-09
Agriculture, forestry and fishing	10.0	0	5.8	4.0	4.9	1.6
Mining & quarrying	3.1	8.2	4.9	8.8	3.3	3.6
Electricity, gas & water supply	6.6	8.7	9.1	11.8	8.2	2.4
Construction	4.8	7.9	5.1	5.3	5.3	3.4
Trade. hotels & restaurants	10.1	7.7	10.3	10.4	10.1	9.0
Transport, storage & Communication	15.3	15.6	14.9	16.3	15.5	9.0
Financing, insurance, real-estate & business services	5.6	8.7	11.4	13.8	11.7	7.8
Community, social and personal services	5.4	6.8	7.1	5.7	6.8	13.1
Total GDP at factor cost	8.5	7.5	9.5	9.7	9.0	6.7

Source: Central Statistical Orginisation

constant prices in 2008-09 was 6.7 per cent as against the 7 per cent projection in the midyear review of the Economy presented in the Parliament on December 23, 2008. The growth of GDP at factor cost (at constant 1999-2000 prices) at 6.7 per cent in 2008-09 nevertheless represents a deceleration from high growth of 9 per cent and 9.7 per cent in 2007-08 and 2006-07 respectively. (Table 13.1) The RBI annual policy statement 2009 presented on July 28, 2009 projects GDP growth at 6 per cent in 2009-10 in 2009-10.

The slowdown in growth of GDP is more clearly visible from the growth rates over successive quarters of 2008- 09. In the first two quarters of 2008-09, the growth in GDP was 7.8 and 7.7 respectively which fell to 5.8 per cent in the third and fourth quarters of 2008-09. The third quarter witnessed a sharp fall in the growth of manufacturing, construction, trade, hotels and restaurants. The last quarter was an added deterioration in manufacturing due to the deepening impact of the global crisis and a slowdown in domestic demand.

V. Strain on Balance of Payments

The overall balance of payments (BoP) situation remained resilient in 2008-09 despite signs of strain in the capital and current accounts, due to the global crisis. During the first three quarters of 2008-09 (April-December 2008), the current account deficit (CAD) was US $ 36.5 billion as against US $ 15.5 billion for the corresponding period in 2007-08.

VI. Reduction in Import-Export

During 2008-09, the growth in exports was robust till August 2008. However, in September 2008, export growth evinced a sharp dip and turned negative in October 2008 and remained negative till the end of the financial year. For the first time in seven years, exports have declined in absolute terms in October 2008.

VII. Reduction in Employment

Employment is worst affected during any financial crisis. So is true with the current global meltdown. This recession has adversely affected the service industry of India mainly the BPO, KPO, IT companies etc. Economic Survey of India gives alarming bell about the on-going effects of the global slowdown on employment and has pressed upon the government the urgency of the major response, especially in the unorganized sector.

VIII. Taxation

The economic slowdown has severely dented the Centre's tax collections with indirect taxes bearing the brunt. The tax-GDP ratio registered a steady increase from 8.97 per cent to 12.56 per cent between 2000-01 and 2007-08. But this trend has been reversed as the tax-GDP ratio has fallen to 10.95 per cent during current fiscal year mainly on account of reduction in Customs and Excise Tax due to effect of economic slowdown.

RESPONSE TO THE CRISIS

The future trajectory of the economic meltdown is not yet clear. However, the Government and the Reserve Bank responded to the challenge strongly and promptly to infuse liquidity and restore confidence in Indian financial markets. The Government introduced stimulus package while the Reserve Bank shifted its policy stance from monetary tightening in response to the elevated inflationary pressures in the first half of 2008-09 to monetary easing in response to easing inflationary pressures and moderation of growth engendered by the crisis. The fiscal and *monetary response to the crisis* has been discussed in the following points:

I. Fiscal Response

The Government launched three fiscal stimulus packages between December 2008 and February 2009. These stimulus packages came on top of an already announced expanded safety-net programme for the rural poor, the farm loan waiver package and payout following the Sixth Pay Commission report, all of which added to stimulating demand. The fiscal stimulus packages and other measures have led to sharp increase in the revenue and fiscal deficits which, in the face of slowing private investment, have cushioned the pace of economic activity.

In order to address these issues, the government has to effectively and carefully take up the following steps :

- Enhance coordination and harmonization of the regulatory apparatus internationally, given the global scope of the recent crises with increased cross border financial integration;
- Supervision and management of liquidity risk and greater transparency in the financial sector to improve better risk assessment by the customers and investors; Improvement in transparency in the structured credit instruments. The rise in macro-economic uncertainty and the financial dislocation of the year 2008 have raised a problem of adjustment in market interest rates in response to changes in policy rates gets reflected with some lag. The Union Budget for 2009-10, presented against the backdrop of persistent global economic slowdown and the associated dampened domestic demand, has placed the fiscal deficit at 6.8 per cent of GDP in 2009-10 with a view to providing the necessary boost to demand and thereby support a faster recovery.

II. Monetary Response

The RBI has taken several measures aimed at infusing rupee as well as foreign exchange liquidity and to maintain credit flow to productive sectors of the economy such as infusing liquidity through interest rate management, risk management and credit management which is described in detail under the following heads :

1. **Interest rate management :** In order to deal with the liquidity crunch and the virtual freezing of international credit, RBI took steps for monetary expansion which gave a cue to the banks to reduce their deposit and lending rates.
2. **Risk management :** There has been a sustained demand from various quarters for exercising regulatory forbearance in regard to extant prudential regulations applicable to the banking sector. As a part of counter-cyclical package, RBI has already made several changes to the current prudential norms for robust risk disclosures, transparency in *restructured products and standard assets* such as:
    - Implementation of Basel II w.e.f. March 2009 by all Scheduled Commercial Banks except RRBs which would promote closer cooperation, information sharing and coordination of policies among sector wise regulators, especially in the context of financial conglomerates.
    - Further guidance to strengthen disclosure requirements under Pillar 3 of Basel II.
    - Reduction in the provisioning requirement for all standard assets to 0.40 per cent;
3. **Credit management :** There was a noticeable decline in the credit demand during 2008-09 which is indicative of slowing economic activity—a major challenge for the banks to ensure healthy flow of credit to the productive sectors of the economy. In order to facilitate demand for credit in the economy the Reserve Bank has taken certain steps such as :
    - Opening a special repo window under the liquidity adjustment facility for banks for on-

lending to the non-banking financial companies, housing finance companies and mutual funds.

- Extending a special refinance facility, which banks can access without any collateral.
- Expanding the lendable resources available to the Small Industries Development Bank of India, the National Housing Bank and the Export-Import Bank of India.

Summary

The global financial recession which started off as a sub-prime crisis of USA has brought all nations including India into its fold. The GDP growth rate which was around nine per cent over the last four years has slowed since the last quarter of 2008 owing to deceleration in employment, export-import, tax-GDP ratio, reduction in capital inflows and significant outflows due to economic slowdown. The demand for bank credit is also slackening despite comfortable liquidity in the system. Higher input costs and dampened demand have dented corporate margins while the uncertainty surrounding the crisis has affected business confidence leading to the crash of Indian stock market and volatility in forex market. Indian financial markets are capable of withstanding the global shock, perhaps somewhat bruised but definitely not battered. India, with its strong internal drivers for growth, may escape the worst consequences of the global financial crisis. In other words, the fundamentals of our economy continue to be strong and robust. The global economic environment continues to remain uncertain, although the rate of contraction in economic activities and the extent of pressures on financial systems eased in the first quarter of 2009-10. Yet, it is not possible to clearly see the path of the crisis and its resolution over the coming months. In this sense, India is not unique as almost every country, whether or not directly affected, has to manage the current economic crisis under uncertainty.India has by-and-large been spared of global financial contagion due to the subprime turmoil for a variety of reasons.

India's growth process has been largely domestic demand driven and its reliance on foreign savings has remained around 1.5 per cent in recent period. It also has a very comfortable level of forex reserves. The credit derivatives market is in an embryonic stage; the originate-to-distribute model in India is not comparable to the ones prevailing in advanced markets; there are restrictions on investments by residents in such products issued abroad; and regulatory guidelines on securitisation do not permit immediate profit recognition. Financial stability in India has been achieved through perseverance of prudential policies which prevent institutions from excessive risk taking, and financial markets from becoming extremely volatile and turbulent.

REFERENCES

1. *Annual Report 2008-09*, Reserve Bank of India
2. Macro-economic and Monetary Developments, *First Quarter Review 2009-10,* Reserve Bank of India
3. Reserve Bank of India (2008), *Annual Policy Statement for the Year 2008-09,* April
4. World Bank (2008), *'Global Development Finance 2008'* June.
5. *Economic Survey,* Government of India
6. http://www.economics.harvard.edu/about/views
7. www.finmin.nic.in
8. www.rbi.org.in
9. Mohan, Rakesh (2006), *"Coping with Liquidity Management in India: A Practitioner's View",* Reserve Bank of India Bulletin, April.

CHAPTER

14

Global Financial Crisis and Its Impact on the Indian Real Estate Sector

*Dr. A. Amruth Prasad Reddy
**Dr. P.V. Varaprabhakar
***Prof. C. Sivarami Reddy

The Origins of the Global Financial Crisis

The crisis which began with the bursting of the housing bubble in the US and high incidence of defaults on sub-prime mortgages early last year has its origins in the loose monetary policy followed under former Chairman of the US Federal Reserve, Alan Greenspan. In a bid to counter the economic slowdown brought on by the dotcom bust of 2000, the US Fed steadfastly lowered interest rates to 1 per cent during the period till 2004 before raising it to 5.25 per cent in 2006. The combination of rising prosperity and low interest rates led to a sharp increase in demand for housing loans even as easy liquidity saw a run up in all asset values, including houses. This encouraged borrowers to assume expensive mortgages in the belief that they would be able to get refinance on more

* Assistant Professor, Dept. of Business Administration, Y.V. University, Kadapa-03, Andhra Pradesh

** Assistant Professor, Dept. of Business Administration, Y.V. University, Kadapa-03, Andhra Pradesh

*** Senior Professor, Dept. of Commerce, S.V.U. College of CM & IS, Tirupati-02, Andhra Pradesh

favourable terms. However, once interest rates began to rise and housing prices started to drop in many parts of the US in 2006-07, refinancing became more difficult. Defaults and foreclosures became commonplace once home prices stopped going up and then started falling.

What made matters worse was that banks and mortgage lenders that had securitised their loans by issuing mortgage-backed securities, based on underlying mortgage payments, suddenly found the value of these securities falling rapidly as defaults rose. Major banks and financial institutions, both in the US and in many other developed countries, that had borrowed and invested hugely in such securities lost heavily. Credit default swaps that were meant to act as insurance against the risk that borrowers will not pay back bank loans and make the financial system less risky (because they allow holders of securitised instruments to offset the risk of holding them) failed to provide the expected comfort. The fear now is that CDS issuers may not be able to fulfill their obligations in case of a default in which case there is a very real danger of the credit crisis worsening.

The first hint of trouble came from the collapse of two Bear Stearns Hedge funds early last. Subsequently a number of other banks and financial institutions also began to show signs of distress. However, matters really came to a head with the bankruptcy of Lehman Brothers, an iconic investment bank, in September 2008.

The US government's failure to rescue Lehman destroyed what little confidence there was among market participants. As inter-bank lending seized up and banks refused to lend each other, funds flow to the larger economy became constrained. Stock markets across the world plummeted on account of rising risk aversion and the resultant flight to safety. Faced with the fear of productive sectors of the economy being denied credit, central banks and governments around the world announced various economic stimulus packages to spur growth and instill confidence in financial markets. These moves have as yet had limited impact in ameliorating the distress.

Is this the 1929 Great Depression Revisited?

Many have compared the present crisis with the 1929 Great Depression and though there are undoubtedly similarities there are a number of differences as well that give us reason to hope the distress will not be on the scale witnessed in the 1930s. In both cases the epicenter is the USA and the proximate cause, indiscriminate borrowing and spending by US citizens, is also the same. The present credit crisis was caused by huge borrowing and spending on homes leading to inflated home values, while the crisis in 1929 was the outcome of increased spending (using borrowed money) on radios, cars and appliances. But there is a key difference. The present US economy is 20 per cent of the world economy; in 1929 it was only 3 per cent. The unemployment rate during 1929 was 5 per cent; it increased to 8.5 per cent in 1933 and further to 15 per cent in 1940. However, the unemployment rate in the US is presently only 6.1 per cent and though it is expected to increase following the failure of several banks and financial institutions, the government has been far more proactive this time round. Policy makers have acted fast to offset the downward momentum with a series of dramatic steps: nationalising banks, guaranteeing deposits, increasing money supply, slashing interest rates. The present Chairman of the US Federal Reserve Ben Bernanke, who has done extensive research on the Great Depression, has been at the forefront of formulating far more aggressive policy interventions together with the US Treasury Secretary, Hank Paulson. The US Fed rate is down to 1 per cent, the Bank of England cut its policy rate by an unprecedented 1.5 percentage points early November while the European Central Bank reduced interest rates by 50 basis points. Hence it is reasonable to expect that the US, and hence the world economy, will have a softer landing this time.

Financial Globalisation: The Indian Approach

The Indian economy is now a relatively open economy, despite the capital account not being fully open. The current account, as measured by the sum of current receipts and current payments, amounted to about 53 per cent of GDP in 2007-08, up from about 19 per cent of GDP in 1991. Similarly, on the capital account, the sum of gross capital inflows and outflows increased from 12 per cent of GDP in 1990-91 to around 64 per cent in 2007-08. With this degree of openness, developments in international markets are bound to affect the Indian economy and policy makers have to be vigilant in order to minimize the impact of adverse international developments on the domestic economy.

As the current global financial crisis has shown, liquidity risks can rise manifold during a crisis and can pose serious downside risks to macro-economic and financial stability. The Reserve Bank had already put in place steps to mitigate liquidity risks at the very short-end, risks at the systemic level and at the institution level as well. Some of the important measures by the Reserve Bank in this regard include:

First, restricting the overnight unsecured market for funds to banks and primary dealers (PD) as well as limits on the borrowing and lending operations of these entities in the overnight inter-bank call money market.

Second, large reliance by banks on borrowed funds can exacerbate vulnerability to external shocks. This has been brought out quite strikingly in the ongoing financial crisis in the global financial markets.

Third, asset liability management guidelines for dealing with overall asset-liability mismatches take into account both on and off balance sheet items.

Finally, guidelines on securitization of standard assets have laid down a detailed policy on provision of liquidity support to Special Purpose Vehicles (SPVs). In order to further strengthen capital requirements, the credit conversion factors, risk weights and provisioning requirements for specific off-balance sheet items including derivatives have been reviewed. Furthermore, in India, complex structures like synthetic securitisation have not been permitted so far. Introduction of such products, when found appropriate, would be guided by the risk management capabilities of the system.

Impact on the Indian Real Estate Sector

The crisis in the US financial market has affected Indian real estate sector adversely. It has made availability of funds scarce and, at the same time, pushed the interest rates high. So, while scarcity of funds will affect the supply side, high interest rate will dwindle the demand.

The sector is already reeling under tremendous pressure as the RBI has increased interest rates to contain inflation, besides restricting the fund flow to the sector . Consultants say that in the present circumstances the real estate prices would go for a sharp correction in the short to medium term. The financial crisis in the global market will affect the availability of funds for the domestic realty sector.

As RBI put constraints on Indian banks from financing real estate companies in the country, the sector was dependent on foreign funds, which used to flow in either through foreign direct investment (FDI) route or through investments from private equity. A senior consultant points out that following the development in US, many of the private equity funds are returning back to their mother countries. In fact, many of these private equity funds were launched by investment banks, which are presently facing an uncertain future. As the real estate prices almost crashed in the US and other developed markets, many of these banks' assets have shrunk to an extent that they can no longer meet their liabilities. This has forced regulators in US to ask these banks to replenish the capital or face bankruptcy. One of the largest US investment banks, Lehman Brothers, has already filed for bankruptcy. This has created a domino effect and other banks are also in for a rough ride.

One of the biggest bulls of Wall Street, Merrill Lynch, was also sold to Bank of America (BOA) to tide over the crisis. A number of other banks in US are placed in a similar situation. Most of the banks want to encash their investments, so that they can meet any shortfall in meeting their liabilities.

In these circumstances, a foreign banker had this to say: "Raising funds in the developed market to invest in Indian real estate sector would not be easy." The investors are also wary in investing in any instruments excepting secured ones like government securities and gold.

This has resulted in a fall in the interest rates on short-term papers to less than half a percent in the US market. At the same time, gold prices surged by over $90 per ounce on Wednesday, following which, on Thursday, gold price in Indian market surged by around ₹ 1100 per ten gram. But, these trends signal a tough time ahead. The availability of funds will be severely constrained in India, particularly in the real estate sector. A large player in the sector said that as the availability of funds from banking sector is restricted, they are forced to arrange money from foreign private equity funds. But now, as this route will also dry up, they will have to borrow from the high net-worth individuals, who lend at high interest rates—at around 20 per cent.

At the same time, the crisis in the global market will affect the demand for real estate. The development in US has affected the global economy, which has forced many of the global majors to either postpone or cut their expansion plans.

According to a source in the industry, global IT major Google has cut its expansion plan substantially in the NCR region. Earlier, the global major expressed its intent to take lease of 5 lakh sq feet of office space. But now, it is learnt, it has cut its requirement to only 300000 sq. feet.

Similarly, German major SAP, which had shown interest to start operations in Gurgaon in the NCR region, has now postponed the plan. A number of small and medium size companies, the source said, have followed the wait-and-watch policy as the global economy faces turmoil and an uncertain future.

This has affected the demand of the real estate space. Global consultancy firms now predict that with the cancellation and postponement of the expansion plan of companies, many of the regions like NCR, Bangalore and Pune will face a situation of oversupply in office space.

The rentals in these areas are projected to fall by 25-30 per cent over the next 12 months. The worsening condition in the demand for office space indicates the slowing down in the economic activities in the country. This will affect the demand for residential space also, which is already at a very low level since the interest rates rose.

A further dip in the demand for real estate will affect the sector very badly. This will starve them of fund. Fund flows from all the possible channels have now been seriously constricted. Funds from banks are already not available. Private equity source are also likely to dry up and demand from end users is also getting affected.

Conclusion

Unless the government comes to the rescue by lowering interest rates so as to boost demand from end users, the sector might face one of the worst crisis in recent times. This will not only affect the sector but could also affect the economic growth in the country, as a whole. Therefore, we must learn from this crisis is that we must be self-reliant. Though WTO propagates free trade, we must adopt safeguarding measures in certain sectors of the economy so that recession in any part of the globe does not affect India.

CHAPTER

15

The Impact of Recession on Indian Financial System and Indian Financial Markets

*M. Lakshmi Pathi Naidu

Introduction

The economic slowdown of the advanced countries which started around mid-2007, as a result of sub-prime crisis in USA, led to the spread of economic crisis across the globe. Many hegemonic financial institutions like Lehman Brothers or Washington Mutual or General Motors collapsed and several became bankrupt in this crisis. Even as recently as six months ago, there was a view that the fallout of the crisis will remain confined only to the financial sector of advanced economies and at the most there would be a shallow effect on emerging economies like India. These expectations, as it now turns out, have been belied. The contagion has traversed from the financial to the real sector; and it now looks like the recession will be deeper and the recovery longer than earlier anticipated. Many economists are now predicting that this *'Great Recession'* of 2008-09 will be the worst global recession since the 1930s.

* Research Scholar and Lecturer, Department of Management, MŞ Ramaiah College of Arts, Science and Commerce, Bangaluru, Karnataka.

The Indian financial system has not been affected in the same way the financial system abroad has been affected for reasons already explained. However, there is the impact of the drying up of liquidity because of the fall in reserves. The inability of Indian firms to raise funds abroad, including trade credit, puts pressure on the domestic banking system for more credit. Is is, in this context, one must view the actions of the Reserve Bank in expanding liquidity. Reduction of the CRR and repo and reverse repo rates are steps in the right direction. It is necessary for the RBI to watch the liquidity situation and take such actions as re necessary from time to time. It is being pointed out that the actions of the RBI have not percolated to the ground level. People point to the slow growth in credit. The role of the Reserve Bank of India is to create an environment in which additional credit can be made available. As far as India is concerned, we will see definite signs of recovery in the second half of 2009-10. fiscal year 2010-11 will see a distinct improvement in growth.

Meaning of Recession

A recession is a decline in a country's gross domestic product (GDP) growth for two or more consecutive quarters of a year. A recession is also preceded by several quarters of slowing down. An economy, which grows over a period of time, tends to slow down the growth as a part of the normal economic cycle.

At the initial stages of recession, where the interest rates were low and there existed a grater demand for houses, hence banks advanced housing loans to people with low credit worthiness with an assumption that housing prices would continue to rise. Later, the financial institutions restructured the debts into financial instruments called Collateralized Debt Obligations and sold them to investors world-wide. In this way the risk was passed on multifold through derivatives trade. Surplus inventory of houses and the subsequent rise in interest rates led to the decline of housing prices in the year

2006-07 which resulted in unaffordable mortgage payments and many people defaulted. The house prices crashed and the mortgage crisis affected many banks, mortgage companies and investment firms world-wide that had invested heavily in sub-prime mortgages. The financial crisis has not only affected United States of America, but also European Union, U.K and Asia.

Surplus inventory of houses and increase in interest rates led to a decline in housing prices in 2006-2007 resulting in an increased defaults and foreclosure activity that collapsed the housing market (Sengupta 2008). Consequently, a large number of properties were up for sale affecting mortgage companies, investment firms and government sponsored enterprises which had invested heavily in sub prime mortgages. Since the collateral debt instruments had been globally distributed, many banks and other financial institutions around the world were affected. Major Banks and other financial institutions around the world have reported losses of approximately US $ 435 billion as on 17th July, 2008 (Onaran 2008). Thus with the failure of a few leading institutions in United States, the entire financial system in the world has been affected.

The Indian Economy too has felt the impact of the crisis to some extent. Though it is difficult to quantify the impact of the crisis on Indian financial system and markets, it is felt that certain sectors of the economy were affected by the spillover effects of the financial crisis.

Methodology

The present study focuses on :

- The impact of the crisis on the Indian Financial system.
- The impact of the crisis on the Indian financial markets.

The data for the study has been collected from secondary sources.

Impact of Recession on Indian Financial System and Markets

Due to globalization, the Indian financial system cannot be insulated from the present financial crisis in the developed economies. The development in the U.S financial sector has affected not only America but also European Union, U.K and Asia. The Indian financial system and markets too has felt the impact of the crisis though not to the same extent but to a little extent. It is not possible to quantify the consequences of the recession on the Indian financial system and markets. However the impact has multi-fold effect.

1. *Information Technology:* With the global financial system getting trapped in the quicksand, there is uncertainty across the Indian Software industry. The U.S. banks have huge running relations with Indian Software Companies. A rough estimate suggests that at least a minimum of 30,000 Indian jobs could be impacted immediately in the wake of happenings in the U.S. financial system. Approximately 61 per cent of the Indian IT Sector revenues are from U.S financial corporations only. The top five Indian players account for 46 per cent of the IT industry revenues. The revenue contribution from U.S clients is approximately 58 per cent. About 30 per cent of the industry revenues are estimated to be from financial services (Atreya—2008). The software companies may face hard days ahead.

2. *Exchange Rate:* In India, the current economic crisis was largely insulated by the reversal of foreign institutional investment (FII), external commercial borrowings (ECB) and trade credit. Its spillovers became visible in September-October 2008 with overseas investors pulling out a record US $ 13.3 billion and fall in the nominal value of the rupee from ₹ 40.36 per US $ in March 2008 to ₹ 51.23 per US $ in March 2009, reflecting at 21.2 per cent depreciation during the fiscal 2008-09. The annual average exchange rate during 2008-09 worked out to ₹ 45.99 per US dollar compared to

₹ 40.26 per US $ in 2007-08 which is the biggest annual loss for the rupee since 1991 crisis.

Hence, sharp fluctuation in the overnight forex rates and the depreciation of the rupee reflects the combined impact of the global credit crunch and the deleveraging process underway in Indian forex market.

3. *Money Market:* The money market consists of credit market, debt market and government securities market. All these markets are in some or other way related to the soundness of banking system as they are regulated by the Reserve Bank of India. According to the Report submitted by the Committee for Financial Sector Assessment (CFSA), set up jointly by the Government and the RBI, our financial system is essentially sound and resilient, and that systemic stability is by and large robust and there are no significant vulnerabilities in the banking system. Yet, NPAs of banks may indeed rise due to slowdown as Reserve Bank has pointed out. Nevertheless, the call money rate went over 20 per cent immediately after the Lehman Brothers' collapse and banks' borrowing from the RBI under daily liquidity adjustment facility overshot ₹ 50,000 crore on several occasions during September-October 2008 under tight liquidity situation.

4. *Slowing GDP:* In the past 5 years, the economy has grown at an average rate of 8-9 per cent. Services which contribute more than half of GDP have grown fastest along with manufacturing which has also done well. But this impressive run of GDP ended in the first quarter of 2008 and is gradually reduced. Even before the global confidence dived, the economy was slowing. According to the revised estimates released by the CSO (May 29, 2009) for the overall growth of GDP at factor cost at constant prices in 2008-09 was 6.7 per cent as against the 7 per cent projection in the midyear review of the Economy presented in the Parliament on December 23, 2008. The growth of GDP at factor cost (at constant 1999-2000 prices) at 6.7 per cent in 2008-09 nevertheless represents a deceleration from high growth of 9 per cent and 9.7 per cent in 2007-08 and 2006-07 respectively.

Table 15.1 : Rate of Growth at Factor cost at 1999-2000 Prices (per cent)

	2003-04	2004-05	2005-06	2006-07	2007-08	2008-09
Agriculture, forestry and fishing	10.0	0	5.8	4.0	4.9	1.6
Mining & quarrying	3.1	8.2	4.9	8.8	3.3	3.6
Manufacturing	6.6	8.7	9.1	11.8	8.2	2.4
Electricity, gas & water supply	4.8	7.9	5.1	5.3	5.3	3.4
Construction	2.0	16.1	16.2	11.8	10.1	7.2
Trade, hotels & restaurants	10.1	7.7	10.3	10.4	10.1	9.0
Transport, storage & communication	15.3	15.6	14.9	16.3	15.5	9.0
Financing, insurance, real estate & business, services	5.6	8.7	11.4	13.8	11.7	7.8
Community, social & personal services	5.4	6.8	7.1	5.7	6.8	13.1
Total GDP at factor cost	**8.5**	**7.5**	**9.5**	**9.7**	**9.0**	**6.7**

Source: Central Statistical Organisation

5. Foreign Exchange Outflow: The most immediate effect of the crisis has been an outflow of foreign institutional investment (FII) from the equity market. There is a serious concern about the likely impact on the economy because of the heavy foreign exchange outflows in the wake of sustained selling by Foreign Institutional Investors in the stock markets and withdrawal of funds by others. The crisis resulted in net outflow of $ 10.1 billion from the equity and debt markets in India till 22nd Oct, 2008 (Kundu 2008). There is even the prospect of emergence of deficit in the balance of payments in the near future.

Table 15.2 : Rate of Growth at Factor Cost at 1999 – 2000 Prices (per cent)

	2007-08				2008-09			
	Q1	Q2	Q3	Q4	Q1	Q2	Q3	Q4
Agriculture, forestry and fishing	4.3	3.9	8.1	2.2	3.0	2.7	–0.8	2.7
Mining & quarrying	0.1	3.8	4.2	4.7	4.6	3.7	4.9	1.6
Manufacturing	10.0	8.2	8.6	6.3	5.5	5.1	0.9	–1.4
Electricity, gas & water supply	6.9	5.9	3.8	4.6	2.7	3.8	3.5	3.6
Construction	11.0	13.4	9.7	6.9	8.4	9.6	4.2	6.8
Trade, hotels, transport & communication	13.1	10.9	11.7	13.8	13.0	12.1	5.9	6.3
Finance, insurance, real estate & business services	12.6	12.4	11.9	10.3	6.9	6.4	8.3	9.5
Community, social & personal services	4.5	7.1	5.5	9.5	8.2	9.0	22.5	12.5
Total GDP	**9.2**	**9.0**	**9.3**	**8.6**	**7.8**	**7.7**	**5.8**	**5.8**

Source: Central Statistical Organisation

6. Investment: The tumbling economy in the U.S is going to dampen the investment flow. It is expected that the capital inflows into the country will dry up. Investments in mega projects, which are under implementation and in the pipeline, are bound to buy more time before injecting funds into infrastructure and other ventures. The buoyancy in the economy is absent in all the sectors. Investment in tourism, hospitality and healthcare has slowed down. Fresh investment flows into India is in doubt.

7. Real Estate: The realty sector is witnessing a sudden slump in demand because of the global economic slowdown. The recession has forced the real estate players to curtail their expansion plans. Many on-going real estate projects are suffering due to lack of capital, both from buyers and bankers.

Some realtors have already defaulted on delivery dates and commitments. The steel producers have decided to resort to production cuts following a decline in demand for the commodity.

*8. **Stock Market:*** The financial crisis affected the stock markets even in India. Foreign institutional investors pulled out close to $ 11 billion from India, dragging the capital market down with it (Lakshman 2008). Stock prices have fallen by 60 per cent. India's stock market index—Sensex touched above 21,000 mark in the month of January, 2008 and has plunged below 10,000 during October 2008 (Kundu 2008). The movement of Sensex shows a positive and significant relation with Foreign Institutional Investment flows into the market. This also has an effect on the Primary Market. Corporate performance of most of the companies remained subdued, and the impact of moderation in demand was visible in the substantial deceleration during the current fiscal year.

Corporate profitability also exhibited negative growth in the last three successive quarters of the year. Indian stock market has tumbled down mainly because of 'the substitution effect' of:

- Drying up of overseas financing for Indian banks and Indian corporates;
- Constraints in raising funds in a bearish domestic capital market; and
- Decline in the internal accruals of the corporates.

Thus, the combined effect of the reversal of portfolio equity flows, the reduced availability of international capital both debt and equity and the perceived increase in the price of equity with lower equity valuations has led to the bearish influence on stock market.

*9. **Exports:*** The recession have an impact on merchandise exports and service exports. The decline in export growth may sharply affect some segments of the Indian Economy. The slowdown in the world economy has affected the garment industry. The orders for factories which are dependent on exports, mainly to the U.S have come down following deferred buying by big apparel brands. Rising unemployment and reduced spending by the Americans have forced some of the leading brands in the U.S. to close down their outlets, which in turn has affected the apparel industry here in India. The global recession will undermine other major export sectors of the Indian economy like sea foods, gems and jewellery.

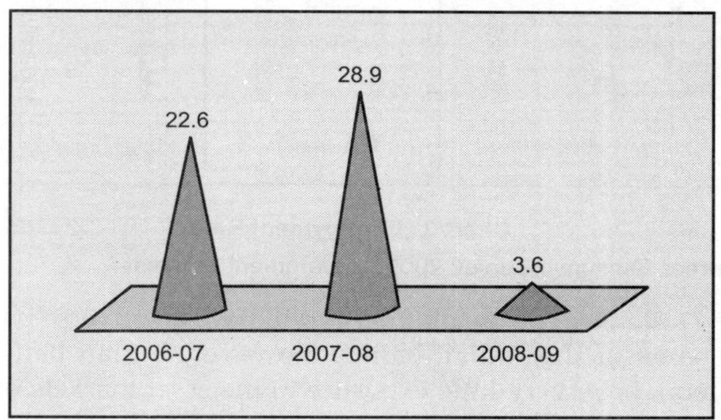

Chart-1 : Export Growth Year-wise

Source: Economic Survey 2009, Government of India

10. Reduction in Employment: Employment is worst affected during any financial crisis. This recession has adversely affected the service industry of India mainly the BPO, KPO, IT companies etc. According to a sample survey by the commerce ministry 109,513 people lost their jobs between August and October 2008, in export-related companies in several sectors, primarily textiles, leather, engineering, gems and jewelry, handicraft and food processing. Economic Survey of India gives alarming bell about the on-going effects of the global slowdown on employment and has pressed upon the government the urgency of the major response, especially in the unorganized sector. There would also be a significant drop in new hiring (*The Hindu,* 2008) All these will change the complexion of the job market.

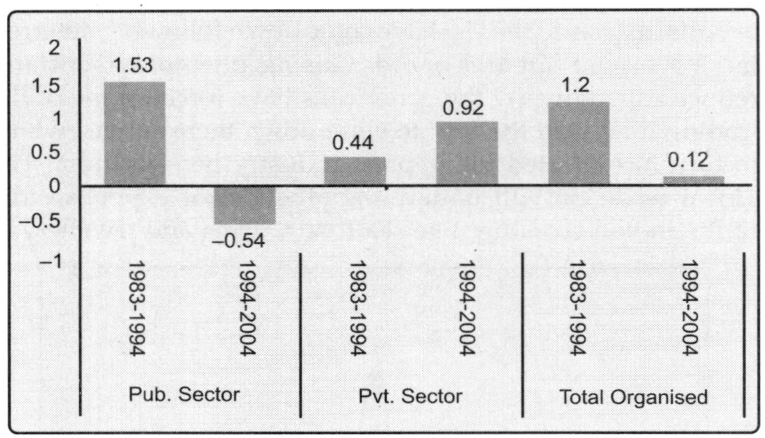

Chart-2 : Employment Rate

Source: Economic Survey 2009, Government of India

11. Banks: The ongoing crisis will have an adverse impact on some of the Indian banks. However, Indian banks in general, have very little exposure to the asset markets of the developed world. Effectively speaking, the Indian banks and financial institutions have not experienced the kind of losses and write-downs that banks and financial institutions in the Western world have faced. Indian banks have very few branches abroad. Our Indian banks are slightly better protected from the financial meltdown, largely because of the greater role of the nationalized banks even today and other controls on domestic finance. Strict regulation and conservative policies adopted by the Reserve Bank of India have ensured that banks in India are relatively insulated.

In India, the impact of the crisis has been deeper than what was estimated by our policy makers although it is less severe than in other emerging market economies. The extent of impact has been restricted due to several reasons such as:

- Indian financial sector particularly our banks have no direct exposure to tainted assets and its off-balance sheet activities have been limited. The credit derivatives market is in an embryonic stage and there are restrictions on investments by residents in such products issued abroad.

- India's growth process has been largely domestic demand driven and its reliance on foreign savings has remained around 1.5 per cent in recent period.
- India's comfortable foreign exchange reserves provide confidence in our ability to manage our balance of payments notwithstanding lower export demand and dampened capital flows.
- Headline inflation, as measured by the wholesale price index (WPI), has declined sharply. Consumer price inflation too has begun to moderate.
- Rural demand continues to be robust due to mandated agricultural lending and social safety-net programmes.
- India's merchandise exports are around 15 per cent of GDP, which is relatively modest.

Despite these mitigating factors, India too has to weather the negative impact of the crisis due to rising two-way trade in goods and services and financial integration with the rest of the world. Today, India is certainly more integrated into the world economy than ten years ago at the time of the Asian crisis as the ratio of total external transactions (gross current account flows plus gross capital flows) to GDP has increased from 46.8 per cent in 1997-98 to 117.4 per cent in 2007-08. Although Indian banks have very limited exposure to the US mortgage market, directly or through derivatives, and to the failed and stressed financial institutions yet Indian economy is experiencing the knock-on effects of the global crisis, through the monetary, financial and real channels – all of which are coming on top of the already expected cyclical moderation in growth.

Taxation

The economic slowdown has severely dented the Centre's tax collections within direct taxes bearing the brunt. The tax-GDP ratio registered a steady increase from 8.97 per cent to 12.56 per cent between 2000-01 and 2007-08. But this trend has been reversed as the tax-GDP ratio has fallen to 10.95 per cent during current fiscal year mainly on account of reduction in Customs and Excise Tax due to effect of economic slowdown.

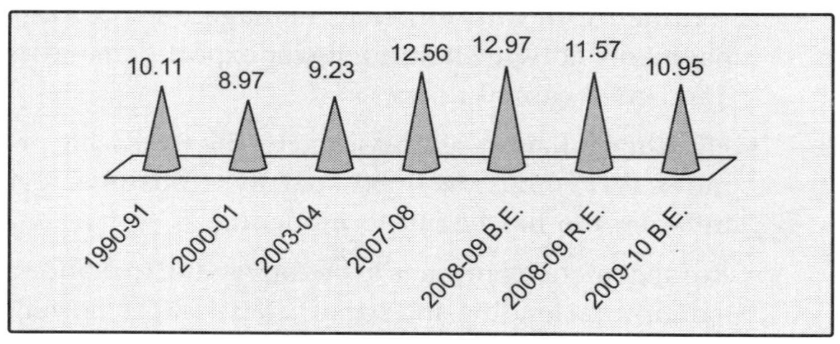

Chart-4 : Reduction in Tax-GDP Ratio

Source: Central Statistical Organisation

Response to the Crisis

The future trajectory of the economic meltdown is not yet clear. However, the Government and the Reserve Bank responded to the challenge strongly and promptly to infuse liquidity and restore confidence in Indian financial markets. The Government introduced stimulus package while the Reserve Bank shifted its policy stance from monetary tightening in response to the elevated inflationary pressures in the first half of 2008-09 to monetary easing in response to easing inflationary pressures and moderation of growth engendered by the crisis.

Results and Discussion

This chapter mainly concentrated on boom in the housing market, speculation, high-risk mortgage loans and lending practices, securitization practices, inaccurate credit ratings and poor regulation.

1. Boom in the Housing Market: Subprime borrowing was a major contributor to an increase in house ownership rates and the demand for housing. This demand helped fuel housing price increase and consumer spending. Some house owners used the increased property value experienced in housing bubble to re-finance their homes with lower interest rates and take second mortgages against the added value to use the funds for consumer spending. Increase in house purchases during the boom period eventually led to surplus inventory of houses, causing house prices to decline, beginning in the summer of 2006.

Easy credit, combined with the assumption that housing prices would continue to appreciate, had encouraged many subprime borrowers to obtain adjustable-rate mortgages which they could not afford after the initial incentive period. Once housing prices started depreciating moderately in many parts of the U.S., re-financing became more difficult. Some house owners were unable to re-finance their loans reset to higher interest rates and payment amounts. Excess supply of houses placed significant downward pressure on prices. As prices declined, more house owners were at risk of default and foreclosure.

2. Speculation: Speculation in real estate was a contributing factor. During 2006, 22 per cent of houses purchased (1.65 million units) were for investment purposes with an additional 14 per cent (1.07 million units) purchased as vacation homes. In other words, nearly 40 per cent of house purchases were not primary residences. Speculators left the market in 2006, which caused investment sales to fall much faster than the primary market.

3. High- Risk Mortgage Loans and Lending Practices: A variety of factors caused lenders to offer higher-risk loans to higher-risk borrowers. The risk premium required by lenders to offer a subprime loan declined. In addition to considering high-risk borrowers, lenders have offered increasingly high-risk loan options and incentives. These high-risk loans included 'No Income, No Job and No Assets loans.' It is criticized that mortgage underwriting practices including automated loan approvals were not subjected to appropriate review and documentation.

4. Securitization Practices: Securitization of housing loans for people with poor credit- not the loans themselves-is also a reason behind the current global credit crisis. Securitization is a structured finance process in which assets, receivables or financial instruments are acquired, pooled together as collateral for the third party investments (Investment Banks). Due to securitization, investor appetite for mortgage-backed securities (MBS), and the tendency of rating agencies to assign investment-grade ratings to MBS, loans with a high risk of default could be originated, packaged and the risk readily transferred to others.

5. Inaccurate Credit Ratings: Credit rating process was faulty. High ratings given by credit rating agencies encouraged the flow of investor funds into mortgage-backed securities helping finance the housing boom. Risk rating agencies were unable to give proper ratings to complex instruments (Gregorio 2008). Several products and financial institutions, including hedge funds, and rating agencies are largely if not completely unregulated.

6. Poor Regulation: The problem has occurred during an extremely accelerated process of financial innovation in market segments that were poorly or ambiguously regulated—mainly in the U.S. The fall of the financial institutions is a reflection of the lax internal controls and the ineffectiveness of regulatory oversight in the context of a large volume of non-transparent assets. It is indeed amazing that there were simply no checks and balances in the financial system to prevent such a crisis and 'not one of the so called pundits' in the field has sounded a word of caution. There are doubts whether the operations of derivatives markets have been as transparent as they should have been or if they have been manipulated.

7. ***Interest Rate Management:*** In order to deal with the liquidity crunch and the virtual freezing of international credit, RBI took steps for monetary expansion which gave a cue to the banks to reduce their deposit and lending rates. The major changes in the interest rate policy of RBI are given below:

- Reduction in the cash reserve ratio (CRR) by 400 basis points from 9.0 per cent in August 2008 to 5 per cent in January 2009;
- Reduction in the repo rate (rate at which RBI lends to the banks) by 425 basis points from 9.0 per cent as on October 19 to 4.75 per cent by July 2009 (the lowest in past 9 years) in order to improve the flow of credit to productive sectors at viable costs so as to sustain the growth momentum.
- In order to make parking of funds with RBI unattractive for banks, the reverse repo rate (RBI's borrowing rate) was reduced by 275 points which currently stands at 3.25 per cent.

Table 15.3 : Changes in Regulatory Rates during 2008-2009

Time Frame	Repo rate	Reverse Repo Rate	CRR
Prior to Oct. 2008	9.0	6.0	6.5
Oct. 20, 2008	8.0	6.0	6.5
Nov. 3, 2008	7.5	6.0	5.5
Dec. 6, 2008	6.5	5.0	5.5
Jan. 2, 2009	5.5	4.0	5.0
July 29, 2009	4.75	3.25	5.0

(**Source:** www.rbi.org.in)

The above said policy changes since mid-September 2008, enabled Reserve Bank of India to infuse ₹ 5,61,700 crore (excluding ₹ 40,000 crore under SLR reduction) in market in order to ensure ample liquidity in the banking system.

Future Outlook for India

To sum up we can say that the global financial recession which started off as a sub-prime crisis of USA has brought all nations including India into its fold. The GDP growth rate which was around nine per cent over the last four years has slowed since the last quarter of 2008 owing to deceleration in employment, export-import, tax-GDP ratio, reduction in capital inflows and significant outflows due to economic slowdown. The demand for bank credit is also slackening despite comfortable liquidity in the system. Higher input costs and dampened demand have dented corporate margins while the uncertainty surrounding the crisis has affected business confidence leading to the crash of Indian stock market and volatility in forex market. Nevertheless, a sound and resilient banking sector, well-functioning financial markets, robust liquidity management and payment and settlement infrastructure, buoyancy of foreign exchange reserves have helped Indian economy to remain largely immune from the contagious effect of global meltdown.

Indian financial markets are capable of withstanding the global shock, perhaps somewhat bruised but definitely not battered. India, with its strong internal drivers for growth, may escape the worst consequences of the global financial crisis. In other words, the fundamentals of our economy continue to be strong and robust. The global economic environment continues to remain uncertain, although the rate of contraction in economic activities and the extent of pressures on financial systems eased in the first quarter of 2009-10. Yet, it is not possible to clearly see the path of the crisis and its resolution over the coming months. In this sense, India is not unique as almost every country, whether or not directly affected, has to manage the current economic crisis under uncertainty.

Conclusion

While the developed world, including the U.S., the Euro Zone and Japan, have plunged into recession, the Indian Economy is being affected by the spill-over effects of the global financial crisis (Chidambaram 2008). Great savings habit among people, strong fundamentals, strong conservative and regulatory regime have saved Indian economy from going out of gear, though significant parts of the economy have slowed down and there is a wide variance of opinion about how long it will continue. It is expected that growth will be moderate in India. The most important lesson that we must learn from the crisis is that we must be self-reliant. Though World Trade Organization (WTO) propagates free trade, we must adopt protectionist measures in certain sectors of the economy so that recession in any part of the globe does not affect our country.

I would like to conclude this chapter in the words of Dr. Rakesh Mohan, former Deputy Governor of RBI, *"As the monetary and fiscal stimuli work their way through, and if calm and confidence are restored in the global markets, we can see economic turnaround later this year. Once calm and confidence are restored in the global markets, economic activity in India will recover sharply. Yet there will be a period of painful adjustment which is inevitable."*

Finally this to conclude the unprecedented economic crisis has definitely taken a toll of India's economic performance. Most likely it has also reduced our potential for economic development in the next 3 or 4 years. However, despite the severity of the global crisis, India's economy has demonstrated considerable resilience, in part, thanks to the strength of our agricultural sector.

REFERENCES

1. Nidhi Choudhari, *Global Recession and Its Impact on Indian Financial Markets*, August 2009, Volume 3, Issue 3/4.
2. www.vcircle.com (Retrieved December 2008)

3. *The Hindu*, *Daily*, October 27, 2008. p.12
4. http://www.macroscan.org (Retrieved October, 2008)
5. http:// www.bis.org (Retrieved October, 2008)
6. *The Hindu*, *Daily*, November, 2008, p. 14
7. http://www.observerindia.com (Retrieved December, 2008)
8. http://www.businessweek.com. (Retrieved October, 2008)
9. *Annual Report 2008-09,* Reserve Bank of India
10. Macroeconomic and Monetary Developments: *First Quarter Review 2009-10,* Reserve Bank of India
11. *Bank Quest,* Vol. 80, January-March 2009, IIBF
12. *Economic Survey,* Government of India
13. http://www.economics.harvard.edu/about/views
14. www.finmin.nic.in
15. www.rbi.org.in

CHAPTER

16

Impact of Global Recession on Indian Manufacturing Sector

*P. Nainar Reddy
**Dr. D. Raghunatha Reddy

Importance

Recession has been defined in the marketing literature as a "process of decreasing demand for raw materials, products and services, including labour" (by Shama, 1978).

Recession refers to a "state in which the demand for a product is less than its former level" (by Kotler 1973). A recession is a decline in a country's gross domestic product (GDP) growth for two or more consecutive quarters of a year. A recession normally takes place when consumers lose confidence in the growth of the economy and spend less. This leads to a decreased demand for goods and services, which in turn leads to a decrease in production, lay-offs and a sharp rise in unemployment. Investors spend less; as they fear stocks values will fall and thus stock markets fall on negative sentiment. *Risk aversion, de-leveraging* and *frozen money markets* and reduced investor interest adversely affect capital and

* Research Scholar, School of Management Studies, JNTUH, Hyderabad, Andhra Pradesh
** Professor, School of Management Studies, JNTUH, Hyderabad, Andhra Pradesh

financial flows, import-export and overall GDP of an economy. This is exactly what happened in US and as a result of contagion effect spread all over the world due to high integration in the global economy.

Many professionals and experts around the world believe that a true economic recession can only be confirmed if GDP (Gross Domestic Product) growth is negative for a period of two or more consecutive quarters. The International Monetary Fund (William A. Niskanen 1998.) takes many factors into account when defining a global recession, but it states that global economic growth of 3 per cent or less is equivalent to a global recession.

Recession is a phenomenon of decreasing demand for raw materials, products, and services. Technically, its beginning, progress, and ending depends on the operational measures used by different researchers and federal agencies. The worst ever financial crisis to have ravaged the United States since the Great Depression of 1930s, has taken a heavy toll on the world's largest economy. There is rise in the number of job layoffs and cost cutting. In fact, all the economies of the world are facing crisis to tackle this global meltdown. The meltdown has led to shock waves across the world, with economy after economy gasping for breath to survive this financial tsunami.

IMPACT OF GLOBAL RECESSION ON INDIAN MANUFACTURING SECTOR

India's manufacturing sector witnessed a decline between April 2007 and March 2008. While 21.73 per cent of all units in the manufacturing sector recorded over 20 per cent growth in 2006-07, the figure declined to 15.38 per cent in 2007-08, according to the Confederation of Indian Industry (CII)-Association of Council (ASCON) Survey.

The study says 30.77 per cent units in the sector recorded 10 to 20 percent growth in 2007-08 against 36.73 per cent in the previous year.

The manufacturing units that recorded over 20 per cent growth were in the categories of sponge iron, power cables, electric motors, power transformers, personal computer, groundnut oil, and transmission line towers.

The manufacturing units that witnessed a moderate growth of up to 10 per cent increased to 37.5 per cent during 2007-08 against 30.61 per cent, while 16.35 per cent recorded less than zero percent growth against 11.22 per cent in the previous financial year.

The categories recording negative growth included fertilizers, machine tools, tractors, the vehicle industry, including three-wheelers and motorcycles.

The survey says the segments like asbestos, cement, ball and roller bearings and vanaspati were all in the moderate growth category.

It is a cause of concern that there is a clear shift of sectors from excellent and high growth category to moderate and negative growth category.

Though growing very fast, the manufacturing sector's contribution to India's GDP is only around 17 per cent, against 25 to 35 per cent in some East Asian economies.

Since manufacturing has been recognized as the main engine of growth for the economy, the CII has prepared an action plan to increase its contribution to the GDP to 25 per cent.

The government's National Manufacturing Competitiveness Council (NMCC) has also prepared a national strategy for manufacturing to increase its share in the GDP.

India's manufacturing sector showed signs of revival and is in on the higher growth trajectory during April-September 2009. There is also a discernible shift in the growth trends from negative and moderate growth category to high and excellent growth category in respect of about 12 per cent of the sectors in April-September 2009 from April-March 2008-

2009. This improvement in manufacturing growth has been a result of the stimulus packages announced by the government.

Around 10 per cent of the manufacturing sector has registered excellent growth rates of more than 20 per cent in April- September 2009 compared to 7 per cent in April-September 2008. Notably, the share of the sectors registering moderate growth rate has significantly declined to 35.8 per cent in April-September 2009 from 42.6 per cent in the corresponding period of the year 2008. The share of the sectors recording negative and moderate growth rates have also declined to 64.21 per cent from 66.36 per cent in the previous corresponding period.

Comparing the first two quarters of the year i.e. April-June 2009 and July-September 2009, it is observed that there is pronounced improvement in the second quarter (i.e. July-Sept 2009). This has been reflected in the substantial decline in the share of the sectors recording negative growth rate from 40 per cent in the first quarter to 19.4 per cent in the second quarter. Moreover, the figures indicate greater tempo of growth for the high growth sectors whose share has increased to 35.5 per cent in the second quarter from 22.7 per cent in the first quarter.

Impact of Global Recession on Indian Car Industry

Indian car industry is one of the most promising car industries across the globe. The country is dealing with many car manufacturers, dealers, and associations in various different countries including U.S. From some countries, India imports cars and car components and to some India exports. With this, the global recession is obvious to have its impact on the Indian car industry.

Though India has witnessed a growing customer base, it has not inoculated them from the global crisis. The crippling liquidity and high interest rates have slowed down the vehicle demand. However, the fall down started in July with a decline of 1.9 per cent and thereafter the industry saw a major slowdown in October 2008.

Business Analysts reported that Indian car market had recorded a continuous growth of about 17.2 per cent over the last few years but in the year 2008, the recession has brought the growth to about 7-8 per cent. Be it Tata Motors or Maruti Suzuki or even Mercedes-Benz, the car market has gone down to a tremendously negative terrain.

Tata has reported that its profit fell from 34.1 per cent to 3.47 billion rupees because of the slower growth in the industrial production. Further, the company has also recorded a 20 per cent decline in the sales as compared to the sales in the year 2007.

Even Maruti Suzuki reported a 7 per cent decline in sales due to rising cost of the materials and a falling rupee value. Even Mahindra and Mahindra, the India's largest Small Utility Vehicles and tractor manufacturer, is not immunized, showing profit fall of 20.6 per cent.

SALES TREND (No. of Vehicles)

Category	2002-03	2003-04	2004-05	2005-06	2006-07	2007-08
Passenger Vehicles	707,198	902,096	1,061,572	1,143,076	1,379,979	1,547,985
Commercial Vehicles	190,682	260,114	318,430	351,041	467,765	486,817
Two Wheelers	4,812,126	5,364,249	6,209,765	7,052,391	7,872,334	7,248,589
Grand Total	**5,710,006**	**6,526,459**	**7,589,767**	**8,546,508**	**9,720,078**	**9,283,391**

PRODUCTION TREND (No. of Vehicles)

Category	2003-04	2004-05	2005-06	2006-07	2007-08
Passenger Vehicles	989,560	1,209,876	1,309,300	1,545,223	1,762,131
Commercial Vehicles	275,040	353,703	391,083	519,982	545,176
Two Wheelers	5,622,741	6,529,829	7,608,697	8,466,666	8,026,049
Grand Total	**6,887,341**	**8,093,408**	**9,309,080**	**10,531,871**	**10,333,356**

Impact of Global Recession on Indian Textile Industry

The textiles and garments industry is the second-largest employer in India after agriculture as it directly employs 35 million people and indirectly provides a livelihood to an additional 88 million.

Industry analysts predict that by the end of April 2009, approximately half a million direct workers from textile, garment and handicraft sectors will lose their jobs. Considering the other people who are indirectly associated with the textile industries, total direct and indirect job losses are expected to reach 6 million.

Two years ago, the Indian textiles industry was supposed to have been on the threshold of rapid growth. Today it is in urgent need for resuscitation. Even the figure of 1.2 million job losses put out by the association, the Confederation of Indian Textiles Industry (CITI), could prove to be an underestimate.

Roughly half the total production of textiles and garments in India is exported, 60 per cent of it to markets in the United States, Japan and the European Union. The recession in the West had adversely impacted these economies the most as a result of which exports from India are projected to fall sharply in the coming months.

Union commerce and industry minister estimated that in the financial year that ended in March 2008, approximately 800,000 garment and textile employees had lost their jobs, almost half of the two million lost in export-oriented industries.

A recent study conducted by the Economic Times newspaper of eleven major textile corporations in India found that while the total debt among the companies has quadrupled in the last six years, their ability to cover debt had not increased since 2003.

Although the index of industrial production IIP had soared by 8.1 per cent, in the last fiscal, big players in the textile sector has reported poor growth figures. Wool, silk and manmade fibre textile production grew mere 4.2 per cent, cotton textiles by 4.1 per cent and textile products including garments just 3.3 per cent.

According to the data provided by the Ministry of Textile, last year, spun yarn output mounted by 4 per cent and cloth production by 3.9 per cent. In the current fiscal, the growth is expected to plunge further.

IMPACT OF GLOBAL RECESSION ON INDIAN SERVICE SECTOR

The service sector, which contributes over 55 per cent to India's economy, has started showing a marked deterioration since October 2008 due to the global financial crisis, credit crunch and higher interest rates during recent months, according to a survey carried out by apex business chamber FICCI.

Segments adversely impacted by the global crisis include financial services, information technology and InfoTech-enabled services, aviation and real estate. The credit crunch and higher interest rates have impacted these areas, it said. While there was moderation in the growth of several segments of services during the first half of the current fiscal, a marked deterioration in performance was seen in many areas from October 2008 onwards, the survey said.

"Many segments in the services sector, particularly those impacted by foreign institutional investors have fared very badly," the survey points out. "The marked slowdown that occurred from October pulled down the cumulative growth rate for the period April- November 2008 compared with the cumulative growth in April-November, 2007. This trend clearly indicates that the services sector that registered a robust growth in the year 2007-08 is beginning to feel the impact of the ongoing economic turmoil and there are signs that in the month's ahead further slowdown cannot be ruled out," the survey observes.

Of 31 sectors covered under the FICCI survey, only three achieved excellent growth of more than 20 per cent during April-November this fiscal. As many as 12 sectors had been rated 'excellent' in the same period of the previous year. Nine sectors showed high growth of 10-20 per cent, compared to 14 last year. The number of areas registering moderate growth up to 10 per cent went up to 13 against mere four a year ago.

As many as six sectors showed negative growth. These were air passenger traffic, fixed line telephone subscribers, assets mobilization by mutual funds, asset under management of mutual funds and insurance premium. APART from fixed line subscribers, these segments had shown an impressive expansion ranging from 20 per cent to 64 per cent last year.

The dipping performance in the services sector comes close on the heels of the manufacturing sector registering a negative growth and this would result in slowdown in the overall economic growth rate. The government has already admitted that the expected rate of economic growth could not come down to seven per cent.

Impact of Global Recession on Indian Tourism

It is official now. For the first time in six years, the number of tourists coming to India has come down - thanks to the global meltdown. And there could be further bad news in the wake of the Mumbai terror attack. (IANS, Dec. 10).

According to official estimates, the number of overseas visitors to the country fell by 2.1 per cent in November 2008 compared to November 2007 - from 532,000 to 521,000.

'The arrivals have fallen for the first time in six years. This is the direct impact of the global meltdown more than the Mumbai terror attack,' a top ministry official told IANS.

About 5.37 million foreign tourists visited India in 2008. The first five months of 2009 showed a sharp decline in the number of foreign tourists arrivals, compared to the same period in 2008, but a slight increase was witnessed in June and July.

India has already started showing signs of early recovery from the impact of global economic meltdown and in December 2009 tourist arrivals grew substantially by 21 per cent registering a growth of over 8 per cent over the arrivals in December 2007 which was a year of high growth.

Impact of Global Recession on the Health of Service Sector Employees

Recession has melted down economies, companies and now employee's health. Over half of the service sector people are suffering from diseases, caused due to stress and overwork. The corporate sectors are taking several measures to cope up with the economic recession. Several companies have reduced the number of employees on board, whereas, several others took the route of cost-cutting, which has resulted into lack of the office-keeping facilities, etc.

The number of working hours has been raised in some companies to 10 hours a day. No increment or least amount of increment is being awarded to the employees. Few of the companies are asking employees to work for reduced salary. Even some sectors, where there is no major impact of recession, like in the knowledge process outsourcing industry, companies have already started exploiting employees by increasing office hours and raising per capita per day productivity target.

At the same time, the costly day-to-day consumption goods are draining money out of the employees at a faster pace. This state of employees along with stress of saving job, is leading to many diseases, such as depression, severe headache, obesity and hypertension. These diseases are afflicting employees sleep and resulting in sleep disorders leading to higher stress and reduced workplace productivity. This scenario is threatening a global adverse health impact among employees. Perhaps the meltdown is not just for economy but for employee's health as well.

MARKETING STRATEGIES TO BATTLE THE RECESSION

Following marketing strategies should be adopted to battle the recession:

1. Focus on core business;
2. Improve process and efficiency;
3. Look for strategic divestment;
4. Have contingency planning;
5. Check for acquisitions and strategic alliances;
6. Advertising and marketing;
7. Research and development;
8. Human factor;
9. Adjust product portfolios;
10. Support distributors;
11. Understand the influence of the economy;
12. Checking out competition;
13. Peg down your business model;
14. Plan marketing strategies;
15. Know your market and your client's needs;
16. Polish your image;
17. Think of your exit strategy.

Conclusion

In the globalize market scenario, the impact of recession at one place/industry/sector percolate down to all the linked industry and this can be truly interpreted from the current market situation which is faced by the world. Businesses are tightening their budgets and many of them are cutting their marketing budget. These times are tough and many companies are even laying off employees, but it is important to understand that cutting the marketing budget can often cause more harm to the growth of the business than one realizes. It is during tough times that one needs to alter the marketing strategy to survive to sell another day. The above mentioned marketing strategies can pay rich dividends - both during and after the recession.

Successful companies do not abandon their marketing strategies in a recession; they adapt them. Studies have shown that companies that continue to market during tough economic times often see growth during those times, where businesses that cut their marketing budget will often see a decrease in sales (Ruddar Datt, 2009).

India, the emerging economy, is affected by the negative influence of the US Subprime Market Crisis. Due this global recession all companies are worried about the future and existence of their business. Whether a global recession occurs or not, there several companies, whose businesses go under simply because of the speculation about a recession. It is incredibly sad but it is a fact and it was happened all throughout the history whenever the recessions have occurred.

We can hopefully conclude that we will get over this recession very soon and once again our global markets will begin to perform.

REFERENCES

1. John Bird, John Fortune, *Sub-Prime Crisis,* February 14, 2008
2. Shares, *Effect of the Global Meltdown on the Indian Economy,* February 1, 2009.
3. Ben Bernanke, U.S.Fed Chairman, *Official Forecasts in Parts of the World*, March 2009.
4. Jan Oberg, TFF Director, *G20 and C5-Connecting the Dots?* April 5, 2009.
5. Reasons for Global Recession: In Plain Simple English, the indian blogger.com,18 Oct, 2008 .
6. *McKinsey Report – Economic Conditions Snapshot,* April 2009.
7. Ruddar Datt, *Mainstream*, Vol XLVII, No 15, March 28, 2009.
8. HR has to Challenge the Challenges, *HRD News Letter,* January 2009 Vol. 24, Issue 10, p. 22.

CHAPTER

17

The Impact of Recession on Indian Financial System and Indian Financial Markets

*P. Subramanyam
**Prof. B. Ramachandra Reddy
***D. Balamuniswamy

Introduction

The economic slowdown of the advanced countries which started around mid-2007, as a result of sub-prime crisis in USA, led to the spread of economic crisis across the globe. Many hegemonic financial institutions like Lehman Brothers or Washington Mutual or General Motors collapsed and several became bankrupt in this crisis. Even as recently as six months ago, there was a view that the fallout of the crisis will remain confined only to the financial sector of advanced economies and at the most there would be a shallow effect on emerging economies like India. These expectations, as it now turns out, have been belied. The contagion has traversed from the financial to the real sector; and it now looks like the recession will be deeper and the recovery longer than earlier anticipated. Many economists are now predicting that this

* Research Scholar, Dept. of Commerce, S.V. University, Tirupati, Andhra Pradesh
** Professor, Dept. of Commerces, S.V. University, Tirupati, Andhra Pradesh
*** Research Scholar, Dept. of Economics, S.V. University, Tirupati, Andhra Pradesh

'Great Recession' of 2008-09 will be the worst global recession since the 1930s.

The Indian financial system has not been affected in the same way the financial system abroad has been affected for reasons already explained. However, there is the impact of the drying up of liquidity because of the fall in reserves. The inability of Indian firms to raise funds abroad, including trade credit, puts pressure on the domestic banking system for more credit. It is, in this context, one must view the actions of the Reserve Bank in expanding liquidity. Reduction of the CRR and repo and reverse repo rates are steps in the right direction. It is necessary for the RBI to watch the liquidity situation and take such actions are necessary from time to time. It is being pointed out that the actions of the RBI have not percolated to the ground level. People point to the slow growth in credit. The role of the Reserve Bank of India is to create an environment in which additional credit can be made available. As far as India is concerned, we will see definite signs of recovery in the second half of 2009-10. fiscal year 2010-11 will see a distinct improvement in growth.

Meaning of Recession

A recession is a decline in a country's gross domestic product (GDP) growth for two or more consecutive quarters of a year. A recession is also preceded by several quarters of slowing down. An economy, which grows over a period of time, tends to slow down the growth as a part of the normal economic cycle.

At the initial stages of recession, where the interest rates were low and there existed a grater demand for houses, hence banks advanced housing loans to people with low credit worthiness with an assumption that housing prices would continue to rise. Later, the financial institutions restructured the debts into financial instruments called Collateralized Debt Obligations and sold them to investors world-wide. In this way the risk was passed on multifold through derivatives trade. Surplus inventory of houses and the subsequent rise in interest rates led to the decline of housing prices in the year 2006-07 which resulted in unaffordable mortgage payments and many people defaulted. The house prices crashed and the mortgage crisis affected many banks, mortgage companies and investment firms world-wide that had invested heavily in sub-prime mortgages. The financial crisis has not only affected United States of America, but also European Union, U.K and Asia.

Surplus inventory of houses and increase in interest rates led to a decline in housing prices in 2006-2007 resulting in an increased defaults and foreclosure activity that collapsed the housing market (Sengupta 2008). Consequently, a large number of properties were up for sale affecting mortgage companies, investment firms and government sponsored enterprises which had invested heavily in sub prime mortgages. Since the collateral debt instruments had been globally distributed, many banks and other financial institutions around the world were affected. Major Banks and other financial institutions around the world have reported losses of approximately US $ 435 billion as on 17th July, 2008 (Onaran 2008). Thus with the failure of a few leading institutions in United States, the entire financial system in the world has been affected.

The Indian Economy too has felt the impact of the crisis to some extent. Though it is difficult to quantify the impact of the crisis on Indian financial system and markets, it is felt that certain sectors of the economy were affected by the spillover effects of the financial crisis.

Methodology

The present study focuses on :

- The impact of the crisis on the Indian Financial system;
- The impact of the crisis on the Indian financial markets.

The data for the study has been collected from secondary sources.

Impact of Recession on Indian Financial System and Markets

Due to globalization, the Indian financial system cannot be insulated from the present financial crisis in the developed economies. The development in the U.S. financial sector has affected not only America but also European Union, U.K. and Asia. The Indian financial system and markets too has felt the impact of the crisis though not to the same extent but to a little extent. It is not possible to quantify the consequences of the recession on the Indian financial system and markets. However the impact has multi-fold effect.

1. Information Technology: With the global financial system getting trapped in the quicksand, there is uncertainty across the Indian Software industry. The U.S. banks have huge running relations with Indian Software Companies. A rough estimate suggests that at least a minimum of 30,000 Indian jobs could be impacted immediately in the wake of happenings in the U.S. financial system. Approximately 61 per cent of the Indian IT Sector revenues are from U.S. financial corporations only. The top five Indian players account for 46 per cent of the IT industry revenues. The revenue contribution from U.S. clients is approximately 58 per cent. About 30 per cent of the industry revenues are estimated to be from financial services (Atreya—2008). The software companies may face hard days ahead.

2. Exchange Rate: In India, the current economic crisis was largely insulated by the reversal of foreign institutional investment (FII), external commercial borrowings (ECB) and trade credit. Its spillovers became visible in September-October 2008 with overseas investors pulling out a record US $ 13.3 billion and fall in the nominal value of the rupee from ₹ 40.36 per US $ in March 2008 to ₹ 51.23 per US $ in March 2009, reflecting at 21.2 per cent depreciation during the fiscal year 2008-09. The annual average exchange rate during 2008-09 worked out to ₹ 45.99 per US dollar compared to ₹ 40.26 per US $ in 2007-08 which is the biggest annual loss for the rupee since 1991 crisis.

Hence, sharp fluctuation in the overnight forex rates and the depreciation of the rupee reflects the combined impact of the global credit crunch and the deleveraging process underway in Indian forex market.

3. Money Market: The money market consists of credit market, debt market and government securities market. All these markets are in some or other way related to the soundness of banking system as they are regulated by the Reserve Bank of India. According to the Report submitted by the Committee for Financial Sector Assessment (CFSA), set up jointly by the Government and the RBI, our financial system is essentially sound and resilient, and that systemic stability is by and large robust and there are no significant vulnerabilities in the banking system. Yet, NPAs of banks may indeed rise due to slowdown as Reserve Bank has pointed out. Nevertheless, the call money rate went over 20 per cent immediately after the Lehman Brothers' collapse and banks' borrowing from the RBI under daily liquidity adjustment facility overshot ₹ 50,000 crore on several occasions during September-October 2008 under tight liquidity situation.

4. Slowing GDP: In the past 5 years, the economy has grown at an average rate of 8-9 per cent. Services which contribute more than half of GDP have grown fastest along with manufacturing which has also done well. But this impressive run of GDP ended in the first quarter of 2008 and is gradually reduced. Even before the global confidence dived, the economy was slowing.

According to the revised estimates released by the CSO (May 29, 2009) for the overall growth of GDP at factor cost at constant prices in 2008-09 was 6.7 per cent as against the 7 per cent projection in the mid-year review of the Economy presented in the Parliament on December 23, 2008. The growth of GDP at factor cost (at constant 1999-2000 prices) at 6.7 per cent in 2008-09 nevertheless represents a deceleration from high growth of 9 per cent and 9.7 per cent in 2007-08 and 2006-07 respectively.

Table 17.1 : Rate of Growth at Factor cost at 1999-2000 Prices (percent)

	2003-04	2004-05	2005-06	2006-07	2007-08	2008-09
Agriculture, Forestry and fishing	10.0	0	5.8	4.0	7.9	1.6
Mining & quarrying	3.1	8.2	4.9	8.8	3.3	3.6
Manufacturing	6.6	8.7	9.1	11.8	8.2	2.4
Electricity gas & water supply	4.8	7.9	5.1	5.3	5.3	3.4
Construction	12.0	16.1	16.2	11.8	10.1	7.2
Trade, hotels & restaurants	10.1	7.7	10.3	10.4	10.1	9.0
Transport, storage & communication	15.3	15.6	14.9	16.3	15.5	9.0
Financing, insurance, real estate & business services	5.6	8.7	11.4	13.8	11.7	7.8
Community, social & personal services	5.4	6.8	7.1	5.7	6.8	13.1
Total GDP at factor cost	8.5	7.5	9.5	9.7	9.0	6.7

Source : Central Statistical Organisation

5. Foreign Exchange Outflow: The most immediate effect of the crisis has been an outflow of foreign institutional investment (FII) from the equity market. There is a serious concern about the likely impact on the economy because of the heavy foreign exchange outflows in the wake of sustained selling by Foreign Institutional Investors in the stock markets and withdrawal of funds by others. The crisis resulted in net outflow of $ 10.lbillion from the equity and debt markets in India till 22nd Oct, 2008 (Kundu 2008). There is even the prospect of emergence of deficit in the balance of payments in the near future.

Table 17.2 : Rate of Growth at Factor Cost at 1999 – 2000 Prices (per cent)

	2007-08				2008-09			
	Q1	Q2	Q3	Q4	Q1	Q2	Q3	Q4
Agriculture, Forestry and fishing	4.3	3.9	8.1	2.2	3.0	2.7	-0.8	2.7
Mining & quarrying	0.1	3.8	4.2	4.7	4.6	3.7	4.9	1.6
Manufacturing	10.0	8.2	8.6	6.3	5.5	5.1	0.9	-1.4
Electricity gas & water supply	6.9	5.9	3.8	4.6	2.7	3.8	3.5	3.6
Construction	11.0	13.4	9.7	6.9	8.4	9.6	4.2	6.8
Trade, hotels, transport & communication	13.1	10.9	11.7	13.8	13.0	12.1	5.9	6.3
Financing, insurance, real estate & business services	12.6	12.4	11.9	10.3	6.9	6.4	8.3	9.5
Community, social & personal services	4.5	7.1	5.5	9.5	8.2	9.0	22.5	12.5
Total GDP at factor cost	9.2	9.1	9.3	8.6	7.8	7.7	5.8	5.8

Source : Central Statistical Organisation

6. Investment: The tumbling economy in the U.S is going to dampen the investment flow. It is expected that the capital inflows into the country will dry up. Investments in mega projects, which are under implementation and in the pipeline, are bound to buy more time before injecting funds into infrastructure and other ventures. The buoyancy in the economy is absent in all the sectors. Investment in tourism, hospitality and healthcare has slowed down. Fresh investment flows into India is in doubt.

7. Real Estate: The realty sector is witnessing a sudden slump in demand because of the global economic slowdown. The recession has forced the real estate players to curtail their expansion plans. Many on-going real estate projects are suffering due to lack of capital, both from buyers and bankers. Some realtors have already defaulted on delivery dates and commitments. The steel producers have decided to resort to production cuts following a decline in demand for the commodity.

8. Stock Market: The financial crisis affected the stock markets even in India. Foreign institutional investors pulled out close to $ 11 billion from India, dragging the capital market down with it (Lakshman 2008). Stock prices have fallen by 60 per cent. India's stock market index—Sensex touched above 21,000 mark in the month of January, 2008 and has plunged below 10,000 during October 2008 (Kundu 2008). The movement of Sensex shows a positive and significant relation with Foreign Institutional Investment flows into the market. This also has an effect on the Primary Market. Corporate performance of most of the companies remained subdued, and the impact of moderation in demand was visible in the substantial deceleration during the current fiscal year.

Corporate profitability also exhibited negative growth in the last three successive quarters of the year. Indian stock market has tumbled down mainly because of 'the substitution effect' of:

- Drying up of overseas financing for Indian banks and Indian corporates;
- Constraints in raising funds in a bearish domestic capital market; and
- Decline in the internal accruals of the corporates.

Thus, the combined effect of the reversal of portfolio equity flows, the reduced availability of international capital both debt and equity and the perceived increase in the price of equity with lower equity valuations has led to the bearish influence on stock market.

9. Exports: The recession have an impact on merchandise exports and service exports. The decline in export growth may sharply affect some segments of the Indian Economy. The slowdown in the world economy has affected the garment industry. The orders for factories which are dependent on exports, mainly to the U.S have come down following deferred buying by big apparel brands. Rising unemployment and reduced spending by the Americans have forced some of the leading brands in the U.S to close down their outlets, which in turn has affected the apparel industry here in India. The global recession will undermine other major export sectors of the Indian economy like sea foods, gems and jewellery.

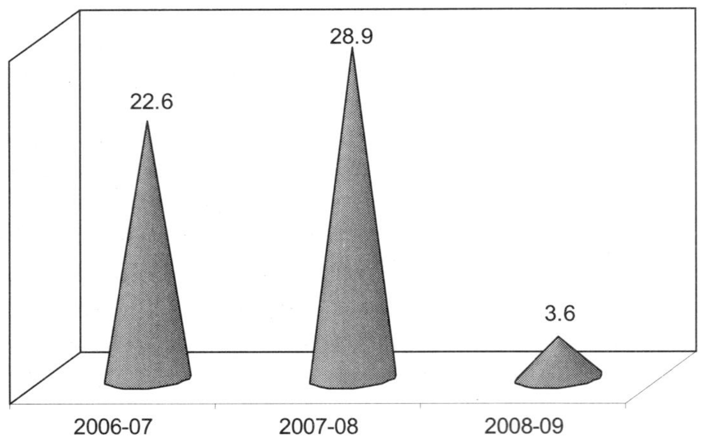

Chart—I : Export Growth Year-wise

(**Source** : Economic Survey 2009, Government of India)

10. Reduction in Employment: Employment is worst affected during any financial crisis. This recession has adversely affected the service industry of India mainly the BPO, KPO, IT companies etc. According to a sample survey by the commerce ministry 109,513 people lost their jobs between August and October 2008, in export related companies in several sectors, primarily textiles, leather, engineering, gems and jewellery, handicraft and food processing. Economic Survey of India gives alarming bell about the on-going effects of the global slowdown on employment and has pressed upon the government the urgency of the major response, especially in the unorganized sector. There would also be a significant drop in new hiring (*The Hindu*, 2008) All these will change the complexion of the job market.

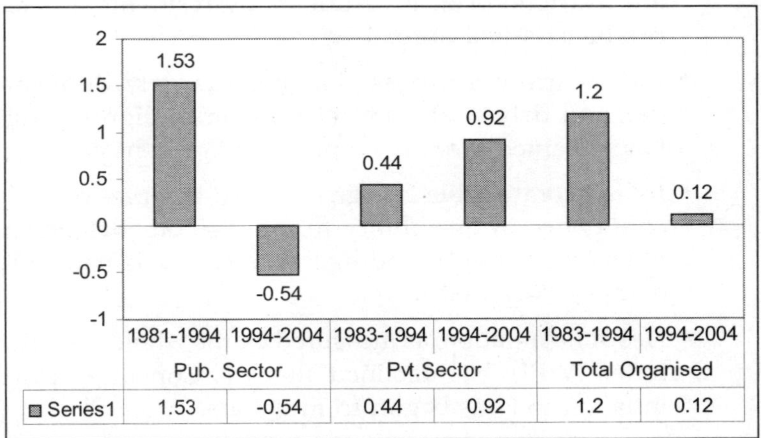

(**Source:** Economic Survey 2009, Government of India)

11. Banks: The ongoing crisis will have an adverse impact on some of the Indian banks. However, Indian banks in general, have very little exposure to the asset markets of the developed world. Effectively speaking, the Indian banks and financial institutions have not experienced the kind of losses and write-downs that banks and financial institutions in the Western world have faced. Indian banks have very few branches abroad. Our Indian banks are slightly better protected from the financial meltdown, largely because of the greater role of the nationalized banks even today and other controls on domestic finance. Strict regulation and conservative policies adopted by the Reserve Bank of India have ensured that banks in India are relatively insulated.

In India, the impact of the crisis has been deeper than what was estimated by our policy makers although it is less severe than in other emerging market economies. The extent of impact has been restricted due to several reasons such as:

- Indian financial sector particularly our banks have no direct exposure to tainted assets and its off-balance sheet activities have been limited. The credit derivatives market is in an embryonic stage and there are restrictions on investments by residents in such products issued abroad.
- India's growth process has been largely domestic demand driven and its reliance on foreign savings has remained around 1.5 per cent in recent period.
- India's comfortable foreign exchange reserves provide confidence in our ability to manage our balance of payments notwithstanding lower export demand and dampened capital flows.
- Headline inflation, as measured by the wholesale price index (WPI), has declined sharply. Consumer price inflation too has begun to moderate.
- Rural demand continues to be robust due to mandated agricultural lending and social safety-net programmes.
- India's merchandise exports are around 15 per cent of GDP, which is relatively modest.

Despite these mitigating factors, India too has to weather the negative impact of the crisis due to rising two-way trade in goods and services and financial integration with the rest of the world. Today, India is certainly more integrated into the world economy than ten years ago at the time of the Asian crisis as the ratio of total external transactions (gross current account flows plus gross capital flows) to GDP has increased from 46.8 per cent in 1997-98 to 117.4 per cent in 2007-08. Although Indian banks have very limited exposure to the US mortgage market, directly or through derivatives, and to the failed and stressed financial institutions yet Indian economy is experiencing the knock on effects of the global crisis, through the monetary, financial and real channels—all of which are coming on top of the already expected cyclical moderation in growth.

12. Taxation : The economic slowdown has severely dented the Centre's tax collections within direct taxes bearing the brunt. The tax-GDP ratio registered a steady increase from 8.97 per cent to 12.56 per cent between 2000-01 and 2007-08. But this trend has been reversed as the tax-GDP ratio has fallen to 10.95 per cent during current fiscal year mainly on account of reduction in Customs and Excise Tax due to effect of economic slowdown.

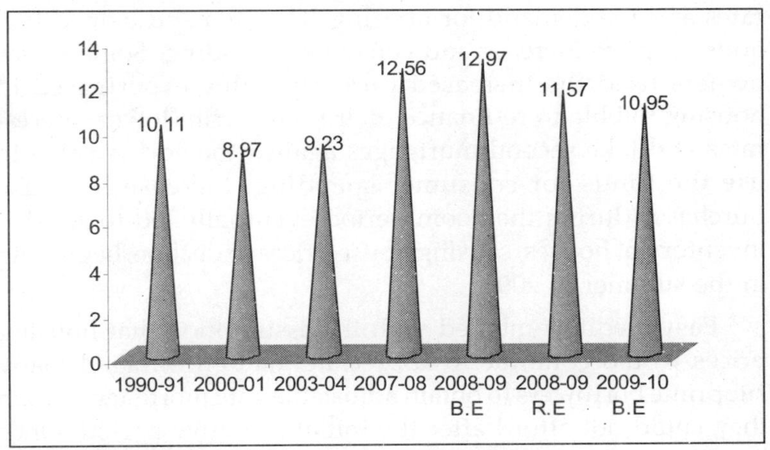

Chart—4 : Reduction in Tax-GDP Ratio
(**Source:** Central Statistical Organisation)

Response to the Crisis

The future trajectory of the economic meltdown is not yet clear. However, the Government and the Reserve Bank responded to the challenge strongly and promptly to infuse liquidity and restore confidence in Indian financial markets. The Government introduced stimulus package while the Reserve Bank shifted its policy stance from monetary tightening in response to the elevated inflationary pressures in the first half of 2008-09 to monetary easing in response to easing inflationary pressures and moderation of growth engendered by the crisis.

Results and Discussion

This chapter mainly concentrated on boom in the housing market, speculation, high-risk mortgage loans and lending practices, securitization practices, inaccurate credit ratings and poor regulation.

1. Boom in the Housing Market: Subprime borrowing was a major contributor to an increase in house ownership rates and the demand for housing. This demand helped fuel housing price increase and consumer spending. Some house owners used the increased property value experienced in housing bubble to re-finance their homes with lower interest rates and take second mortgages against the added value to use the funds for consumer spending. Increase in house purchases during the boom period eventually led to surplus inventory of houses, causing house prices to decline, beginning in the summer of 2006.

Easy credit, combined with the assumption that housing prices would continue to appreciate, had encouraged many subprime borrowers to obtain adjustable-rate mortgages which they could not afford after the initial incentive period. Once housing prices started depreciating moderately in many parts of the U.S, re-financing became more difficult. Some house owners were unable to re-finance their loans reset to higher interest rates and payment amounts. Excess supply of houses placed significant downward pressure on prices. As prices declined, more house owners were at risk of default and foreclosure.

2. Speculation: Speculation in real estate was a contributing factor. During 2006, 22 per cent of houses purchased (1.65 million units) were for investment purposes with an additional 14 per cent (1.07 million units) purchased as vacation homes. In other words, nearly 40 per cent of house purchases were not primary residences. Speculators left the market in 2006, which caused investment sales to fall much faster than the primary market.

3. High- Risk Mortgage : Loans and Lending Practices: A variety of factors caused lenders to offer higher-risk loans to higher-risk borrowers. The risk premium required by lenders to offer a subprime loan declined. In addition to considering high-risk borrowers, lenders have offered increasingly high-risk loan options and incentives. These high-risk loans included 'No Income, No Job and No Assets loans.' It is criticized that mortgage underwriting practices including automated loan approvals were not subjected to appropriate review and documentation.

4. Securitization Practices: Securitization of housing loans for people with poor credit—not the loans themselves—is also a reason behind the current global credit crisis. Securitization is a structured finance process in which assets, receivables or financial instruments are acquired, pooled together as collateral for the third party investments (Investment Banks). Due to securitization, investor appetite for mortgage-backed securities (MBS), and the tendency of rating agencies to assign investment-grade, ratings to MBS, loans with a high risk of default could be originated, packaged and the risk readily transferred to others.

5. Inaccurate Credit Ratings: Credit rating process was faulty. High ratings given by credit rating agencies encouraged the flow of investor funds into mortgage-backed securities helping finance the housing boom. Risk rating agencies were unable to give proper ratings to complex instruments (Gregorio 2008). Several products and financial institutions, including hedge funds, and rating agencies are largely if not completely unregulated.

6. Poor Regulation: The problem has occurred during an extremely accelerated process of financial innovation in market segments that were poorly or ambiguously regulated—mainly in the U.S. The fall of the financial institutions is a reflection of the lax internal controls and the ineffectiveness of regulatory oversight in the context of a large volume of non-transparent assets. It is indeed amazing that there were simply no checks and balances in the financial system to prevent such a crisis and 'not one of the so called pundits' in the field has sounded a word of caution. There are doubts whether the operations of derivatives markets have been as transparent as they should have been or if they have been manipulated.

7. Interest Rate Management: In order to deal with the liquidity crunch and the virtual freezing of international credit, RBI took steps for monetary expansion which gave a cue to the banks to reduce their deposit and lending rates. The major changes in the interest rate policy of RBI are given below:

- Reduction in the cash reserve ratio (CRR) by 400 basis points from 9.0 per cent in August 2008 to 5 per cent in January 2009.
- Reduction in the repo rate (rate at which RBI lends to the banks) by 425 basis points from 9.0 per cent as on October 19 to 4.75 per cent by July 2009 (the lowest in past 9 years) in order to improve the flow of credit to productivesectors at viable costs so as to sustain the growth momentum.
- In order to make parking of funds with RBI unattractive for banks, the reverse repo rate (RBI's borrowing rate) was reduced by 275 points which currently stands at 3.25 per cent.

Table 17.3 : Changes in Regulatory Rates during 2008-2009

Time Frame	Repo rate	Reverse Repo Rate	CRR
Prior to Oct. 2008	9.0	6.0	6.5
Oct. 20, 2008	8.0	6.0	6.5
Nov. 3, 2008	7.5	6.0	5.5
Dec. 6, 2008	6.5	5.0	5.5
Jan. 2, 2009	5.5	4.0	5.0
July 29, 2009	4.75	3.25	5.0

Source: www.rbi.org.in

The above said policy changes since mid-September 2008, enabled Reserve Bank of India to infuse ₹ 5,61,700 crore (excluding ₹ 40,000 crore under SLR reduction) in market in order to ensure ample liquidity in the banking system.

Future Outlook for India

To sum up we can say that the global financial recession which started off as a sub-prime crisis of USA has brought all nations including India into its fold. The GDP growth rate which was around nine per cent over the last four years has slowed since the last quarter of 2008 owing to deceleration in employment, export-import, tax-GDP ratio, reduction in capital inflows and significant outflows due to economic slowdown. The demand for bank credit is also slackening despite comfortable liquidity in the system. Higher input costs and dampened demand have dented corporate margins while the uncertainty surrounding the crisis has affected business confidence leading to the crash of Indian stock market and volatility in forex market. Nevertheless, a sound and resilient banking sector, well-functioning financial markets, robust liquidity management and payment and settlement infrastructure, buoyancy of foreign exchange reserves have helped Indian economy to remain largely immune from the contagious effect of global meltdown.

Indian financial markets are capable of withstanding the global shock, perhaps somewhat bruised but definitely not battered. India, with its strong internal drivers for growth, may escape the worst consequences of the global financial crisis. In other words, the fundamentals of our economy continue to be strong and robust. The global economic environment continues to remain uncertain, although the rate of contraction in economic activities and the extent of pressures on financial systems eased in the first quarter of 2009-10. Yet, it is not possible to clearly see the path of the crisis and its resolution over the coming months. In this sense, India is not unique as almost every country, whether or not directly affected, has to manage the current economic crisis under uncertainty.

Conclusion

While the developed world, including the U.S, the Euro Zone and Japan, have plunged into recession, the Indian Economy is being affected by the spill-over effects of the global financial crisis (Chidambaram 2008). Great savings habit among people, strong fundamentals, strong conservative and regulatory regime have saved Indian economy from going out of gear, though significant parts of the economy have slowed down and there is a wide variance of opinion about how long it will continue. It is expected that growth will be moderate in India. The most important lesson that we must learn from the crisis is that we must be self-reliant. Though World Trade Organization (WTO) propagates free trade, we must adopt protectionist measures in certain sectors of the economy so that recession in any part of the globe does not affect our country.

I would like to conclude the chapter in the words of Dr. Rakesh Mohan, former Deputy Governor of RBI, "As the monetary and fiscal stimuli work their way through, and if calm and confidence are restored in the global markets, we can see economic turnaround later this year. Once calm and confidence are restored in the global markets, economic activity in India will recover sharply. Yet there will be a period of painful adjustment which is inevitable."

Finally this to conclude the unprecedented economic crisis has definitely taken a toll of India's economic performance. Most likely it has also reduced our potential for economic development in the next 3 or 4 years. However, despite the severity of the global crisis, India's economy has demonstrated considerable resilience, in part, thanks to the strength of our agricultural sector.

REFERENCES

1. Nidhi Choudhari, *Global Recession and Its Impact on Indian Financial Markets,* August 2009, Vol. 3, Issue 3, 4.
2. www.vcircle.com> (Retrieved December 2008)
3. *The Hindu, Daily,* October 27, 2008, p.12
4. http://www.macroscan.org (Retrieved October, 2008)
5. http:Il www.bis.org (Retrieved October, 2008)
6. *The Hindu,* Daily, November, 2008, p. 14
7. http://www.observerindia.com, (Retrieved December, 2008)
8. http://www.businessweek.com, (Retrieved October 2008)
9. *Annual Report 2008-09*, Reseive Bank of India
10. Macroeconomic and Monetary Developments: First Quarter Review
11. 2009-10, Reserve Bank of India
12. *Bank Quest* Vol. 80 January- March 2009, IIBF
13. *Economic Survey*, Government of India
14. http://www.economics.harvard.edu/about/views
15. 14, www.finmin.nic.in
16. www.rbi.org.in

CHAPTER

18

Impact of Global Financial Crisis in US, China and India

*Dr. G. Narasimhulu
**Dr. P. Kothandarami Reddy

The Prelude

With globalization, America's economy and the rest of the world have become increasingly interwoven. The ratio of rising debt to GDP has fuelled US growth in the past several decades (it went from 240% in 1990 to 340% in 2007). With total debt/GDP suddenly flattening, the US has plunged into recession. Once US debt GDP has fallen, the world is in grip of recession, because US accounts for at least 20 per cent of world consumer market. This year, what began as a problem in one sector of the U.S. housing market-mortgages for borrowers with poor credit histories has infected credit markets world-wide. That's because global financial institutions repackaged those American mortgages as sophisticated securities and sold them to banks, corporations and local governments around the globe. Under the impact of US sub-prime crisis, European economy is facing appreciable slowdown and becoming sluggish. As a result of this the rate

* Lecturer, SKIT, Srikalahasti, Chittoor District, Andhra Pradesh
** Associate Professor, Academic Staff College, S.V. University, Tirupati, Andhra Pradesh

of unemployment is on the rise. Owing to Ibis situation, the properties are being sold at a compromising rate.

Why This Crisis

It is said that the predicament is attributable to the overflowing greed of some banks and Mortgage Institutions for making sudden super profits bypassing prudential norms. So there is stockpiling of goods leading to recession. If there is no off-take of goods in the market, tile capitalists stop production. So industries get closed rendering millions jobless. On the other hand, with scope for maximum profit dwindling, the capitalist owners try to cut production cost by drastically reducing manpower and opt for a few higher technology-driven productions. So unemployment soars. Bereft of employment, income of the households dips even lower causing further squeezing of the market for the capitalists. This is the vicious cycle of capitalism now in its death throes[1].

About Common People

Common people who are the worst victims of the crisis. Under the pretext of being entangled in the crisis, most of the organizations are going for massive retrenchment. Twenty Six Thousand employees of Lehman Brothers are slated to lose their jobs. According to International Labour Organization, with the crisis hitting hardest such sectors as construction, automotive, tourism, finance, services and real estate, world unemployment could increase by an estimated 20 million. Many organizations have already announced substantial wage cut for their employees. The number of working poor living on less than a dollar a day, it is envisaged, could rise by some 40 million and those at 2 dollars a day by more than 100 million. This is going to wreak havoc in the life of the toiling millions not only in US but in all the imperialist-capitalist countries.

Will China and India Maintain Their Growth Levels?

Statistics indicate that manufacturing in China decreased sharply in October. According to the BBC Chinese network, China's exports are shrinking because of fewer orders. The recession in North America and Europe is causing China's export industry to face a difficult situation. Besides fewer orders, the export industry is concentrated along the coast of China, and China is also facing rising labour costs. Many toy manufacturers were forced to close down between January and July before the Western crisis. Seven-thousand workers lost their jobs. China's economic growth will fall into the single-digit range this year. This will be the first time that China's economic growth has slid into a single-digit in the past six years. Unemployment has become the greatest concern of the Chinese people. Given the above picture of China, India's investment scenario is healthy, in the more comprehensive sense. India's GDP growth is projected at around 7-8 per cent, with inflation showing signs of slowing down. The factors behind the growth rate healthy investment levels, expanding consumer demand and government's policies aimed at boosting growth. Besides this, the relief in various taxes, the scrapping of import duty on essential commodities will in turn help in reducing inflation[2].

Impact on Outsourcing Industry

With Barack Obama elected as the 44th President of the US, every Indian is wondering if his victory will affect the Indian outsourcing industry. The million-dollar outsourcing industry in India is beholden to the US for its survival. Although the BPO (Business Process Outsourcing) companies are receiving a good number projects from the European countries, there is no denying that we still largely depend on the US companies when it comes to outsourcing. Over 80 per cent of the BPOs and call centers in India are regulated by the US companies. During his election campaign, Barack Obama had made some controversial remarks on outsourcing of American jobs to

India. If he stands on what he said, then it will spell doom for Indian outsourcing industry.

But actually he is not likely to go to that extent. On another occasion, he did indicate that he would make the US economy strong again by expanding opportunities outward rather than clamping down on outsourcing to countries like India and China. Outsourcing, in fact, is here to stay. There may be a slowdown. But the outsourcing industry will not collapse. The value of the business was estimated to be $47.8 bn in 2007, 10 times higher than what it was a decade ago, with a projected growth rate of 28 per cent every year[3]. India commands 5-6 per cent share of the outsourcing industry in the world, which is a substantial chunk.

Impact on Indian Economy

Serious dimensions of international financial crisis are becoming apparent with successive bailouts of major investment banks, topped by takeover of principal mortgage institutions, leading to layoffs and pile up of inventories. International money market is nearly frozen, resulting in acute credit crunch. Total loss in stock values world over since the beginning of 2008 has been nearly $30 tn. Total cost to the US could go to over $2 tn since the crisis is not likely to end soon.

Indian corporates, slowly but surely, are being sucked into the global financial storm. In India, inflow of foreign capital is drying up and domestic credit has become expensive, resulting in decline in growth of industrial output. The apparent slowdown of the US economy is bothering economists all over the globe. Emerging economies such as India and China are well aware of their dependence on the US economy and are bracing themselves for the impending impact. The global economy has slowed since the second half of 2007 against the backdrop of the financial turmoil and a deepening US downturn. Developments in the advanced industrial economies pose major challenges. First, a pronounced slowdown in the US is hurting the Emerging Market Economies (EMEs) which, although remarkably resilient so far, still depend significantly on external demand. Second, tighter conditions in global financial markets are constraining EMEs with large current account deficits, particularly those relying on more volatile portfolio financing. Countries heavily dependent on cross-border bank borrowing are greatly affected.

As the global financial crisis began unfolding in the first nine months of 2008, the foreign institutional investors pulled out close to $10 bn from India, dragging the capital market down with it. The liquidity crisis, coupled with the credit squeeze and a weak currency, is hurting various sectors. Banks have reduced home and auto loans. Car loans account for 70 per cent of consumer auto purchases at present, down from 85 per cent a year ago. Meanwhile, consumers are deferring other purchases, while financiers have been logging a drop in loan disbursals. The corporate sector is struggling too with its expansion plans and merger activity being pushed to the back burner. The weak rupee is of little help to exporters. Just last November the textile and apparel industry was reeling from an 11 per cent appreciation of the rupee, as US and European clients were negotiating contracts and looking for cheaper alternatives to source garments. This time though the rupee has depreciated 21 per cent in the past nine months, the industry is still struggling. The gains from a weak rupee are offset by rising input costs, for example, cotton prices have increased 30 per cent in the past one year. The high cost of borrowing and the financial turmoil in their main export markets in the US and Europe is affecting Indian exports. The IT sector, which should have been a beneficiary of the weak rupee is also concerned about its future due to the meltdown. The US still accounts for more than half of the global revenues for major Indian players in IT sector[4].

Conclusion

There has been a significant and positive change in the way India has been managing its external sector with respect to changes in the global scenario. Appropriate exchange rate and good external debt management are some of the positive traits of the Indian economy. New policies and mature governance have helped India face numerous global crises and yet maintain an enviable growth rate. While most economists worldwide believe that the slowdown of the US economy will impact the global economy, with countries like India and China being hit the hardest, a sizeable number of Indian entrepreneurs and economists believe in India's ability to withstand global upheavals. Six months into the current turmoil, the overall impact has been manageable and most developing countries are performing well, but a worst case scenario cannot be ruled out. India's growth story is funded more by domestic savings than by foreign investments. The economy's expansion is not dependent on foreign fund inflows that much. The increase in the domestic savings rate has been higher than the increase in the domestic investments since 2003. A high rate of investment growth is required to spur the economy into a trajectory of high growth. But once it plateaus at a higher level essentially with domestic savings, there is no need for higher foreign savings to sustain it. Even if net capital inflows fall by half in 2008, India's macro-economy will not be affected, as domestic savings levels are intact. There, however, could be some impact on different sectors at the micro level.

So far as India is concerned, Prime Minister Manmohan Singh concluded his speech at the Sumitt of 20 to welcome any 'initiative' of the IMF to establish a new liquidity facility, only raising the question whether IMF was 'adequately funded' to manage the global crisis. This was combined with the hope that the World Bank would double its annual aid to India in the coming two-three years. But his main anxiety at this gathering seems to have been to defend the 'globalization' of the capitalist order in the 'open' economies in the developing world. He pleaded for private investment, including foreign direct investment for the development of the infrastructure and economic growth in the developing countries. In his entire speech, there was no word for what India could do by itself for equitable growth in India in the present hard times of global recession. He seemed to rely entirely on foreign aid, institutional and private investment rather than self-reliant domestic effort to face the worsening economic crisis in India and the World.

REFERNCES

1. *Monthly Public Opinion Surveys,* December 2008, p. 3.
2. *Management Accountant*, November 2008, p. 44.
3. *The Analyst,* January 2009, pp. 22-23
4. *Economic Times,* 6th February, 2009

CHAPTER

19

Global Financial Crisis and Its Impact on Indian Economy

*Dr. B. Parameswara Reddy
**C. Lakshmikantha Reddy

Introduction

The world economy has changed dramatically since September 2008. What began as a downturn in the US housing sector is now a global crisis, spreading to both rich and poor economies. Many people believe that this may go down in history as the worst crisis since the Great Depression of the 1930s. Developing countries at first sheltered from the worst elements of the turmoil are now much more vulnerable, with dwindling capital flows, huge withdrawals of capital leading to losses in equity markets, and skyrocketing interest rates. GDP growth in developing countries only recently expected to increase by 6.4 per cent in 2009 is now likely to be only 4.5 per cent, according to economists at the World Bank. And rich countries are now expected to contract by 0.1 per cent next year. *"The global financial crisis, coming so soon after the food and fuel crises, is likely to hurt the poor most in developing countries,"* said World

* Post-Doctoral Scholar, Dept. of Commerce, Sri Venkateswara University, Tirupathi-517502, Andhra Pradesh
** Research Scholar, Dept. of Economics, Sri Venkateswara University, Tirupathi-517502, Andhra Pradesh

Bank Group President Robert B. Zoellick, "*Working with the IMF, UN agencies, and regional development banks and others, the World Bank Group is helping both governments and the private sector through lending, equity investments, innovative new tools, and safety net programmes.*" The World Bank Group's response to this crisis includes increased lending for crisis-hit developing countries likely to nearly triple from US $13.5 billion last year to more than US $35 billion present year as well as accelerated grants and virtually interest free long term loans to the world's 78 poorest countries, 39 of which are in Africa.

Besides extending help to cash strapped governments, the group is boosting support to the private sector through four initiatives by the International Finance Corporation (IFC), and providing much needed liquidity in developing country banking markets through the Multilateral Investment Guarantee Agency (MIGA). The crash of the Wall Street has had its repercussions on the whole world. Even the superpower of the world, the United States of America, could not be resistant from the evil aspects of capitalism.Essentially, what transpired that a massive company like Merrill Lynch and a major investment bank, Lehman Brothers, collapsed? Fannie Mae and Freddie Mac, giant government sponsored mortgage lenders, were also debt-ridden. How come the insurance giant, American Insurance Group, renowned for insuring others, could not insure itself? It all happened mainly because of the housing bubble in the US. The banks kept giving loans to people who were not even credit worthy enough to pay it back. With more and more people borrowing money, the banks were accumulating increasing funds. Every thing seemed rosy at that time. The Republican government under George Bush did not put enough regulations on the banks. Consequently out of greed, the banks kept lending money and people kept on borrowing. The economic analysts knew that this doom was coming. So the crash was not a shock, because it was something that was anticipated by the government. Finally when the doomsday came, it hit the financial markets across the world. This is a globalizing world, or for some, it is even an Americanization of the world. After all, the US does enjoy 1/4th of the world Gross Domestic Product (GDP) and so a recession in the US has hampered the growth of other countries too. Economies across the world found it hard to sail through. All the stock markets of the world felt the heat, from the DOW and the Nikkei, to our very own NIFTY. Even the United Kingdom could not remain unscathed. Ireland is also suffering from terrible recession. As far as India is concerned, our former finance minister, Mr. P.Chidambaram, first chose to pretend to be unassailed by the US meltdown, but it was actually a façade. Foreign Institutional Investors (FIIs) have disinvested around $10 billion from the Indian shores. Our economy was already writhing under the travails of inflation and as if this was not enough, recession has jolted our markets. Exports in the month of October were 12 per cent lower than their rate in October 2007. The Indian rupee has hit an all-time low in comparison to the dollar. This means that even though our exports are bringing in more foreign exchange, our imports have become costlier. Moreover, our export orders are reducing. Thus, our local markets have to pay the price. Foreign companies like Walmart, Target, Gap etc., which have their rudimentary units in India, are asking their Indian partners to pay less to the workers on account of the growing recession. Therefore, the incomes of skilled artisans have plunged. In urban areas, job lay-offs are happening. The Jet Airways lay-offs struck the headlines of many newspapers. Our government has finally realized that we were affected too. So the same government that was reducing liquidity in the economy some months back, has reversed its policies. The Government has started bringing in more and more liquidity. The repo rate, the rate at which the Reserve Bank of India (RBI) grants loans to other banks, was reduced. The Cash Reserve Ratio—the ratio of money which banks have to store with the RBI, was also pushed down. In this way, the credit needs were somehow met. The US salvaged its sagging economy by the Paulson plan. It injected $700 billion to buy the bankrupt companies. It again gathered much flak because while in the time of prosperity the companies enjoyed their profits alone, the bailout plan was made out of the taxes of the common man. The companies had anticipated this debacle and so the CEO's had already been bloating on heavy salaries. So, 'profits were privatized, losses were socialized' unjustifiably. In India, things are bad, but are certainly better than in many other countries. This happened because ours is a mixed economy; we have both public and private sector undertakings and therefore, capitalists here do not find a free flow. As even as our economy is affected, it is not in so bad a plight as that of other nations. Our economy is still expected to have one of the strongest growth rates, as was suggested by Usha Thorat, RBI deputy governor. Besides this, the global recession has also declined the soaring oil prices and this has certainly benefited India. The recession is nowhere expected to end in the coming months, but the governments across the world have to somehow contain this crash. The best that we can expect from this defeat is to only learn not to repeat the same mistakes again.

Global Recession: Replica of Great Depression?

Most of the economists are concerned that the current global crisis might turn into something grave like the great depression of 1929 or even worse. In order to avoid that, the central banks round the world are taking steps to create more liquidity in their respective economies without realizing that this may aggravate the problem. Before making a new economic policy, it is important to see the past implications of that policy.

It was an artificial economic boom that was responsible for the great depression of 1929. For the entire decade before that, most of the companies throughout the world saw unprecedented rise in their profits. The economic growth came to a halt after the giant companies started facing losses due to lack of demand. It was the biggest recession in the history which lasted for a decade ruining world's biggest economies of US and Europe. It all started when the US economy was becoming increasingly unstable due to widening disparity of income between the rich and the poor class which resulted in an oversupply of goods as people did not have income to buy those goods. Easy availability of credit and more investment were thought of to be the immediate solutions by the fed (the central bank of United States). Cash reserve ratio, statutory liquidity ratio and repo rates were all brought down in order to induce liquidity in the economy. This way artificial demand was created. However, most of the people were unable to repay the debts. The demand for the goods declined as most of the income of the people went to repay debts. Consequently, the investors' confidence declined which reduced the production of luxury goods as well. The effect poured on to other nations as well.

The world economy was trapped in an unusual vicious circle. Something like this happened again in the 1990s when most of the banks got into home loans and mortgages. As the real estate prices were rising, this became an easy way for lenders to create money. The optimism led the banks to take up risky loans as well. The banks and investment companies got into the business of trading risk. Yet again, the same crisis of confidence approached when people found it increasingly difficult to repay the long-term debts. Some of the world's largest banks like Lehman Brothers found themselves bankrupt. It did not take long to percolate the effect onto other companies as well. The giant companies like Sony, Motorola, DLF, AIG, Indian Inc, TCS, General Motors, etc have suffered heavy losses; millions have lost their jobs and the solutions to bring the declining growth rates back on the track are no where in the sight. The importance of two most significant sectors—infrastructure and agriculture—is often understated. It is the growth in these two sectors which brings about rise in demand for all other industries (by increasing wages for a large number of people) and thus, higher overall economic growth. But not much attention is paid to these key sectors while policy formation. The rise in food production in US also played a major role in taking the economy out of recession. The governments should not ignore the agricultural sector completely. It is the high time that the governments invest in infrastructure wherever necessary. In order to avoid the situation becoming more precarious like the Great Depression, more 'aggressive' policies are needed immediately.

Sub Prime Crisis

As interest rates started falling due to excess liquidity, house prices rose rapidly, creating a pool of wealth in the hands of Americans, which they unlocked by contracting mortgage loans. It benefited them in two ways—they got huge liquidity at inflated housing prices and interest rates that were practically lowest in the last twenty years. This became a virtuous cycle, which resulted in very high consumer spending, obviously fuelling global growth. As interest rates started rising in the US due to inflation concerns, this virtuous cycle came to a standstill and the demand for houses started tapering. This resulted in lower prices for houses and many were unable to cover the mortgage loans. It has now hit the entire banking industry in the US and the virtuous cycle is becoming a vicious cycle. This subprime crisis has inevitably become an election issue, and the Democratic presidential candidates have outlined plans to address it. *Obama's* stand, which avoids direct government spending, is more conservative and impractical, as compared to Clinton's, who has promised to allocate federal reserves to resolve the crisis. What does all this mean for the Indian capital market? For one, the flow of capital coming to the Indian stock market will be reduced.

India was always considered one of the robust emerging markets, but definitely with certain political and economic risks. These risks, in recent times, were not priced into equity valuations as the excess liquidity was chasing emerging market exposures and India became the investor's darling, after China. Now with the subprime crisis, excess liquidity will vanish and the market will correct for the price of risks. Let us also look at domestic fundamentals. Indian markets will see a correction because of high oil prices, high interest rates, slowing down of exports because of the slowing down of the US economy and rupee appreciation. This will definitely have an impact on the GDP growth rate. The stock market has, in the recent past, rallied largely because of global cues and has almost completely ignored the local issues. With liquidity drying up, the market will now focus on local issues, including political uncertainties and corporate earnings. It is natural to expect that, finally, fundamentals will rule over technicalities, and the market will look at ground realities. A slowdown can be observed in the automobile sector, some slowing down is already being witnessed in the real-estate segment and, with exports coming down, and it will not be too long before we see the same in textiles, jewellers and other areas as well. Perhaps a similar story will unfold in the next couple of months for these lenders who have lent big money into the subprime markets. One or more banks will fold, just like Enron did, resulting in a huge crisis of confidence. It would be naive to wish away this major problem inflicting the global markets and to presume that the Indian market is decoupled. If the global super-tanker US, which has a 25 per cent share of global GDP, slows down it will definitely have an impact on the Indian economy. Only time can decide which policy becomes successful. More importantly, no one can predict a change of plans in the Oval office.

Raising from the Depth of 2007 Crisis

The Global Financial Crisis of 2007 has been an outcome of several businesses concerned and finance related backdrops. This was probably the worst of the economic crashes that the world has witnessed after the 'The Great Depression' of 1930. Several theories have been contrived to examine the roots to this upheaval, and the consequential measures to combat the heavy downfall; market based and regulatory solutions, that can potentially balance the trade flow temporarily. Many calculative concepts devised by experts and economists to suggest that the overall situation will start recuperating by the year 2010. This deduction came in after a steady inflation was observed in oil and food prices, which owe to a huge uncertainty of the economy's turns in the period of 2009 to 2012. Due to the inflation, several countries, including the USA and Euro zone countries like France and the UK, had been clawed by the widespread recession. However, it has been predicted that these developed countries, especially, will experience a brighter financial flow in 2010, as opposed to several markets that will be seeing a much worse negative growth. For example, the housing and credit markets in the USA and Euro zone are beginning to enhance, and it is estimated that the GDP growth will reach 2 per cent, in contrast to what it was in 2009. A similar statistical analysis reveals that the upcoming economies of today; China and India, had experienced an equally drastic scenario in the period of 2008 to 2009. Nevertheless, according to experts, an unwavering growth is on the cards for the Asian markets, which is expected to lift from 7.7 per cent in 2009 to 8.4 per cent in 2010, and eventually stabilizing at 8.5 per cent by 2012. A more threatening series of risks, which although may temporarily indicate signs of optimism but further damage the current economic equations, are the currency markets and the exposure to bad credit.

The US Dollar, for instance, enjoyed an all time high in 2008 against the UK Pound, but because of inflation and, it had affected trading blocs. Furthermore, all this imposed an upward pressure on US interest rates. Another potential risk is the unearthing of 'bad credit' in the global market. This can firstly, lead to the recovery of the market, and secondly, slow down the lending to consumers and businesses. (This can lead to two outcomes. Firstly, recovery of the market and secondly, it can slow down the lending to consumers and businesses.) While there is a definite scope for foreseeing a state of betterment in the upcoming years, however, an uncertainty towards the declining market scales still persist, and therefore, it may be too early to comment on the economic recovery. On the contrary, owing to the uncertainty, it can also be said that probably the complete impact of recession hasn't affected the markets as yet, and there may be more to follow. Some economists, despite the Great Depression of 1930, call this as the worst nightmare for markets worldwide in the last century. In spite of the presumed recuperation, markets are still feeling the heat of a fall-down. For developed nations such as USA and the UK, GDP growth will occur from 2009 and will come to a steady margin by 2012. For developing countries, on the contrary, there will be a definite slow down in the financial growth over the same period. As for the prices, unpredictability in the inflation levels, especially in the prices of oil and food, will act as pivotal forecasts in determining future statistics.

US Sneezes, India Catches Cold

Before the financial crisis broke out, it was generally believed that the corporate sector was in the pink of health. As the credit and liquidity crunch has intensified, the vulnerabilities have come trembling out. To a great extent, the current economic turmoil is a fall out of the global economic crisis, which in turn, is the outcome of US sub prime crisis. However, what had begun as a financial crisis is now a crisis in real economies of the world and India is no exception. Contrary to what was believed earlier, the Indian economy is not immune from development in the global economies. There is no panic, but it cannot be denied that a lot of uncertainties have been created with the sharp reduction of the GDP and industrial growth rates, steep and continuous fall in stock prices, erosion of export growth and depreciation of the rupee. All this has created a crisis of confidence. Elaborating on the fall out of crisis for countries in Asia, Mr. Manmohan Singh, Prime minister of India said that the anticipated economic slow down in the US and Europe would affect exports and lending. *"The growth rates in these countries are likely to be affected. This will affect exports of developing countries"*—he said. He further said that international financial institutions were reluctant to lend and that this would cause problems in the balance of payments and flow of funds, from developed to developing countries. A comprehensive policy response is required to prevent such a collapse and limit the damage to the Indian economy. The response so far has been to loosen the monetary tap and to get banks to lower the lending rates.

This slowdown has hit the mid and small sized companies harder compared to the bigger firms. When the latest financial results for the quarter ending September 2008 has been disapproving for Indian Inc. as a whole, an ETIG study reveals that it is only the larger companies that have managed to register growth in profits. The Prime minister and Finance minister have been busy meeting captains of Indian industries. The message from the government seems to be that everything will be done to ensure funds for industries. In return, Indian industries must refrain from effecting big layoffs. This approach makes sense only if the government thinks that the crisis will blow over in six months or so. This is a dangerous approach to take, because half hearted measures could result in crisis taking more than two years to play out. And action to arrest a fall in confidence cannot be confined to monetary policy. We need a strong fiscal response. This does not imply a cut in indirect taxes only. That can only have a limited impact on the economy. People may have the money but they lack the confidence to spend. Confidence can be bolstered only through massive government spending and the creation of new jobs. This means spending on infrastructure. We are not just talking about airports, but rural roads etc., that create employment and can be planned and executed. According to Montek Singh Ahluwalia, deputy chairman of the Planning Commission, for the current fiscal growth may even fall below the RBI estimates of 7.5 to 8.1, *"we should be planning for as low as 7 per cent this year. However we can expect inflation to come down further. This would give greater flexibility in monetary policy. Infusion of liquidity would ease interest rates and spur investment and growth"* he said. The present crisis poses a challenge, but it also creates a major opportunity to address the long neglected issues of the financial structure. If tackled properly, the present crisis could turn out to a blessing just as the balance of payments crisis in 1991 was. It could lay the foundation for much stronger growth once the crisis is resolved.

Effects of Global Meltdown on Indian Economy

"Whatever is going to happen, will happen; just don't let it happen to you" The year 2008, one of the worst years in the world's economic history, experienced a major global meltdown. This global meltdown led to job lay-offs across the world. It claimed its first casualty in Los Angeles with a 45 year old NRI killing 5 members of his family before taking his own life. According to the Labour Department's report, the unemployment rolls swelled by 2.2 million, over the last year, to 9.5 million. Different Indian associates and CEOs of multinational companies have started feeling the heat. The recent downturn is weighing on the minds of employers. Although India has not been directly impacted by the global financial crisis, we should be cautious about the indirect knock-on effect of the global crisis. According to the GET report, over 50 million could lose their jobs by 2009 worldwide. The worst thing is that as we live in an agrarian economy where the unemployment rate is already high and 60 per cent of the population is still dependent on agriculture, the rate of unemployment is rising further due to these worldwide lay-offs as most of the students of India go abroad for job purposes. Going further, not only the labour market, but also the financial market, IT/ITes, export and manufacturing sectors have been affected adversely. The IT/ITes sector is the major component of India's growth because the share in GDP given by agriculture has been taken up by the services sector in recent past. The global meltdown is not only affecting the services sector, even the industrial sector has been affected adversely.

Major projects and expansion plans are being reviewed by the corporate sector and they have started focussing on reducing costs and borrowings. The first half of the year 2009 is considered as the worst period. Despite all these problems, the biggest problem that still exists from the past is 'Information asymmetry'. It would be fine if our Government or the members of the major corporate sector don't know the problem or where to find the answer, but the truth is that they know both and are waiting for other countries to take steps. The most important challenge faced by our Government during this time is to ensure a balance between inflation and growth. If our economy experiences high growth rates, it will lead to major exports from our nation which will affect our domestic market and if economy experiences a decline in the inflation rate, it will lead to major imports to our country which will affect the government budget. Though the impact of global financial crisis on India is stronger than expected, it will be the first to recover if the Government takes correct decisions and changes the established fiscal and monetary policies. The wholesale price index and the consumer price index need to be watched. The Government should ensure continuous credit flow at a low rate of interest to the private sector and especially to small and medium enterprises for their expansion and the growth projects. Low rate of interest is not the only way of boosting the economic growth. The Government should also initiate measures to address the mutual funds and non-banking financial companies. They should also keep an eye on the market manipulators and the institutional speculators, as when most individual investors lose when the market falls, the institutional speculators make money when there are financial speculative transactions. Hence, it can be seen that although we have been hit hard, but 'Every black cloud has a silver lining'; with stern steps being taken in the right direction, we shall soon come out of this crisis without much damage.

India and the Global Economic down turn

One of the grave issues of recent days is the global economic crisis which has not only affected the developed nations but has had far reaching effects on the developing countries too. The 2008/2009 recession is seeing private consumption fall for the first time in nearly 20 years. According to World Bank, the global economy is going to shrink by 2.9 per cent this year. The US has seen the highest level of unemployment at 9.5 per cent since 1983. It is a well known fact that governments are apprehensive regarding the future of most of the economies which are greatly dependent on the US for foreign investments. As a consequence of the global liquidity squeeze, Indian banks and corporates have found their overseas financing drying up, forcing corporates to shift their credit demand to the domestic banking sector. 500,000 people were rendered jobless between October to December 2008. Eight major sectors like textile and garment industry, metals and metal products, Information Technology and BPO, automobiles, gems and jewellery, transportation, construction and mining industries were included in the survey by the ministry of Labour and Employment. Inflation in India had turned negative for the first time in more than 30 years, official figures had shown. 30-50 per cent of the business in garment industry has fall—exports have fallen by a much higher 4.8 per cent as compared to the other sectors and there are a number of job losses too. However, against all odds, India has managed to achieve 6.1 per cent GDP (Gross Domestic Product) growth in the first quarter (April-June) of the fiscal year. This makes India the second fastest growing major economy after China. Much of this can be attributed by the consumer confidence investors had in the Indian markets even through these bad times. According to the Nielsen Global Consumer Confidence, which polled 26,000 consumers across the globe, "India ranks foremost in consumer confidence as investors have been safeguarded by India's relatively nascent financial markets." Secondly and importantly it was the conservative policies adapted by the Indian Banking system which kept India relatively protected from the impact of the recession. New York Times credits the tough lending standards Y.V Reddy imposed on the Indian banks as RBI (Reserve Bank of India) Governor for saving the entire Indian baking system from the massive sub-prime and liquidity crisis of 2008 and beyond. As Governor, he saw his job as making sure Indian banks did not get too caught up in the bubble mentality. He banned the use of bank loans for the purchase of raw land, and sharply curtailed securitizations and derivatives, and essentially prohibited off-balance sheet financing. Saving for the future instead of spending on short-term desires is a tendency imbibed in the psyche of the Indian masses. Before thinking at an individual level, the expenditure is always thought collectively in terms of family which makes the entire money-making system unique in India. The government too works on the principle of welfare of the people rather than profit-making. It is this element of the Indian culture maybe which has saved it from the affinity towards insatiability and self-interest prevailing in the West which further facilitated the common objective of working together in times of crisis. For the past two years, the number of youngsters opting for education abroad has fallen drastically. They have become aware of the inimitable opportunities they can get in India itself, thus instigating the idea of giving their inputs towards the development of their own country rather than draining their calibre for another one. Even though the crisis slowed the rate of growth of the economy in the country, it has given a message to the world of the resilience power the economy can manifest in times of adversity.

The Ongoing Global Financial Crisis

The ongoing financial crisis became prominent since September 2008 after the failure of few big financial American firms due to subprime mortgage crisis in the US, although its signs were visible early that year. A negative aspect of Globalisation was soon visible when the US financial crunch hit other markets as well and it rapidly evolved into a global credit crisis and deflation. That resulted in a number of European bank failures and decline in various stock indexes. This led to reduction in the market value of equities and commodities worldwide. The crumbling figure in the Wall Street is affecting markets all over the world. The mess that began due to fast, unregulated mortgage lending in the US has now become a perilous crisis and markets worldwide have lost the confidence of the investors. There is a fear amongst investors and depositors, bankers as well as regulators since no easy solution seems to be in sight. United Kingdom's Prime Minister, Gordon Brown acknowledges this when he says, "This is not a time for conventional thinking or outdated dogma but for fresh and innovative intervention that gets to the heart of the problem."

Federal banks have tried all possible options. Most Reserve Banks have cut down on interest rates. On January 8, 2009 the Bank of England cut down base rate to 1.5 per cent, the lowest in the Central Bank's history since its inception in 1694. The economy is also being affected by cuts in capital spending. Finance is one of the most important of all industries. All major banks have their networks spread wide across seas and continents. Thus when banks run into trouble, it's not clear who should actually help. Generally the favoured practice has been the direct government intervention. The US Congress announced a $700 billion rescue package, referred by many as 'socialism for the rich'. But this is not always a viable option. US itself is not in a position to announce similar package for the automobile industry. And then there are many small or third world countries where these big banks have their balance sheets far exceeding their gross domestic products. Industry watchers predict a 'bleak 2009' for the Global Economy. According to International Monetary Fund (IMF) US economy will grow only 0.1 per cent in 2009. Europe, China and India are also expected to have very slow growth rates. Thus nobody will be able to take over the US as the world economy, but that will drag down everyone else. Dennis Snower, president of Germany's Kiel Institute for the World Economy, believes, "Governments are making the same mistake....They're trying to deal with the crisis on a piecemeal basis." Robert Zoellick, president of the World Bank, too agrees that the problem has now become a global phenomenon and so only a multinational solution can work. "While American eyes are on the intersection of the Wall and Main Streets, there is much more to the story," he says. "The response to these crises will have to be larger and global."

Ideological differences, as also other hostilities, however are proving great impediments in tackling this global problem. Governments are fast realizing this and so a sense of 'intimate cooperation' has developed among nations. Economists worldwide are stressing on the need to re-examine the free-market system. French president Nicholas Sarkozy has even spoken of the 'new balance' in market economy between the market and the state. American President George Bush, however, still supports the free market system. He has reiterated that "capitalism is not perfect, it can subject to excess to excesses and abuse, but it's the most efficient way of structuring the economy." China, which still calls its economy 'socialism with market characteristics' has welcomed

America's bailout plans and emphasize that greater market check is necessary for regulation. Indian Prime Minister (and current Finance Minister as well) hinted as early as in September itself that India can't remain unaffected by the global financial crisis for long. But looking back at the year passed, the year has not been as bad as it could have got and certainly the Indian economy has not been as affected as many feared. India has often been described as an elephant who does not know its potentials. The year 2008 has not been as bad for the economy but markets are at ebb. Even Reliance Industries had to cut down on its expenditure and postpone future adventures. But with inflation now coming to below 6 mark and slash in petroleum price, costs of most commodities are now in control. But if India wants to play a major role in the world economy, then it needs to take some bold steps and cut down on subsidies. But with the Left becoming a formidable force in recent years and the general election ahead the government here is taking every step cautiously. No doubt the financial crisis has affected those maximum that seemed to have the soundest economy-USA, Germany, Japan. In last two years more than a million homes have been lost to foreclosure in US alone and experts believe that another 1.5 million are on the verge of foreclosure. The third world countries have suffered so miserably that it's becoming difficult for them to come back on their own. The IMF is already lending money to Hungary, Iceland and Pakistan and several other are pleading for aids. World leaders thus need to augment at least $500 billion to IMF. China has offered about $200 billion and one expects similar goodwill gestures from countries with huge reserves, like Japan, Saudi Arabia.

No country, as of now, appears to take over America as the leader of the world economy. But one thing is sure, the ongoing crisis will give rise to a slightly 'balance' system with many players coming to foreground. Dollar thus will lose its initial monopolistic credence. Euros and Yen too will grow in value and that will have political implications as well.

Stabilizing the Financial Sector

'A new agenda is now emerging for financial sector policymaking,' said Asli Demirguc-Kunt, Senior Research Manager, Finance, in the World Bank's Development Research Group. *"This crisis is prompting a reassessment of certain principles and practices in financial sector policymaking. There could be important changes in the structure and oversight of financial systems worldwide."* To prevent shifts of deposits to state-owned banks, developing countries may now need to provide some sort of underwriting of banking system deposits, but deposit insurance should be designed carefully because such measures take large scale fiscal resources to be credible and may introduce incentives for excessive borrowing. Governments will also need to strike a balance between maintaining financial stability and encouraging financial innovation. The need to kick-start lending to the real sector once again following the credit squeeze may lead several countries to upgrade the role of development banks and the use of directed lines of credit and credit guarantee schemes, as well as to involve themselves in the resource allocation decisions of recently-nationalized banks. This projection depends on country circumstances.

Conclusion

"It is very important that countries come together to face the crisis in a coordinated way," said Justin Lin, World Bank Chief Economist, speaking at the Korea Development Institute in Seoul in October 2008. *"But whatever the detail of the multilateral effort, the point is that the scale of the problem demands greater creativity. We cannot be constrained by institutional structures and approaches designed for a world before financial globalization."* A stronger financial system will also require effective collateral registration and enforcement systems, well-functioning payments and settlement systems, and well designed corporate governance structures, say World Bank Policy analysts.

REFERENCES

1. www.theviewpaper.net
2. www.weforum.net
3. www.worldbank.org
4. GET Report
5. IMF Report
6. World Economic Outlook (WEO) Crisis and Recovery, April 2009.

CHAPTER

20

The Impact of Global Financial Recession on Indian Banking System

*B.V. Ananth Ram
**Dr. M. Gurumohan Reddy

Introduction

The economic slowdown of the advanced countries which started around mid-2007, as a result of Sub-prime crisis in USA, led to the spread of economic crisis across the world. Many largest financial institutions like Lehman Brothers, Merril Lynch, Wallstreet collapsed and several institutions in UK became bankrupt in this crisis. The contagion will be deeper and the recovery longer than earlier expected. This will be the worst global recession since 1930s.

Meaning of Recession

A recession is a decline in a country's Gross Domestic Product (GDP) growth for two or more consecutive quarters of a year. An economy which grows over a period of time, tends to slowdown the growth as a part of the normal economic cycle. A recession normally occurs when consumers lose confidence

* M. Com, Faculty of Commerce, S.K.S.C. Degree College, Proddatur, Andhra Pradesh
** M.A., Ph.D., Faculty of Economics, S.K.S.C., Degree College, Proddatur, Andhra Pradesh

in the growth of the economy and spend less. This leads to a decline in production, a sharp rise in unemployment. Investors refuse to invest, as they fear stock values will fall and thus stock markets fall on negative sentiment.

Background of Recession

Any Country that has even a remotely similar modern economic structure has suffered to some degree of economic recession.

The United States suffered its first recession back in the years between 1797 and 1800. It was primarily caused by the deflating effects of the Bank of England as they crossed the ocean to American soil.

The second recession confirmed occurred in the years between 1807 and 1814 and was called the depression of 1807. This depression was primarily caused by the Embargo Act of 1807, signed into effect by then President Thomos Jefferson.

The third recession which was considered the first mega financial crisis occurred in the year 1819. This panic brought hits widespread fare closures, failing banks, huge unemployment veta and a gigantic slump in manufacturing and agriculture that caused havoc among Americans.

The economic recession in America continued with the panic of 1837. This recession can really be attributed to failing banks, which were becoming popular at the time.

The panic of 1857 came with the failure of the Ohio Life Insurance and Trust Company which affected the European confidence bubble in the US.

In the year 2001, the collapse of the dot.com bubble as well as the attacks on September 11th on the World Trace Centre towers in New York city, America was hit by 2000s recession.

And lastly, America has been hit by what has been called with the largest hits taken by citigroup($55.1 billion) and Merril Lynch($ 52.2 billion). US-based firms have been suffered by $260 billion, $227 billion by European firms and a $ 24 billion by Asian ones.

The crisis has also seen Lehman Brothers—the fourth largest investment bank in the US file for bankruptcy. Merril Lunch has been bought out by Bank of America. Freddic Mac and Fennie Mac, the giant mortgage companies of US, has been National to prevent them from going under.

The above said crisis during 2007 occurred owing to unregulated environment and heavy buying of mortgage backed securities (MBS) of sub-prime loans given to NINJA category by major American and European banks(Lehman Brothers , Merril Lynch, AIG etc). The problem got worsened as mortgage backed securities (MBS), which by that time had become parts of CDO's of giant investment banks of US and Europe.

The American Federal Reserve announced a US package of $800 Billions to revive the economic system.

Impact on Indian Banking Sector

The Indian Banking sector comprises 80 scheduled commercial banks (SCBs), 27 public sector banks (SBI and its six associates, 19 nationalised banks and the IDBI Bank Ltd.), 7 new private sector banks, 15 old private sector banks and 31 foreign banks.

The impact of the recession on the Indian Banking sector is less severe, than in other emerging market economies. It is evident from the following facts.

Indian Banks have no direct exposure to tainted assets (assets impaired by financial crisis) and its off-balance sheet activities have been limited. The off – balance sheet operations of the SCBs, which include forward exchange contracts, guarantees, acceptances, endorsements etc., had decreased to 26.4 per cent during 2008-2009 as compared to last year.

The Balance sheets of SCBs in India remained unchanged against the effect of global financial recession and its effects on Indian economy.

It is noteworthy that contrary to the trend in some advanced countries, the leverage ratio in India has remained high reflecting the strength of the Indian Banking System. The leverage ratio for Indian banks has risen from 4.1 per cent in March 2001 to 6.3 per cent by march 2009.

The capital to Risk-weighted Assets Ratio (CRAR) of SCBs, a measure of the capacity of the banking system to absorb unexpected losses, improved this year to 13.2 per cent as on March, 2009 from 13.0 per cent as on March, 2008. The rise in CRAR was mainly due to maintenance of high growth rate Tier II capital of banks.

Indian Banks recovered a higher amount of NPAs during 2008-09 than that during the previous year. The total amount recovered and written-off at ₹ 38,828 crore in 2008-09.

Return on Assets (RoA) is an indicator of efficiency with which banks deploy their assets. During 2008-09, RoA of SCBs increased moderately to 1.02 per cent from 0.99 per cent in 2007-08.

Return on Equity (RoE), is an indicator of efficiency with which capital is used by banking institutions. The RoE of SCBs increased to 13.2 per cent during 2008-09 from 12.5 per cent in 2007-08.

Exposure of Banks

The performance of Indian Banks has been slightly affected through the global recession in the following aspects.

Mark-to-Market Losses (MTM Losses)

Indian Banks have been exposed to Mark-to-Market losses of around ₹ 410 crore due to their investments in instruments (CDOs) of troubled US Financial institutions like Lehman Brothers and AIG.

MTM is based on the market value of underlying securities and keep varying. MTM is a notional loss but it would be appeared in the balance sheet.

75 per cent of these losses is accounted by ICICI bank alone (₹ 309 crore approx.) Besides, some state-owned banks

had exposure to these instruments (CDOs) to the tune of ₹ 234 crore.

The London subsidiary of ICICI bank had exposed to the tune of US $80 million. The investment by the subsidiary constitutes less than 1 per cent of the total assets of the subsidiary and less than 0.1 per cent of the consolidated total assets of the ICICI Group.

Sub-prime Lending Losses (B-Paper Lending Losses)

The ICICI bank had been hit by the international sub-prime mortgage crisis. ICICI bank has lost nearly US $264 million (₹ 1050 crore) in January, 2008. The loss was due to the fall in the value of securities in the global market.

The main cause of the sub-prime crisis is the amount of loans given to the domestic borrowers in United States with low repayment capacities. The borrowers were unable to repay the loans due to the slowdown of the US economy, which led to the fall in the value of the securities.

Credit Cut Back

The recession has shown its effect on retail advances of the banks. Retail advances include Housing Loans, Auto Loans, Consumer Durable Loans, Credit Card Loans and other Personal Loans. The retail credit growth of banks decreased from 17.1 per cent on March, 2008 to 4.0 per cent on March, 2009.

According to RBI figures the rate of growth Auto Loans fell from 6.6 per cent at the end of March, 2008 to –4.6 per cent and the end of March, 2009.

Loans to Consumer durables purchases reduced from ₹ 7296 crore at the end of March, 2007 to ₹ 4802 crore at the end of March, 2008 and again slightly increased to ₹ 5431 crore at the end of March, 2009.

Retail advances stood at 19.8 per cent of the total loans and advances of SCBs during 2008-09 and 23.2 per cent during 2007-08.

Table 20.1 : Retail Credit Growth of Banks

(Amount in Rs. corre)

Item	Outstanding as at end March		Percentage variation	
	2008	2009	2007-08	2008-09
Housing Loans	2,52,932	2,63,235	12.7	4.1
Consumer Durables	4,802	5,431	–34.2	13.1
Credit Card Receivables	27,437	29,941	49.8	9.1
Auto Loans	87,998	83,915	6.6	–4.6
Other Personal Loans	1,97,607	2,11,294	27.5	6.9
Total Retail Loans (1 to 5)	5,70,776 (24.5)	5,93,815 (21.3)	17.1	4.0
Total Loans and Advances of SCBs	23,32,032	27,93,572	23.2	19.8

Note: Figures in parentheses represent percentage share in total loans and advances.

Source: Off-site Returns (domestic, unaudited and provisional).

Reduction in the growth of retail advances of banks was mainly on account of slowdown in credit for housing loans, auto loans, credit card receivables and other personal loans.

Government Measures

The Government of India adopted the following measures to overcome the financial crisis.

The Government has launched three fiscal stimulus packages between December 2008 and February 2009 to promote liquidity in the banking system.

The Government has urged banks to lower interest rates. Several public sector banks have already announced plans on reducing their prime lending rates.

To lift the economy out of the recession, the government announced a package of ₹ 350000 crore in the first instance on December 7. the main areas to benefit were Housing, Textiles, Infrastructure, Exports, Small and Medium Enterprises (SMEs).

A small relief package of ₹ 325 Crore was announced by Commerce and Industry Minister Kamalnath on February 26, 2009.

Banks have been asked to increase credit for productive purposes and ensure credit quality of the barrowers.

The RBI bring down the cash reserve ratio(CRR) from 9 per cent to 5.5 per cent, reduce the key policy interest rate(Repo rate) from 9 per cent to 7.5 per cent and statutory liquidity ratio(SLR) to 24 per cent of the net demand and time liabilities of the banks.

Prudential Measures

The following measures are recommended in order to curtail the effect of recession:

Indian banks need to develop a culture of risk management at the institutional level. It should be made mandatory to maintain higher capital standards, stricter liquidity and leverage ratios and a more cautious approach to risk.

All the banks should maintain a minimum of 9 per cent capital to Risk-Weighted Assets Ratio (CRAR) to cover unexpected losses as suggested by Basel II.

The banks should carefully analyse the financial credentials/viabilities of the borrowers on a consolidated basis while assessing the loan requirements of large builders.

The RBI should maintain an accommodative monetary policy for increasing growth rate and also to revive the banking system.

The Indian economy should concentrate on developing the domestic market.

The Indian physical package of ₹ 35000 Crore ($7.3 Billion approximately) is a small measure to boost the Indian economy. It is due to this reason that the industry wants a much bigger package as against this insufficient amount of allocation.

The policy makers in the Ministry of Finance, Commerce, Industry and Rural Development should get together to ensure that the planned expenditure—budgeted and sanctioned in the two stimulus packages is quickly implemented in the productive manner.

State Governments must improve the share of their implementation and co-operate with the Central Government to improve various infrastructure projects.

Employers should cut wages of the employees to reduce costs, rather than retrenching workers and thus leads to unemployment.

REFERENCES

1. *Annual Report 2008-09,* Reserve Bank of India.
2. www.recession.org
3. www.hindubusinnessline.org
4. www.rbi.org
5. *Indian Economic Survey*—2009-10

CHAPTER

21

The Global Crisis and Indian Finance

*Dr. P. Venugopal
**Dr. K. Sudarsan
***C. Uday Kumar Raju
****Prof. D.

A financial crisis refers to a loss of confidence in a country's currency or other financial assets causing international investors to withdraw their funds from the country. Financial crisis is applied broadly to a variety of situations in which some financial institutions or assets suddenly lose a large part of their value. In the 19th and early 20th centuries, many financial crises were associated with banking panics, and many recessions coincided with these panics. Other situations that are often called financial crises include stock market crashes and the bursting of other financial bubbles, currency crises, and sovereign defaults. Economists have offered theories about how financial crises develop and how they could be prevented, however, financial crises are still a regular occurrence around the world. The current financial crisis in the U.S has originated in the indiscriminate lending of housing loans in that country's sub-prime mortgage market. Among

* Research Scholar, Dept. of Commerce, S.V. University, Tirupati
** Research Scholar, Dept. of Commerce, S.V. University, Tirupati
*** Research Scholar, Dept. of Commerce, S.V. University, Tirupati
**** Faculty Member, Dept. of Commerce, S.V. University, Tirupati

the clients were the investors with poor credit histories or insufficient financial resources.

Sub-prime lending has resulted in high levels of defaults. The banks were laying huge bets with each other over loans and assets. Complex transactions were designed to move risk and disguise the sliding value of assets. As the investors are risk averse, they realized the situation, losses occurred, and the market as a whole plummeted. This led to a deep credit crunch in the U.S., the effect of which was felt across the globe. Investor confidence has eroded. Lehman's collapse marked at the very least a powerful symbol of a new low in confidence, and the reverberations continued. America's financial system ailed in its two crucial responsibilities: managing risk and allocating capital. It was all done in the name of innovation, and any regulatory initiative was fought away with claims that it would suppress that innovation. They were innovating, all right, but not in ways that made the economy stronger. Today we are all facing the repercussions of the crises.

Financial Crises: Impact on India

Due to globalization, the Indian economy cannot be insulated from the present financial crisis in the developed economies. The development in the U.S financial sector has affected not only America but also European Union, U.K and Asia. The Indian economy too has felt the impact of the crisis though not to the same extent. It is premature to try to quantify the consequences of the crisis on the Indian economy. However the impact will be multi-fold.

Indian Stock Market

An eventful week of great turbulence has begun in the global financial scenario as stock prices dipped across much of the globe on news that investment bankers, Lehman Brothers Holdings filed for bankruptcy and Merrill Lynch & Co's forced sale to Bank of America. The investments in Indian firms by these U.S. investment bankers are a major worry for Indian investors. Indian stock market has seen its worst time with the global financial crises. Foreign institutional investors pulled out close to $ 11 billion from India, dragging the capital market down with it. Stock prices have fallen by 60 per cent. India's stock market index—Sensex—touched above 21,000 mark in the month of January, 2008 and has plunged below 10,000 during October 2008.The movement of Sensex shows a positive and significant relation with Foreign Institutional Investment flows into the market. This also has an effect on the Primary Market. In 2007-08, the net Foreign Institutional Investment inflows into India amounted to $20.3 billion. As compared to this, they pulled out $11.1 billion during the first nine-and-a-half months of the calendar year 2008, of which $8.3 billion occurred over the first six-and-a-half months of the financial year 2008-09. As a result, the Sensex fell from its closing peak of 20,873 on January 8, 2008, to less than 10,000 by October 17, 2008 (Chart 21.1).

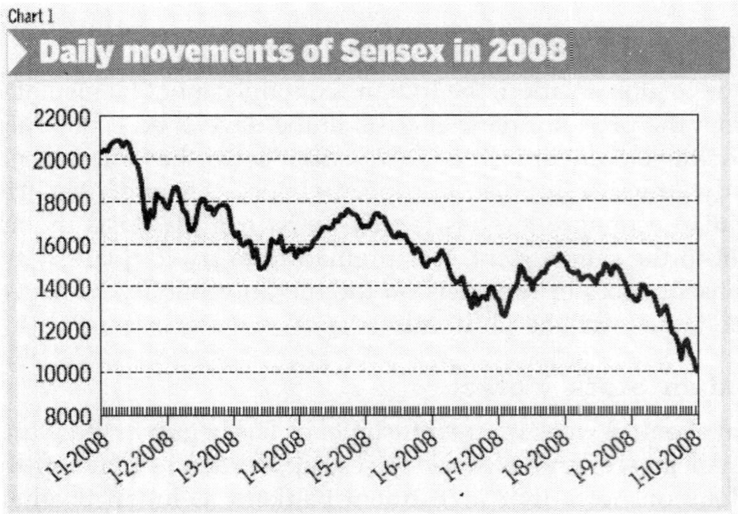

Chart 21.1

Role of Foreign Investors

How much of all this is due to the behaviour of foreign investors, rather than domestic investors? Chart 21.2 tracks the changes in total foreign investment, split up into direct investment and portfolio investment, over the period since April 2007. It is evident that both have shown a trend of increase followed by decline. FDI has been more stable with relatively moderate fluctuations (even though it does include some portfolio-type investments that get categorised as foreign direct investment). It peaked in February 2008 and thereafter has been coming down but is still positive.

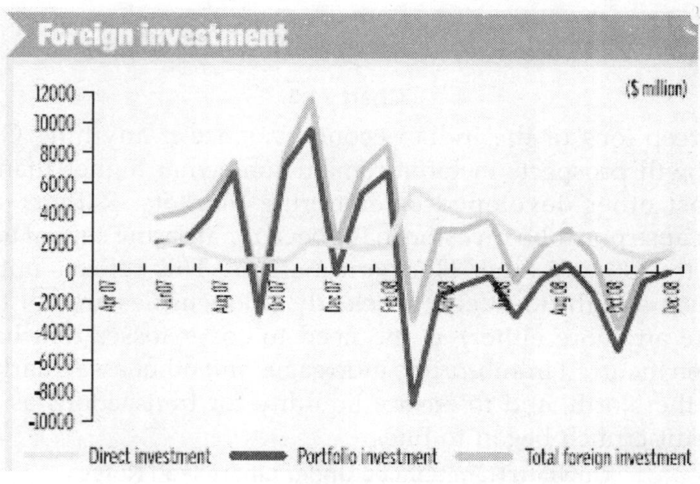

Chart 21.2

Portfolio investment (which includes both FII investment in the domestic share market and GDRs/ADRs) has been extremely volatile and largely negative (indicating net outflows) since the beginning of 2008, and this has dominated the overall foreign investment trend.

As a result, as Chart 21.3 shows, the cumulative value of the stock of Indian equity held by FIIs fell quite sharply, by 24 per cent between May 2008 and February 2009. This is not likely to be due to any dramatically changed investor

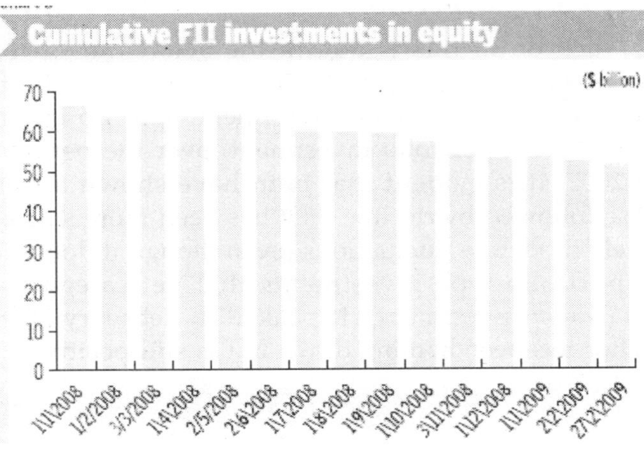

Chart 21.3

perceptions of the Indian economy, since if anything GDP growth prospects in India remain somewhat higher than in most other developed or emerging markets. Rather, it is because portfolio investors have been repatriating capital back to the US and other Northern markets. This reflects not so much a flight to safety (for clearly US securities are not that safe anymore either) as the need to cover losses that have been incurred in sub-prime mortgages and other asset markets in the North, and to ensure liquidity for transactions as the credit crunch began to bite.

Outward Remittances Under Liberalised Rules

($ million)

	2004-05	2005-06	2006-07	2007-08	Apr-Jul '08
Deposit	9.1	23.2	19.7	1.0	12.8
Purchase of immovable property	0.5	19.0	8.5	39.5	26.9
Investment in equity/debt	—	—	20.7	144.7	54.4
Gifts, donations and others	0	0	23.9	232.3	126.6
Total	**9.6**	**25.0**	**72.8**	**440.5**	**220.7**

Chart 21.4

Whatever the causes, the impact on the domestic stock market has been sharp and direct. Since the Indian stock market is still relatively shallow, and FII activities play a disproportionately strong role in determining the movement of the indices, it is not surprising that this outward flow has been associated with the overall decline in stock market valuations.

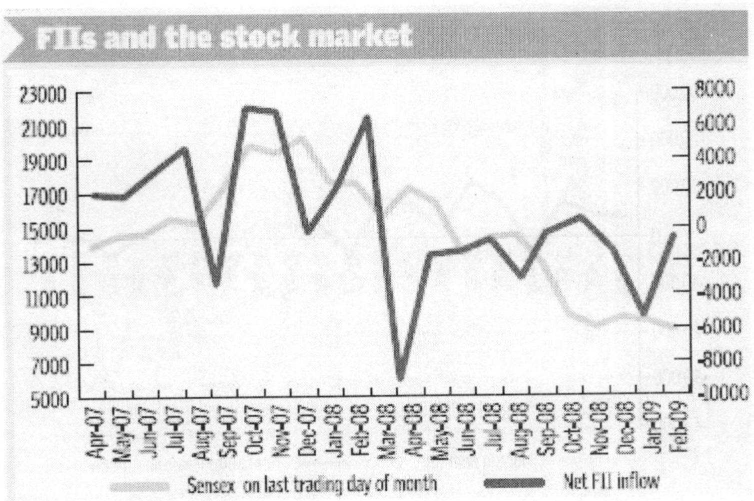

Chart 21.5

As Chart 21.5 shows, the Sensex has moved generally in the same direction as net FII inflows. In fact, movements in the latter have been much sharper and more volatile, suggesting that domestic investors have played a more stabilising role over this period.

Overall foreign investment flows (including not just FII but direct investment) have also, predictably, played a role in determining the level of external reserves. Chart 21.6 shows the pattern of aggregate net foreign investment and change in reserves since April 2007. Once again the two move together. In this case, however, foreign investment has been less volatile than the change in reserves, suggesting that other components of the balance of payments have been important as well. The changes in external commercial borrowing are likely to have been significant. In addition, the possibilities of domestic investors moving their funds out should not be underestimated. As the Table shows, the recently liberalised rules for capital outflow by domestic residents have led to outflows that are not insignificant, even if still relatively small.

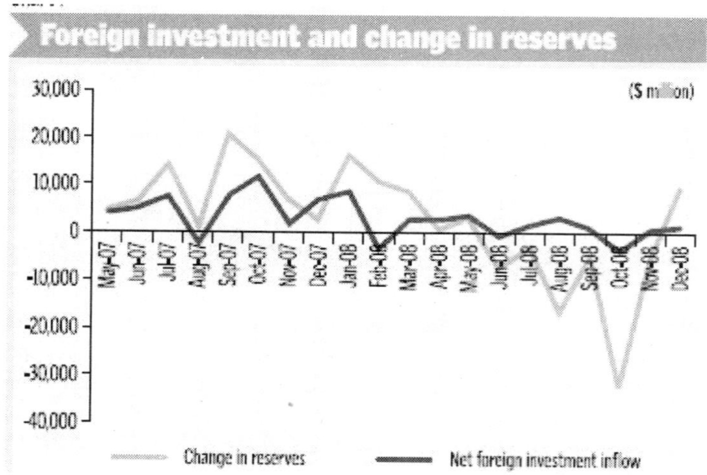

Chart 21.6

Liberalised rules for capital account transactions by Indian residents seem to be increasing the vulnerability that derives from India's dependence on foreign investment flows. This an aspect of India's external payments that policy must address, especially since there are constraints set by WTO membership on using tariffs and quantitative restrictions on reducing foreign exchange outflows that occur on account of imports.

Banks

So far the RBI has claimed that the exposure of Indian banks to assets impaired by the financial crisis is small. According to reports, the RBI had estimated that as a result of exposure to collateralised debt obligations and credit default swaps, the combined mark-to-market losses of Indian banks at the end of July was around $450 million.

Given the aggressive strategies adopted by the private sector banks, the MTM losses incurred by public sector banks were estimated at $90 million, while that for private banks was around $360 million. As yet these losses are on paper, but the RBI believes that even if they are to be provided for, these banks are well capitalised and can easily take the hit. Such assurances have neither reduced fears of those exposed to these banks or to investors holding shares in these banks. These fears are compounded by those of the minority in metropolitan areas dealing with foreign banks that have expanded their presence in India, whose global exposure to toxic assets must be substantial. What is disconcerting is the limited information available on the risks to which depositors and investors are subject. Only time will tell how significant this factor will be in making India vulnerable to the global crisis.

A third indirect fallout of the global crisis and its ripples in India is in the form of the losses sustained by non-bank financial institutions (especially mutual funds) and corporates, as a result of their exposure to domestic stock and currency markets. Such losses are expected to be large, as signaled by the decision of the RBI to allow banks to provide loans to mutual funds against certificates of deposit (CDs) or buyback their own CDs before maturity. These losses are bound to render some institutions fragile, with implications that would become clear only in the coming months.

A fourth effect is that, in this uncertain environment, banks and financial institutions concerned about their balance sheets, have been cutting back on credit, especially the huge volume of housing, automobile and retail credit provided to individuals. According to RBI figures, the rate of growth of auto loans fell from close to 30 per cent over the year ending June 30, 2008, to as low as 1.2 per cent.

Table 21.1 : Retail Credit Growth

	Year up to June (in Rs. Cr)		Year growth (%)
	2007	2008	
Housing Loan	2,30,700	2,59,000	12.27
Personal Loan	1,61,000	1,93,000	19.88
Auto Loans	86,000	87,000	1.16
Credit Card Receivable	21,000	30,000	42.86
Consumer durables	6,000	4,000	-33.33

Loans to finance consumer durables purchases fell from around ₹ 6,000 crore in the year to June 2007, to a little over ₹ 4,000 crore up to June this year. Direct housing loans, which had increased by 25 per cent during 2006-07, decelerated to 11 per cent growth in 2007-08 and 12 per cent over the year ending June 2008. It is only in an area like credit-card receivables, where banks are unable to control the growth of credit that expansion was, at 43 per cent, quite high over the year ending June 2008, even though it was lower than the 50 per cent recorded over the previous year. It is known that credit-financed housing investment and credit-financed consumption have been important drivers of growth in recent years, and underpin the 9 per cent growth trajectory India has been experiencing. The reticence of lenders to increase their exposure in markets to which they are already overexposed and the fears of increasing payment commitments in an uncertain economic environment on the part of potential borrowers are bound to curtail debt-financed consumption and investment. This could slow growth significantly.

Finally, the recession generated by the financial crisis in the advanced economies as a group and the US in particular, will adversely affect India's exports, especially its exports of software and IT-enabled services, more than 60 per cent of which are directed to the US. International banks and financial institutions in the US and EU are important sources of demand for such services, and the difficulties they face will result in some curtailment of their demand. Further, the nationalisation of many of these banks is likely to increase the pressure to reduce outsourcing in order to keep jobs in the developed countries. And the slowing of growth outside of the financial sector too will have implications for both merchandise and services exports. The net result would be a smaller export stimulus and a widening trade deficit.

Real Estate

One of the casualties of the crisis is the real estate. The crisis will hit the Indian real estate sector hard. The realty sector is witnessing a sudden slump in demand because of the global economic slowdown. The recession has forced the real estate players to curtail their expansion plans. Many on-going real estate projects are suffering due to lack of capital, both from buyers and bankers. Some realtors have already defaulted on delivery dates and commitments. The steel producers have decided to resort to production cuts following a decline in demand for the commodity.

India's Exports

The worldwide financial crisis has caused up to 70 per cent fall in India's exports. Handicrafts exports fell by 70 per cent. Other sectors like tea and carpets were also down by 20 per cent and 32 per cent, respectively. The Indian government is now attempting lifting export curbs on steel and some agro products. Overall export growth went down to just over 10 per cent from 26.9 per cent. Two of India's largest markers, European Union and the US, are both in the throes of financial crisis. Bulk cargo shipping rates have also come down by nearly 50 per cent.

Rupee Value

Rupee value against the US dollar has weakened dramatically. One reason might be the foreign fund inflow into India that was so prominent in the last couple of years, has turned negative. Financial institutional investors have deleveraged globally. Part of the reason has been the crunch they have faced in home markets, and part of it has been the flight to safety of US treasury paper. This net FII flow has been the single most important reason for the Rupee's fall. The Dollar has also strengthened against most currencies globally, not due to any strength of the US economy, but due to a 'flight to safety' of global capital. The US Dollar has been the world's reserve currency for several decades now. The Rupee's fall against other major currencies has been less pronounced, as seen in the Figure below.

Increase in Unemployment

One danger is of a dip in the employment market. The global financial crisis could increase unemployment. Layoffs and wage cuts are certain to take place in many companies where young employees are working in Business Process Outsourcing and Information Technology sectors. With job losses, the gap between the rich and the poor will be widened. It is estimated that there would be downsizing in many other fields as companies cut costs. The International Labour Organization predicted that millions of jobs will be lost by the end of 2009 due to the crisis—mostly in "construction, real estate, financial services, and the auto sector." The Global Wage Report 2008-09 of International Labour Organization warns that tensions are likely to intensify over the issue of wages. There would also be a significant drop in new hiring. All these will change the complexion of the job market.

Currently, India is facing a challenge. It is not a new phenomenon as India has faced challenges in the past and has overcome them. Our nation has strength to overcome the current challenges. It is very essential that Indian public rise to the occasion and convert the challenge in to an opportunity to establish new highs. This is the time for unity of purpose and resolute action.

CHAPTER

22

Global Financial Crisis and Its Impact on the Indian IT Sector

*S. Srinivasa Rao
**T. Anil Kumar

Genesis of Global Financial Crisis

The proximate cause of the current financial turbulence is attributed to the sub-prime mortgage sector in the USA. At a fundamental level, however, the crisis could be ascribed to the persistence of large global imbalances, which, in turn, were the outcome of long periods of excessively loose monetary policy in the major advanced economies during the early part of this decade.

Global imbalances have been manifested through a substantial increase in the current account deficit of the US mirrored by the substantial surplus in Asia, particularly in China, and in oil exporting countries in the Middle East and Russia (Lane, 2009). These imbalances in the current account are often seen as the consequence of the relative inflexibility of the currency regimes in China and some other EMEs.

* Faculty in Management, Dept. of Business Administration, TJPS, PG College, Guntur, Andhra Pradesh
** Faculty in Management, Dept. of Business Administration, Y.V. University, Kadapa, Andhra Pradesh

According to Portes (2009), global macroeconomic imbalances were the major underlying cause of the crisis. These saving-investment imbalances and consequent huge cross-border financial flows put great stress on the financial intermediation process. The global imbalances interacted with the flaws in financial markets and instruments to generate the specific features of the crisis.

The current US financial crisis has been variously compared with the 1907 banking/credit crisis, the Great Depression and the dotcom bust. It's been quite a roller-coaster ride for the world economy with financial services dominating the headlines world over-companies writing down losses, companies merging, acquiring, and going bust. The latest saga including Lehman, Merrill and AIG has unnerved the financial world and created serious concerns among their business partners, especially the Indian IT players.

IMPACT ON INDIAN IT SECTOR

The financial crisis in the advanced economies and the likely slowdown in these economies could have some impact on the IT sector. According to the latest assessment by the NASSCOM, the software trade association, the current developments with respect to the US financial markets are very eventful, and may have a direct impact on the IT industry and likely to create a downstream impact on other sectors of the US economy and world-wide markets. About 15 per cent to 18 per cent of the business coming to Indian outsourcers includes projects from banking, insurance, and the financial services sector which is now uncertain.

The current crisis parallels the 2001-2002 bust especially for India's IT (export) sector. Approximately 61 per cent of the Indian IT sector's revenues are from US clients. If you just take the top five India players who account for 46 per cent of the IT industry's revenues, the revenue contribution from US clients is approximately 58 per cent. About 30 per cent of the industry revenues are estimated to be from financial services. In addition, from a qualitative standpoint, the tentacles of the financial sector business are quite well-entrenched and have significant structural impact as well.

The size and maturity of the IT industry today are far ahead of the 2001 days, and the current model has signs of 'irreversibility' and long-term competitive advantage. While GE invented the industry along with India's biggest IT outsourcing firms, the US financial services and insurance sector (BFSI) was one of the earliest adopters of the outsourcing trend in a big way.

The US BFSI players created large outsourcing chunks, made Indian IT players learn from their experience, negotiated aggressively on pricing, pushed for service level commitments, and rewarded with more work to all who excelled in taking on their challenges. Between 1999 and 2008, the share of US financial services revenue as a per cent of total revenues for the Top 3 Indian players thus went up from 25 per cent to 38 per cent.

In the minds of the BFSI US players, Indian companies were flexible, delivered good quality (resources), and gave a key lever in managing their SG&A and time to market by freeing up more critical IT resources. They were essentially partners in taking some of the fixed costs out of their SG&A. Partnering in the operating business areas was still far away and is a tad far even today. It is ironic that this crisis would have had a worse impact, if Indian firms had partnered with the financial services entities much more closely, tying up their invoices with the clients' business outcomes. A recent study by Forrester reveals that 43 per cent of Western companies are cutting back their IT spend and nearly 30 per cent are scrutinizing IT projects for better returns. Some of this can lead to offshoring, but the impact of overall reduction in discretionary IT spends, including offshore work, cannot be denied. The slowing U.S. economy has seen 70 per cent of firms negotiating lower rates with suppliers and nearly 60 per cent are cutting back on contractors. With budgets squeezed, just over 40 per cent of companies plan to increase their use of offshore vendors.

The US financial crisis puts a question mark on growth for Indian IT in the short-to-medium-term. At the time of Q1 results, we saw growth numbers that were revised down by 2-3 per cent after sentiment started building up against the US financial sector. A worse downward revision is expected this quarter as well, though some larger players like TCS and Satyam have officially denied any possible impact on growth. Going by Infy numbers, a gloomy forecast can be expected.

However, there are some offsetting factors softening the revenue slowdown—favorable Rupee-Dollar exchange rate, growth de-risking through Europe, growth in non-financial verticals, and growth through countercyclical new business (countercyclical to US slowdown). There may still be some hope of revenue growth from new avenues, albeit resulting from the current crisis.

Merger activity is going to provide new outsourcing opportunities(as Infy confirmed), as newly-merged entities may have to look at additional or new providers to support the integration work and a broader global presence—especially when you take into account the huge size of combined international operations. In addition to the M&A activity, financial institutions will be looking to reduce their SG&A costs quickly, which will opt for outsourced solutions that impact the bottom-line—i.e. F&A BPO and some ITO and possibly some HRO deals, where there is quick remediation of staff.

A quick look at some numbers—taking the Q1 guidance numbers in Dollar terms and the FY09 guidance provided post the Q1 results, we can arrive at the implied QoQ growth for the next 3 quarters required to achieve these numbers. The numbers as given in the table seem quite high, especially if seen with the lens of the current crisis. Hence, growth projections are tough to do in the current situation. However, the depreciating Rupee gives them additional Rupee growth to hit the numbers, assuming lower hedging.

Brace for large top line impact from several industry players and especially those with financial services expIt is very difficult to replace fixed costs with variable costs at short notice of say a month. Hence, the focus will have to move to across-the-board fixed cost-cutting since making the costs esp. overheads and support costs variable at short notice is impossible.

Pricing has been difficult in this sector compared to other sectors: On an average, the US financial sector has driven bulk volumes through lower onsite pricing, higher offshoring and aggressive volume discounts. It is safe to infer that BFSI application business margins especially in the top companies are a few percentage points below the higher margin verticals like, say, energy. Hence, a replacement of financial services business with business from other verticals is likely to positively impact the bottom-line. A speedy replacement is however, easier said than done.

Exchange Rate : The Rupee-Dollar exchange rate benefit for a company that would have done zero-hedging, is in the range of 10-12 per cent. However, if we analyse the top few firms, the median seems to be around an offset benefit of around 2-3 per cent on the bottom-line, assuming some hedging.

The Rupee has depreciated since the last quarter by more than 10 per cent which has had a positive effect on both top line and the bottom-line in Rupee terms.

This is to an extent countered by the significant hedging done by the IT biggies, the ramifications of which translated into forex losses for them in the June quarter. This may bite them again this quarter. For example, TCS has hedged about US$ 2.2 billion for the year at ₹ 45/US$. According to the June quarter results transcript, at ₹ 45/US$, the mark-to-market loss on this would be about US$100 million. And, considering the Rupee has moved beyond ₹ 47/US$ into the first week of October, this can be far worse.

There is also another issue with this currency pantomime facing firms like Infosys, which derives 28 per cent of its revenues from the Euro, British Pound and Australian Dollar. The US$ has also been appreciating against these currencies. These earnings translated into US$ will have a negative 2 per cent impact on the company's numbers. Taking these factors in to consideration, the currency depreciation does not paint as rosy Wages are stabilizing and overall will have a positive impact on profitability due to lower attrition and hence lower recruitment costs. Wages as a per cent of top line also go down due to depreciation and labour market conditions. Similarly, pushing higher variability into wages can bring more benefits. And so will managing bench more aggressively and employee performance management programmes.

• ***Efficiencies :*** Indian IT companies continue to be made of the same DNA as during the dotcom days, and measures to shore up efficiencies are already underway since we saw the exchange rate hit 39 to the Dollar. Some of those gains are permanent since the processes have not been rolled back after the Rupee started depreciating. Potential measures are voluntary salary cuts, complete moratorium on salary raises, travel reduction, tightening of promotion spends, just-in-time hiring, hire-after-contract, etc.

• G&A levers like payables, facilities costs, transportation and some of the internal IT spends can aid more cost efficiencies. Relooking at the Selling, General and Administration (SG&A) expenses, with a view to be conservative would help, especially the second Tier IT firms. There is a difference of about 10 per cent between the SG&A of the top firms and the mid-level ones. Some conscious pruning on this front will only aid the bottom-line to move upwards (hard because of lack of economies of scale, but some aspects like making costs more variable and postponing some of the support and operational spending, are achievable).

While we have looked mainly at IT, the ITES sector is joined at the hip with IT industry, but with its own flavours. The impact in financial services operations will be much larger, but, over the medium to long term, there will be a huge gain for them from the increase in outsourcing and offshoring in the financial sector. However, short-term pain alongside the US slowdown is inevitable.

Conclusion and Opportunities for India's IT Sector

While there are growth-related challenges in the short-to-medium term, there seem to be some opportunities for managing the bottom-line for the rest of the year. The macroeconomic environment is depressing and has impacted the overall confidence in the sector from a market perspective. A US recession has not started but if it does, in all probability, it will last through 2009 and more, making this period a challenging one for growth.

Despite the foreboding current financial crisis, the opportunities are:

- Make the growth *vs.* profitability trade-off early on during the slowdown (which is now). Profitability levers are still available if growth is sacrificed where required, and managed well.

- Utilize some of the unavoidable fixed costs for implementing investment ideas that have been on the backburner and could not be kicked off due to high utilization.

- Look for M&A opportunities in US, both in financial sector and non-financial sector, especially where the option is to hold cash *vs* acquire.

  1. Financial sector companies: Distressed assets in the mortgage and other financial services industry are available to be picked up by Indian cos—the assets are laden with debt and a lack of good forecasts on future business;

2. IT companies to look for IP and product related investments especially in the US;
3. BPO's, especially captives, with significant financial services exposure are available for investments for Indian players.

• Focus on operational efficiencies—efficiencies that can help shore up the bottom line especially in an attractive labour market and an environment of budget/spend uncertainty.

All in all, the environment looks weakest in a long while, and yet there remain pockets of opportunity. These areas, if tapped intelligently, would enable the IT firms to ease the blow of this financial crisis and help them tide through the tough times. The crisis has now spread globally, and further reduces room to maneuver.

CHAPTER

23

Global Financial Crisis *vs* Indian Economy

*Dr. B. Yuvaraja Reddy
**Dr. Y. Mallikarjun Rao

"Every action has equal and opposite reaction".

—*Newton's third law*

Introduction

The economy tends to move in various phases i.e. from expansion to peak and then peak to recession. Along the way there will be a 'Phase to recovery' and once again it tends to peak. This is because of two reasons such as Greed during expansion and suffering during recession.

The term financial crisis is applied broadly to a variety of situations in which some financial institutions or assets suddenly lose a large part of their value. In the 19th and early 20th centuries, many financial crises were associated with banking panics and many recessions coincided with these panics. Other situations that are often called financial crises

* Lecturer in Commerce, Department of Commerce, S.G.S. Arts College, Tirupati, Andhra Pradesh
** Head of the Department, Department of Commerce, S.G.S. Arts College, Tirupati, Andhra Pradesh

include stock market crashes and the bursting of other financial bubbles, currency crises and sovereign defaults. The current financial crisis is the worst of its kind since the great depression of 1930s. It became prominently visible in September 2008 with the failure of several large US-based financial firms. The global financial meltdown meant disaster for the world economy in general and for the US and the European economies in particular. But surprisingly, when world's developed economies are suffering, developing countries like India and China are still spending money on many projects. Do we need to believe that Indian growth story is over? The answer is a big no. India is still to enter its golden phase of growth. This is the time for India to march on and look for opportunities to make its presence felt on the global economic map.

The Indian Approach in Current Scenario

Today India stands tall to face this financial crunch with many advantages and strengths. One of its major strengths is its nuclear technology, which will aid India to battle out its biggest problem-power.

Cautioning against the use of the word 'recession' for Indian economy, Finance Minister P.Chidambaram says India's growth would moderate in this difficult year, but would still be second-fastest in the world at the rate of 7-8 per cent. According to him a recession is defined as two successive quarters of contraction of GDP. He wishes to emphasize that India is nowhere near a recession. We may expect a moderation in growth rate in the current year to a level between 7 and 8 per cent. India would still be the second-fastest growing economy in the world, Chidambaram says.

Giving a positive projection on the country's economic scenario, Prime Minister Manmohan Singh said India could regain its annual growth rate of 8 per cent to 9 per cent as the world's economy could recover partially from the present crisis by September this year.

According to the Planning Commission Deputy Chairman, Montek Singh Ahluwalia, the global financial turmoil will not have any significant impact on the country's financial system as India is not exposed to the new and innovative financial instruments that triggered the meltdown. We have not been as exposed to these new and innovative instruments, which have been the source of financial distress internationally as some developed countries have been. So the direct impact on the Indian financial system is not going to be significant at all.

There will be indirect effect as regards India. The country is fortunate to have large foreign exchange reserves and, hence, it would be able to tide over any short-term disruption in capital inflows. The strengths of the Indian economy are substantial and capital inflows would eventually resume the normal course. As far as economic growth is concerned, the downturn in the world economy is going to have an impact on India and, unlike in 2008, the country would not register 9 per cent growth rate during the current fiscal year. Still, the growth rate could fall below 8 per cent at 7.7 per cent, as predicted by the Prime Minister's Economic Advisory Council.

Comparison of Indian Economy with Most Powerful World Economies

The world's most powerful economies suffered during the financial crisis. On the other hand India was able to spend a lot of money on launching of Chandrayana—I. US Economy struggled to overcome financial crisis at that time. It is evidenced that Bankruptcy of Lehman Brothers, Merging of Merrill Lynch with Bank of America, Wachovia auctioning by Citi Group, Washington Mutual Operations being taken over by FDIC etc. are a few of the struggles faced by US Economy during that period. But some Indian companies showed success reports at that time. It implies that Indian economy is better placed during financial crises.

Weaknesses of the Economy

The major role of financial crunch is that it exposes the political, structural and financial weaknesses of an economy. The primary reason for financial weakness is that the entire world's economy gets disturbed. It leads to or affects the capital flows and results in shrinkage in liquidity throughout the world. But its role in Indian economy is very minor. In other words, Indian economy is least affected when compared with the most powerful economies of. World like US Economy, European Economy etc. Financial crisis explores efficiency in the financial market, transparency and accountability of new or reformed organizations, opportunity for creating new jobs and technologies, sufficient fund for investment in R&D innovation and education.

India should endeavour to make the regulatory system more sophisticated to ensure that the country does not run into regulator gaps that led to the present global financial crisis. Our country pursued economic reforms in a calibrated manner and escaped the fallout of global financial crisis. Therefore, this expose of weaknesses will definitely help India's fast growing economy in the long run.

Performance Appraisal is Gaining Ground

During financial crisis, many companies did not achieve their primary motive of profit maximization. That is because of customer expectations, global competition, costs of goods and, services and above all because of financial crisis. That reflects on performance of employees', companies are beginning to discover the powerful link that exists between employee performance and financial success. Many companies depend more on human resources to lower operating costs, and improve financial position. Implementation of performance appraisal programmes leads to noticeable development in employee performance. Earlier as the job opportunity was more for the people, the role of performance appraisal was less. As a result, everyone is trying to perform at 100 per cent level at his or her jobs. Only the fear of losing job improves the performance of the employees.

Best Place in Outsourcing

India continues to be the best place or top destination for outsourcing as salary costs in India are extremely competitive and Indian outsourcing firms have now matured into true global companies that can offer best services at competitive prices. India is coming under the list of top outsourcing destinations such as China, Brazil, Mexico, Malaysia etc. India has the second lowest in its BPO salary base of $7,500-$8500 is followed by China. Another advantage that India has is that India is one of the largest producers of English-speaking graduates including management and engineering graduates. Such a huge number of graduates will definitely result in offering higher value-added services to the customers, which is very weak in China as the number of youth is less.

Opportunities for International Trade

The world economy begins to grow again and demand returns to foreign markets. Today countries all over the world are interested in trading with India. It will have a great impact on our foreign direct investment in many areas in India which increase the foreign exchange reserves and sustain the Indian economy.

Global Meltdown and Its Impact on the Indian Economy

The growing recession affected the world's most powerful economies like US, the European Union (EU) and Japan. This was the result of large-scale defaults in the developed countries. In India, due to the global meltdown or financial crisis, it was found that the Foreign Direct Investment (FDI) started drying up which influences the investment pattern of the Indian economy. Indian economy registered a growth rate of about seven per cent during 2008-09 and the same was expected to be at six per cent in 2009-10. That teaches a lesson to India which must exercise caution while liberalizing its financial sector. RBI Governor, Subbarao, said that Indian banks are safe, at a time when the Western banking industry is queuing up for bailouts. Suddenly Indian banks reap the benefit of the Non-Resident Indian (NRI) deposits, which would look for a safe haven back home.

The industries most affected by weakening demand were airlines, hotels and real estate. Besides this, Indian exports suffered a setback and there was a setback in the production of export-oriented sectors. The government advised the sectors of weakening demand to reduce prices. It provided some relief by cutting down excise duties, but such simplistic solutions were doomed to failure. Weakening demand led to producers cutting production. To reduce the impact of the crisis, firms reduced their workforce, to reduce costs. This led to increase in unemployment but the total impact on the economy was not very large. Industrial production and manufacturing output declined to five per cent in the last quarter of 2008-09. Consequently, a vicious cycle of weak demand and falling output developed in the Indian economy.

A weakening of demand in the US affected our IT and Business Process Outsourcing (BPO) sector and the loss of opportunities for young persons seeking employment at lucrative salaries abroad. India's famous IT sector, which earned about $ 50 billion as annual revenue, is expected to lose 50 per cent of its total revenues. This would reduce the cushion to set off the deficit in balance of trade and, thus, enlarge our balance of payments deficit. It has been now estimated that sluggish demand for exports would result in a loss of 10 million jobs in the export sector alone.

To lift the economy out of the recession the Government announced a package of ₹ 35,000 crores in the first instance on December 7, 2008. The main areas to benefit were the following:

(*a*) **Housing :** A refinance facility of ₹ 4000 crores was provided to the National Housing Bank. Following this, public sector banks announced schemes to provide small home loan seekers loans at reduced rates to step up demand in retail housing sector.

(*b*) **Textiles :** Due to declining orders from the world's largest market, the United States, the textile sector has been seriously affected. An allocation of ₹ 1400 crores has been made to clear the entire backlog in the Technology Upgradation Fund (TUF) scheme.

(*c*) **Infrastructure :** The government has been proclaiming that infrastructure is the engine of growth. To boost the infrastructure, the India Infrastructure Finance Company Ltd. (IIFCL) has been authorised to raise ₹ 14,000 crores through tax-free bonds. These funds will be used to finance infrastructure, more especially, highways and ports. It may be mentioned that 'refinance' refers to the replacement of an existing debt obligation with a debt obligation bearing better terms, meaning thereby, at lower rates or a changed repayment schedule. The IIFCL will be permitted to raise further resources by the issue of such bonds so that a public-private partnership (PPP) programme of ₹ 1,00,000 crores in the highway sector is promoted.

(*d*) **Exports :** Exports which accounted for 22 per cent of the GDP are expected to fall by 12 per cent. The government's fiscal package provides an interest rate subsidy of two per cent on exports for the labour–intensive sectors such as textiles, handicrafts, leather and gems and jewellery, but the Federation of Indian Export Organization (FIEO) felt the measures are not enough as they will not make the exports price-competitive and, therefore, will not boost exports. G.K. Pillai, the Commerce Secretary, has estimated a loss of 1.5 million jobs in the export sector alone during 2008-09 on account of the $15 billion decline in the expected exports.

(e) **Small and Medium Enterprises (SMEs) :** The government has announced a guarantee cover of 50 per cent for loans between ₹ 50 lakhs to ₹ 1 crore for SMEs. The government will instruct state-owned companies to ensure prompt payment of bills of SMEs so that they do not suffer on account of delay in the payment of their bills.

In short, the fiscal package is aimed at boosting growth in exports, real estate, auto, textiles and small and medium enterprises. The aim is to encourage growth and boost employment which have been threatened by the recession in the world economy, more especially in the United States.

The package has also provided finances to the non-banking finance companies (NBFCs), but there is serious lack of skill with the NBFCs on project appraisals and to ascertain the credit-worthiness of the borrowers and the accompanying project risks. There has to be a national campaign for training the NBFCs in project appraisals. It needs to be emphasised that implementation holds the key to bail out of the Indian economy from the economic crisis.

The predictions range between somewhat optimistic to fairly pessimistic. The Deputy Chairman of the Planning Commission, shri Montek Singh Ahluwalia, says the stimulus package part two is the part of the government strategy to deal with the situation as it evolves. The fiscal and monetary measures taken under the second package are targeted to increase liquidity for pushing up demand, addressing the concerns of the industries and provide incentives to exporters who have been hit by the recessionary conditions. He said that he was confident that despite the gloomy international economic situation India will register a growth rate of 7 per cent but fiscal deficit will be higher than anticipated on account of the stimulus packages announced. The RBI in its report says there are downsize risks from India's increasing global integration such as the sustained outflow of capital, financial contagion and slowing world growth.

Conclusion

The global financial meltdown meant disaster for the world economy in general and for the US and the European economies in particular. But surprisingly, when world's developed economies are suffering, developing countries like India and China are still spending money on many projects. India is still to enter its golden phase of growth. Today India stands tall to face this financial crunch with many advantages and strengths. One of its major strengths is its nuclear technology, which will aid India to battle out its biggest problem—power. India would still be the second-fastest growing economy in the world, Chidambaram says. The world's most powerful economies suffered during the financial crisis. Therefore, expose of weaknesses will definitely help India's fast growing economy in the long run.

CHAPTER

24

Sustainbility of Indian Economy Despite Global Financial Meltdown

*Prof. P.V. Narasaiah

Introduction

The term 'global financial meltdown' is a recognition of the globalize economy as we have today. In some fifteen to twenty years ago, it was possible to single out a country (economy) that would isolate itself from the vagaries of the world economy. Within the period under reference, there were no wide world web, no cable news network (CNN) and other like it, few interconnectivity of banks and stock exchange markets. All these have changed positively unifying the world and making it a global village.

Financial meltdown has much to do with the crash of stock/share prices in the various stock exchange markets of countries. There is a linkage between the collapse of both the mortgage investments and auto industry in the US and the Wall Street crisis. These companies and their positive performance till the crunch came down on them was due to investor's confidence in their ability to manage their activities and return dividends to their investments.

*Department of Commerce, S.V. University, Tirupati, Andhra Pradesh

Once the companies publicly declared the state of their insolvency and the huge loses experienced by them, the investors' confidence was eroded. The result was a stampede where both small and large investors wanted to off load their shares in the market. In line with the principle of demand and supply, as more shares are off loaded into the market, the prices dropped as far investors showed interest in investing.

The economy works like a web and what affects one affects the other. Banks would have extended loans which are being serviced monthly by these companies. Their inability to pay as the loans fall due would automatically affect the banking industry's liquidity. This will result to situations where the banks can no longer honour cash or credit obligations to their customers and the cyclical effect continues to the detriment of the economy and in the case of the US to that of the world economy.

Global Outlook

The global economic outlook deteriorated sharply over the last quarter. In a sign of the ferocity of the downturn, the IMF made a marked downward revision of its estimate for global growth in 2009 in purchasing power parity terms—from its forecast of 3.0 per cent made in October 2008 to 0.5 per cent in January 2009. In market exchange rate terms, the downturn is sharper—global GDP is projected to actually shrink by 0.6 per cent. With all the advanced economies—the United States, Europe and Japan—having firmly gone into recession, the contagion of the crisis from the financial sector to the real sector has been unforgiving and total. Recent evidence suggests that contractionary forces are strong: demand has slumped, production is plunging, job losses are rising and credit markets remain in seizure. Most worryingly, world trade—the main channel through which the downturn will get transmitted on the way forward—is projected to contract by 2.8 per cent in 2009.

Emerging Economies

Contrary to the 'decoupling theory', emerging economies too have been hit by the crisis. The decoupling theory, which was intellectually fashionable even as late as a year ago, held that even if advanced economies went into a downturn, emerging economies will remain unscathed because of their substantial foreign exchange reserves, improved policy framework, robust corporate balance sheets and relatively healthy banking sector. In a rapidly globalizing world, the 'decoupling theory' was never totally persuasive. Given the evidence of the last few months—capital flow reversals, sharp widening of spreads on sovereign and corporate debt and abrupt currency depreciations—the 'decoupling theory' stands totally invalidated. Reinforcing the notion that in a globalized world no country can be an island, growth prospects of emerging economies have been undermined by the cascading financial crisis with, of course, considerable variation across countries.

Why Has India Been Hit By the Crisis?

There is, at least in some quarters, dismay that India has been hit by the crisis. This dismay stems from two arguments:

The *first* argument goes as follows. The Indian banking system has had no direct exposure to the sub-prime mortgage assets or to the failed institutions. It has very limited off-balance sheet activities or securitized assets. In fact, our banks continue to remain safe and healthy. So, the enigma is how can India be caught up in a crisis when it has nothing much to do with any of the maladies that are at the core of the crisis.

The *second* reason for dismay is that India's recent growth has been driven predominantly by domestic consumption and domestic investment. External demand, as measured by merchandize exports, accounts for less than 15 per cent of our GDP. The question then is, even if there is a global downturn, why should India be affected when its dependence on external demand is so limited?

The answer to both the above frequently-asked questions lies in globalization. First, India's integration into the world economy over the last decade has been remarkably rapid. Integration into the world implies more than just exports. Going by the common measure of globalization, India's two-way trade (merchandize exports plus imports), as a proportion of GDP, grew from 21.2 per cent in 1997-98, the year of the Asian crisis, to 34.7 per cent in 2007-08.

Second, India's financial integration with the world has been as deep as India's trade globalization, if not deeper. If we take an expanded measure of globalization, that is the ratio of total external transactions (gross current account flows plus gross capital flows) to GDP, this ratio has more than doubled from 46.8 per cent in 1997-98 to 117.4 per cent in 2007-08.

Importantly, the Indian corporate sector's access to external funding has markedly increased in the last five years. Some numbers will help illustrate the point. In the five-year period 2003-08, the share of investment in India's GDP rose by 11 percentage points. Corporate savings financed roughly half of this, but a significant portion of the balance financing came from external sources. While funds were available domestically, they were expensive relative to foreign funding.

How Has India Been Hit By the Crisis?

The contagion of the crisis has spread to India through all the channels—the financial channel, the real channel, and importantly, as happens in all financial crises, the confidence channel.

Let us first look at the financial channel. India's financial markets—equity markets, money markets, forex markets and credit markets—had all come under pressure from a number of directions. First, as a consequence of the global liquidity squeeze, Indian banks and corporates found their overseas financing drying up, forcing corporates to shift their credit demand to the domestic banking sector. Also, in their frantic search for substitute financing, corporates withdrew their investments from domestic money market mutual funds putting redemption pressure on the mutual funds and down the line on non-banking financial companies (NBFCs) where the MFs had invested a significant portion of their funds. This substitution of overseas financing by domestic financing brought both money markets and credit markets under pressure.

How Have We Responded to the Challenge?

Let me now turn to how we responded to the crisis. The failure of Lehman Brothers in mid-September was followed in quick succession by several other large financial institutions coming under severe stress. This made financial markets around the world uncertain and unsettled. This contagion, as I explained above, spread to emerging economies, and to India too. Both the government and the Reserve Bank of India responded to the challenge in close coordination and consultation. The main plank of the government response was fiscal stimulus while the Reserve Bank's action comprised monetary accommodation and counter cyclical regulatory forbearance.

Monetary Policy Response

The Reserve Bank's policy response was aimed at containing the contagion from the outside—to keep the domestic money and credit markets functioning normally and see that the liquidity stress did not trigger solvency cascades. In particular, we targeted three objectives: first, to maintain a comfortable rupee liquidity position; second, to augment foreign exchange liquidity; and third, to maintain a policy framework that would keep credit delivery on track so as to arrest the moderation in growth. This marked a reversal of Reserve Bank's policy stance from monetary tightening in response to heightened inflationary pressures of the previous period to monetary easing in response to easing inflationary pressures and moderation in growth in the current cycle. Our measures to meet the above objectives came in several policy packages starting mid-September 2008, on occasion in response to unanticipated global developments and at other times in anticipation of the impact of potential global developments on the Indian markets.

Government's Fiscal Stimulus

Over the last five years, both the Central and State governments in India have made a serious effort to reverse the fiscal excesses of the past. At the heart of these efforts was the Fiscal Responsibility and Budget Management (FRBM) Act which mandated a calibrated road map to fiscal sustainability. However, recognizing the depth and extraordinary impact of this crisis, the Central Government invoked the emergency provisions of the FRBM Act to seek relaxation from the fiscal targets and launched two fiscal stimulus packages in December 2008 and January 2009. These fiscal stimulus packages, together amounting to about 3 per cent of GDP, included additional public spending, particularly capital expenditure, government guaranteed funds for infrastructure spending, cuts in indirect taxes, expanded guarantee cover for credit to micro and small enterprises, and additional support to exporters. These stimulus packages came on top of an already announced expanded safety-net for rural poor, a farm loan waiver package and salary increases for government staff, all of which too should stimulate demand.

Impact of Monetary Measures

Taken together, the measures put in place since mid-September 2008 have ensured that the Indian financial markets continue to function in an orderly manner. The cumulative amount of primary liquidity potentially available to the financial system through these measures is over US$ 75 bln or 7 per cent of GDP. This sizeable easing has ensured a comfortable liquidity position starting mid-November 2008 as evidenced by a number of indicators including the weighted-average call money rate, the overnight money market rate and the yield on the 10-year benchmark government security. Taking the signal from the policy rate cut, many of the big banks have reduced their benchmark prime lending rates. Bank credit has expanded too, faster than it did last year. However, Reserve Bank's rough calculations show that the overall flow of resources to the commercial sector is less than what it was last year. This is because, even though bank credit has expanded, it has not fully offset the decline in non-bank flow of resources to the commercial sector.

Evaluating the Response

In evaluating the response to the crisis, it is important to remember that although the origins of the crisis are common around the world, the crisis has impacted different economies differently. Importantly, in advanced economies where it originated, the crisis spread from the financial sector to the real sector. In emerging economies, the transmission of external shocks to domestic vulnerabilities has typically been from the real sector to the financial sector. Countries have accordingly responded to the crisis depending on their specific country circumstances. Thus, even as policy responses across countries are broadly similar, their precise design, quantum, sequencing and timing have varied. In particular, while policy responses in advanced economies have had to contend with both the unfolding financial crisis and deepening recession, in India, our response has been predominantly driven by the need to arrest moderation in economic growth.

Strengths of Indian Economy

After several decades of sluggish growth, the Indian economy is now amongst the fastest growing economy in the world.

Economic growth is currently 8-9 per cent, second only to China.

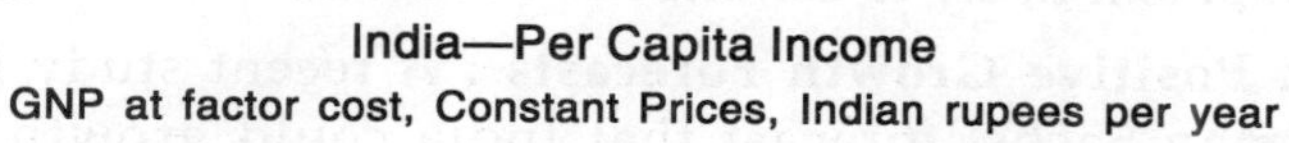

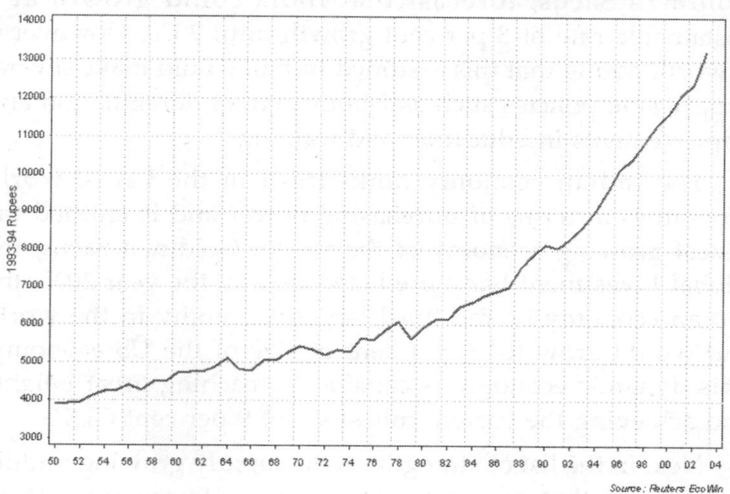

Despite several problems facing the Indian economy many economists point to potential strengths of the Indian economy which could enable it to continue to benefit from high levels of economic growth in the future.

1. Demographics of India are favourable : India still has a positive birth rate meaning that the size of the workforce will continue to grow for the foreseeable future. (unlike India) A rising workforce helps to increase saving and investment. It also enables increased productivity.

2. There is much scope for increases in efficiency : The infrastructure of India is so bad in places that even moderate improvements could lead to significant improvements in the productive capacity of the economy.

3. India is well placed to benefit from globalisation and outsourcing : A legacy of the British Empire is that India has one of the largest English speaking populations in the world. For labour intensive industries like call centres India is an obvious target for outsourcing. This is an economic development likely to continue in the future.

4. Positive Growth Forecasts : A recent study from Goldman Sachs, forecast that India could growth at a sustainable rate of 8 per cent growth until 2020. However it is worth noting that this assumed Indian would make several supply side policies such as labour market deregulation and improvements in education and training.

The Indian economy ranks third in the list of world economies in terms of purchasing power and is entitled the fastest growing economy of the world. Goldman Sachs, the Global Investment Bank predicted that by the year 2035, the Indian economy be the third largest economy in the world and would grow to 60 per cent of size of the US economy. This dynamic economy is capable of reaching great heights and achieving the current milestone of 9 per cent GDP.

Next in the list of strengths is the rapidly growing middle class section that possesses a strong desire to consume. Thus, the Indian economy can easily maintain a preferential balance between its productivity and consumption.

Next comes, the rich natural resource base that comprises of valuable resources like coal, iron ore, water, limestone, granite, Manganese, Mica, Chromites, Bauxite, Titanium ore, Natural gas, Petroleum, Diamonds and Thorium. These energy resources promise a significant future potential for the Indian economy.

Some other strengths of the Indian economy are the growing education system, English language proficiency, strong tertiary education, great record of software development, government support and policies, process quality focus, skilled workforce, cost advantage, entrepreneurship, reverse brain drain, expansion of existing relationships, leverage relationships in West to access overseas markets and Indian domestic-market growth.

India GDP Growth Rate

The Gross Domestic Product (GDP) in India expanded at an annual rate of 7.20 per cent in the last quarter. India Gross Domestic Product is worth 1217 billion dollars or 1.96 per cent of the world economy, according to the World Bank. India's diverse economy encompasses traditional village farming, modern agriculture, handicrafts, a wide range of modern industries, and a multitude of services. Services are the major source of economic growth, accounting for more than half of India's output with less than one third of its labour force. The economy has posted an average growth rate of more than 7 per cent in the decade since 1997, reducing poverty by about 10 percentage points. This page includes: India GDP Growth Rate chart, historical data and news.

Country	Interest Rate	Growth Rate	Inflation Rate	Jobless Rate	Current Account	Exchange Rate
India	3.25%	7.20%	14.97%	7.32%		

India's Economy May Overheat in 2010

In the third quarter of 2009, India's economy expanded 7.9 per cent. And although it is expected that in the last three months of 2009, the third largest economy in Asia might have recorded growth over 8 per cent, the beginning of 2010 may surprise us on the negative side.

Indeed, recent data is indicating that GDP growth in the last quarter of 2009 may beat expectations. For example, since June industrial production has been accelerating, recording 11.7 per cent growth in November, the fastest in two years and exports grew 18 per cent in November. Yet, the stunning performance of the Indian economy has a lot to do with a significant fiscal stimulus and loose monetary policy. In fact, it is estimated that government contributed around 50 per cent of total GDP growth in the year to September. In addition, lower interest rates have supported domestic demand for consumer durables.

However, despite some positive data, the rising inflation is a growing concern. Indeed, a weaker monsoon has pushed price of food significantly higher in the last few months. This price pressure combined with strong industrial production may soon lead to interest rate hikes and tighten credit availability. Also, there is another danger by the corner. It is likely that due to extensive spending, Indian government may record huge fiscal deficit in the year to March. And in order to balance the budget the authorities may decide to increase taxes thus crowding our private investments.

International Monetary Fund (IMF) has revealed that the economic growth rate of India is likely to decline by 6.9 per cent in the year 2009. As per IMF this demotion is inevitable as the Asian countries are not totally immune to the financial crisis in the US and its subsequent fallout. IMF's World Economic Outlook (WEO) claimed that India's gross domestic product (GDP) growth rate, which was 9.3 per cent in 2007, will slope down to 7.8 per cent by the end of 2008 and end up to 6.9 per cent in 2009. The Economic Outlook (WEO) of IMF has been released in Washington on October 8, 2008.

The report further claimed that Asia's economic growth rate is also likely to suffer in the coming year. The GDP growth rate of Asia is likely to decline to 7.7 per cent in 2008 and turn out to be 7.1 per cent in 2009. Due to the September market turbulence, the global financial market has suffered a major setback and is becoming weak day by day. The ailing financial market is also unable to attract the investors. IMF also said that during 2005-07, the global stock markets have declined drastically and India has also not been spared from it.

Inflation in India

India's 2008 Economic Survey Report targeted a drop in India's Inflation Rate—but with food, oil and commodity price rises worldwide, the opposite is happening.

According to the 2008 Economic Survey Report, India's inflation rate was targeted by the Reserve Bank of India (RBI) to be 4.1 per cent, down from a rate of 5.77 per cent in 2007. Inflation rates for many investment goods have decreased dramatically in recent years. The price of basic goods such as lentils, vegetables, fruits and poultry were expected to slow their rise. The price of various manufactured goods also fell in 2007, and this contributed to a reduced inflation rate.

However, the beginning of 2008 has seen a dramatic rise in the price of rice and other basic food stuffs. There has also been a no-less alarming rise in the price of oil and gas. When coupled with rises in the price of the majority of commodities, higher inflation was the only likely outcome.

Indeed, by July 2008, the key Indian Inflation Rate, the Wholesale Price Index, has risen above 11 per cent, its highest rate in 13 years. This is more than 6 per cent higher than a year earlier and almost three times the RBI's target of 4.1 per cent.

Inflation has climbed steadily during the year, reaching 8.75 per cent at the end of May. There was an alarming increase in June, when the figure jumped to 11 per cent. This was driven in part by a reduction in government fuel subsidies, which have lifted gasoline prices by an average 10 per cent.

The Indian method for calculating inflation, the Wholesale Price Index, is different to the rest of world. Each week, the wholesale price of a set of 435 goods is calculated by the Indian Government. Since these are wholesale prices, the actual prices paid by consumers are far higher.

In times of rising inflation this also means that cost of living increases are much higher for the populace. Cooking gas prices, for example, have increased by around 20 per cent in 2008.

With most of India's vast population living close to—or below—the poverty line, inflation acts as a 'Poor Man's Tax'. This effect is amplified when food prices rise, since food represents more than half of the expenditure of this group.The dramatic increase in inflation will have both economic and political implications for the government, with an election due within the year.

Economic growth in emerging markets has slowed but is far from over. With the BRIC countries (Brazil, Russia, India and China) alone accounting for more than 3 billion people, and with these people consuming more resources every year, it is likely that higher inflation rates will be with us for a good while yet—and that is worrying news for the Government of India.

Inflation is Caused Due to Several Economic Factors

- When the government of a country print money in excess, prices increase to keep up with the increase in currency, leading to inflation.
- Increase in production and labour costs, have a direct impact on the price of the final product, resulting in inflation.
- When countries borrow money, they have to cope with the interest burden. This interest burden results in inflation.
- High taxes on consumer products, can also lead to inflation.
- Demands pull inflation, wherein the economy demands more goods and services than what is produced.
- Cost push inflation or supply shock inflation, wherein non-availability of a commodity would lead to increase in prices.

Inflation in Indian Economy

India after independence has had a more stable record with respect to inflation than most other developing countries. Since 1950, the inflation in Indian economy has been in single digits for most of the years:

Between 1950-1960 : The inflation on an average was at 2.00%

Between 1960-1970 : The inflation on an average was at 7.2%

Between 1970-1980 : The inflation on an average was at 8.5%.

Inflation At Present

Inflation in India a menace a few years ago is at a 30 year low. The inflation ended at a low of 0.61 per cent in the week ended May 9, 2009 this after reaching a 16 year high of 12.91 per cent in August 2008, bringing in a sigh of relief to policymakers.

SPECIFIC MEASURES TAKEN BY INDIAN GOVERNMENT TO STRENGTHEN INDIAN ECONOMY

Chasing a ballooning fiscal deficit; which is expected to take a further beating after the hike in prices of petroleum products, the govemment has announced a series of belt-tightening measures, to be implemented with immediate effect, including a 10 per cent cut in all non-plan, non-salary expenditure of all government departments. Incidentally, the guidelines cover not only Central government departments but also extended to state governments and public sector units.

The Finance Ministry mandarins say the austerity measures are being introduced as they fear government's fiscal deficit could cross the targeted limit of 5.1 per cent of GDP by as much as half a percentage point as government spending has been burgeoning even as revenue has been falling short of targets.

The Finance Ministry order also banned the creation of new jobs in the government sector, abolition of posts lying vacant for more than a year. The government departments have also been asked to cut existing jobs by up to 10 per cent wherever possible.

Foreign travel allowance is being cut by 25 per cent for all officials, senior and junior. Travel on study tours and seminars are being banned while unavoidable foreign travel will see smaller delegations. The cuts, officials insisted, covered the political executives as well and was not just limited to the bureaucracy. New rules also ban the purchases of new cars and other vehicles by the government and calls upon all departments to spend 10 per cent less on-fuel bil1s. The departments are also being told to organise fewer and less lavish conferences and seminars.

The Finance Ministry officials estimate these measures should save as much as ₹ 1,500 crore for the government. The government has currently overshot expenditure allocations by as much as 8-10 per cent. Officials said this overspending was at the root of the problem.

Customs duty collections have also been low, compounding the cash-strapped government's woes. In the wake of oil price hike and its recessionary impact on industry, the government can expect even lower revenue collections in the months ahead, Finance Ministry officials added.

Conclusion

The strength of the indian economy lies in its domestic investment and domestic consumption. The Government's timely initiative through its monetary and fiscal policies have helped the indian economy to withstand the pressures of global recession. The indian government's response to the recession is noteworthy and for many a world economy a lesson. Despite the argument whether the advantage is because of the inherent features of the country and the economy or a thoroughly planned initiative of the Government, out Government also has a lesson towards global recession. Ultimately it is the inherent strength of the economy, lesser dependence on the global economies, domestic consumption and investments and timely initiatives which would ensure a sustainable economy in the doldrums of recession.

REFERENCES

1. Roy, Tirthankar (2000). *The Economic History of India*. Oxford University Press. ISBN 0-19-565154-5
2. Sankaran, S (1994). *Indian Economy: Problems, Policies and Development*. Margham
3. The Journal of Economy Watch, www.economywatch.com
4. Reserve Bank of India 2007, Hand book of Indian Economy

CHAPTER

India in Global Recession

*Dr. R. Praveen Kumar Reddy
**K. Nirmal Kumar Reddy

With the liberalization of Indian economy the gates are wide open for free flow of labour, capital, technical know how to all parts of the world. During the last few years after continuous growth in many sectors the world entered into a recession phase which was witnessed with the filing of bankruptcy petitions by world famous companies like Lehman Brothers, Bear Sterns, AIG, General Motor Company etc.,. Liberalization policy in India not only resulted in growth of IT, ITES and real estate sectors but also shock waves when the American economy was affected. The extent of impact has been restricted due to several reasons such as :

- Indian financial sector particularly our banks have no direct exposure to tainted assets and its off-balance sheet activities have been limited. The credit derivatives market is in an embryonic stage and there

* M.Com., Ph.D., Junior Lecturer in Commerce, Govt. Junior College, Nimmanapalli, Andhra Pradesh

** M. Com., M.Phill., Junior Lecturer in Commerce, Aditya Junior College, Madanapalli, Andhra Pradesh

are restrictions on investments by residents in such products issued abroad.

- India's growth process has been largely domestic demand driven and its reliance on foreign savings has remained around 1.5 per cent in recent period.
- India's comfortable foreign exchange reserves provide confidence in our ability to manage our balance of payments notwithstanding lower export demand and dampened capital flows.
- Headline inflation, as measured by the wholesale price index (WPI), has declined sharply.
- Rural demand continues to be robust due to mandated agricultural lending and social safety-net programmes.
- India's merchandise exports are around 15 per cent of GDP, which is relatively modest.

Sub-prime crisis and bankruptcy of Lehman Brothers 2007-09: Beginning in the United States in December 2007 (and with much greater intensity since September 2008, according to the National Bureau of Economic Research, much of the industrialized world has been undergoing a recession, a pronounced deceleration of economic activity. This global recession has been taking place in an economic environment characterized by various imbalances and was sparked by the outbreak of the financial crisis of 2007–2010. With the collapse of Lehman Brothers September 15, 2008 and other Wall Street icons, there was growing recession which affected the US, the European Union (EU) and Japan. This was the result of large scale defaults in the US housing market as the banks went on providing risky loans without adequate security and the repaying capacity of the borrower. The principal source of transmission of the crisis has been the real sector, generally referred to as the 'Main Street'. This crisis engulfed the United States in the form of creeping recession and this worsened the situation. As a consequence, US demand for imports from other countries indicated a decline.

The basic cause of the crisis was largely an unregulated environment, mortgage lending to sub prime borrowers. Since the borrowers did not have adequate repaying capacity and also because sub prime borrowing had to pay two-to-three percentage points higher rate of interest and they have a history of default, the situation became worse. But once the housing market collapsed, the lender institutions saw their balance-sheets go into red.

Late 2000s recession: Although the late-2000s recession has at times been referred to as 'The Great Recession,' this same phrase has been used to refer to every recession of the several preceding decades. With the collapse of Lehman Brothers September 15, 2008 and other Wall Street icons, there was growing recession which affected the US, the European Union (EU) and Japan. As a consequence, US demand for imports from other countries indicated a decline. A redeeming feature of the current crisis is that its magnitude is much lesser than that of the Great Depression of the 1930s when unemployment rate in the United States exceeded 25 per cent. Currently, it stands at 6.5 per cent and is predicted to remain around eight per cent in 2009.

GLOBAL MELTDOWN IN THE INDIAN CONTEXT:

India is not de-linked from the world, and the financial meltdown has certainly impacted us. In the age of globalization, no country can remains isolated from the fluctuations of world economy. Heavy losses suffered by major International Banks is going to affect all countries of the world as these financial institutes have their investment interest in almost all countries.

As of now India is facing heat on three grounds: (1) Our Share Markets are falling everyday; (2) Rupee is weakening against dollars; and (3) Our banks are facing severe cash crunch resulting in shortage of liquidity in the market. Actually all the above three problems are interconnected and have their roots in the above-mentioned global crisis. For the last two years, our stock market was creating a new summit which was mainly due to heavy investments by Foreign Institutional Investors (FIIs). However, when the parent companies of these investors (based mainly in US and Europe) found themselves in a severe credit tumult as a result of sub-prime mess, the only option left with these investors was to withdraw their money from Indian Stock Markets to meet liabilities at home. FIIs were the main buyers of Indian Stocks and their exit from the market is certain to wreak havoc in the market. FIIs who were on a buying spree last year, are now in the mood of selling their stocks in India. As a result our Share Markets were touching new lows everyday.

Since, the money, which FIIs get after selling their stocks, needs to be converted into dollars before they can sent it home, the demand for dollars suddenly increased. As more and more FIIs are buying dollars, the rupee is loosing its strength against dollar. As long as demands for dollars remain high, the rupee will keep loosing its strength against dollar.

Our companies in India have most outsourcing deals from the US. Even our exports to US have increased over the years. Exports for January have declined by 22 per cent. There is a decline in the employment market due to the recession in the West. There has been a significant drop in the new hiring which is a cause of great concern for us. Some companies have laid off their employees and there have been cut in promotions, compensation and perks of the employees. Companies in the private sector and government sector are hesitant to take up new projects. And they are working on existing projects only. Projections indicate that up to one crore persons could lose their jobs in the correct fiscal ending March. The one crore figure has been compiled by Federation of Indian Export Organizations (FIEO), which says that it has carried out an intensive survey. The textile, garment and handicraft industry are worse effected. Together, they are going to lose four million jobs by April 2009, according to the FIEO survey. There has also been a decline in the tourist inflow lately. The real estate has also a problem of tight liquidity situations, where the developers are finding it hard to raise finances. IT industries, financial sectors, real estate owners, car industry, investment banking and other industries as well are confronting heavy loss due to the fall down of global economy. Federation of Indian Chambers of Commerce and Industry (FICCI) found that faced with the global recession, inventories industries like garment, gems, textiles, chemicals and jewellers had cut production by 10 per cent to 50 per cent. A global depression is likely to result in a fall in demand of all types of consumer goods. In 2007-08, India sold 13.5 per cent of its goods to foreign buyers. A fall in demand is likely to affect the growth rate this year. Our export may get affected badly.

The current financial crisis has also started directly affecting Indian Industries. For the past few years, the two most preferred method of raising money by the companies were Stock Markets and external borrowings on low interest rates. Stock Markets were falling everyday and it was not possible to raise money there. Regarding external borrowing from world markets, this option has also become difficult (McKinsey Report, 2009).

In the last fiscal year alone, India borrowed $29 billion from foreign lenders and got $34 billion of foreign direct investment. A global recession has hurt external demand. International lenders who have become extremely risk aversive can limit access to international capital. If that happens, both India's financial markets and the real economy will be hurt in the process. Suddenly, the 9 per cent growth target does not seem that 'doable' any more; we should be happy to clock 7 per cent this fiscal year and the next.

Although the impact of recession on Indian economy is limited but still India witnessed some fluctuations which can be clearly understood by these:

1. Stock market reached a 20,000 mark within a short span of time. It also reached 7000 mark in line with

the decline of global markets. This was augmented by the outflow of funds from the system by FIIS. Reduced availability of international capital and increase in price of equity has led to bearish trend.

2. Indian Forex Market showed wide fluctuations with decreasing of rupee value against dollar due to global credit crunch.
3. The annual GDP growth rate which saw a steady growth of around 9 per cent suddenly reduced due to impact of recession which was revised to 6 per cent as per RBIs latest policy statement.
4. There was growth of exports till Aug 2008. But it turned negative after October 2008 due to the effect of recession.
5. Recession has adversely affected service industry there by slowing down the rate of growth in textiles, jewellery, food processing industries.
6. The tax GDP ratio which showed a growth from 8.97 to 12.56 per cent showed a reverse trend to 10.95 per cent during fiscal year due to economic slowdown.

India's Response to Recession

The Government of India introduced stimulus package to overcome financial crisis. The RBI took policy decisions for easing liquidity. These can be discussed as follows :

- **Fiscal Response** : The GOI launched 3 stimulus packages in addition to existing safety net programme for the rural poor, farm loan waiver package and the increasing of salaries of Central Government employees. These packages led to sharp increase in revenue and fiscal deficits which slowed down the economic activities. Tight regulatory and supervisionary measures have also been introduced.

- **Monetary Response:** The RBI through its actions like reducing CRR, Repo, SLR and reverse repo rates infused ₹ 6,00,000 crores in order to ensure liquidity into the banking system. It also issued strict orders for implementation of Basel II norms and provisioning norms for all types of standard assets. It also took several measures for free flow of credit into the Indian market.

Conclusion

The global financial crisis bought almost all the countries into its fold. The GDP slowdown since the last quarter of 2008, slow employment growth and capital outflows are seen in this period. Higher input costs took away the corporate profit margins. India has a little impact of recession due to sound banking sector, good regulatory framework and enough forex reserves. The growth of Indian market can be further triggered by boosting up the confidence in investors. We should not follow whatever is suitable for abroad countries. We should slowly study and introduce financial instruments with strict monitoring. Efforts should increase for satisfying huge domestic market and for product innovation. The government should concentrate much on agriculture and manufacturing sectors which are in slow pace. It should remove the packages to IT, automobile and pharma sector.

REFERENCES

1. *Annual Report 2008-09,* Reserve Bank of India.
2. *Macroeconomic and Monetary Developments: First Quarter Review 2009-10,* Reserve Bank of India.
3. *Bank Quest* Vol. 80 January-March 2009, IIBF.
4. Chidambaram P 2008. Spill-over Effects of Global Crisis Will Be Tackled. *The Hindu, Daily*, November 19, 2008, p. 15.
5. Venkitaramanan S 2008. Global Financial Crisis: Reflections on Its Impact on India. *The Hindu*, Daily,October 10, 2008, p. 11.

CHAPTER

26

Impact of Financial Crisis—2009-10

*Dr. Morusu Sivasankar

While the global financial crisis has beset the world with adversities and challenges, the black cloud does offer a silver lining to emerging countries like India and China to emerge as strong contender's pecking order of world economic power. The effect of global financial crisis on Indian financial system has been limited. However, the cumulative impact of all these were a slowing down of out-put and employment. Despite the slow down, India is still the second fastest growing economy in the world. The strength is also reflected in the increased financial crisis over last year's numbers. Across the world, foreign direct investment has been increasing dramatically since the beginning of nineties. Most of the countries in the world have recognized foreign capital role in the relevance to rapid economic and industrial development. It contributes in many important ways to the process of economic growth and industrialization. It can act as a catalyst for domestic industrial development. Further, it helps in

* Post-doctoral fellow, Department of Commerce, Sri Venkateswara University, College of Commerce and Management, Computer Science, Tirupati-517 502, Andhra Pradesh

speeding up economic activity and brings with it service productive factors such as technical know-how and managerial experience, which are equally essential for the economic development of financial sector. This chapter envisages the impact of crisis on the financial sector in USA and opportunities as well as challenges confronting with the global financial crisis.

Financial Crisis of 2007–2010

The *financial crisis of 2007–present* is a global financial crisis triggered by a liquidity shortfall in the United States banking system. It has resulted in the collapse of large financial institutions, the 'bail out' of banks by national governments and downturns in stock markets around the world. It is considered by many economists to be the worst financial crisis since the Great Depression of the 1930s. It contributed to the failure of key businesses, declines in consumer wealth estimated in the trillions of U.S. dollars, substantial financial commitments incurred by governments, and a significant decline in economic activity. Many causes have been proposed, with varying weight assigned by experts. Both market-based and regulatory solutions have been implemented or are under consideration, while significant risks remain for the world economy over the 2010–2011 periods. Although this economic period has at times been referred to as 'the Great Recession,' this same phrase has been used to refer to every recession of the several preceding decades.

The collapse of a global housing bubble, which peaked in the U.S. in 2006, caused the values of securities tied to real estate pricing to plummet thereafter, damaging financial institutions globally. Questions regarding bank solvency, declines in credit availability, and damaged investor confidence had an impact on global stock markets, where securities suffered large losses during late 2008 and early 2009. Economies worldwide slowed during this period as credit tightened and international trade declined. Critics argued that credit rating agencies and investors failed to accurately price

could not refinance to avoid the higher payments associated with rising interest rates and began to default. During 2007, lenders began foreclosure proceedings on nearly 1.3 million properties, a 79 per cent increase over 2006. This increased to 2.3 million in 2008, an 81 per cent increase vs. 2007. By August 2008, 9.2 per cent of all U.S. mortgages outstanding were either delinquent or in foreclosure By September 2009, this had risen to 14.4 per cent.

Easy Credit Conditions

Lower interest rates encourage borrowing. From 2000 to 2003, the Federal Reserve lowered the federal funds rate target from 6.5 per cent to 1.0 per cent. This was done to soften the effects of the collapse of the dot-com bubble and of the September 2001 terrorist attacks, and to combat the perceived risk of deflation.

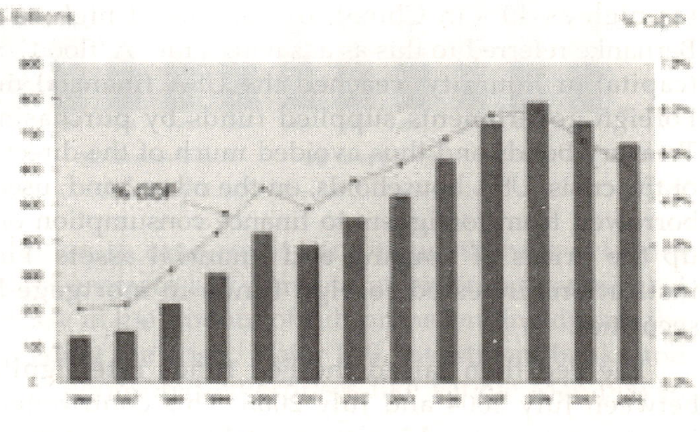

U.S. Current Account or Trade Deficit

Additional downward pressure on interest rates was created by the USA's high and rising current account (trade) deficit, which peaked along with the housing bubble in 2006. Ben

which permitted the largest five investment banks to dramatically increase their financial leverage and aggressively expand their issuance of mortgage-backed securities. This applied additional competitive pressure to Fannie Mae and Freddie Mac, which further expanded their riskier lending. Sub-prime mortgage payment delinquency rates remained in the 10-15 per cent range from 1998 to 2006, then began to increase rapidly, rising to 25 per cent by early 2008.

Some, like American Enterprise Institute fellow Peter J. Wallison, believe the roots of the crisis can be traced directly to sub-prime lending by Fannie Mae and Freddie Mac, which are government sponsored entities. On 30 September 1999, *The New York Times* reported that the Clinton Administration pushed for sub-prime lending:

Fannie Mae, the nation's biggest underwriter of home mortgages, has been under increasing pressure from the Clinton Administration to expand mortgage loans among low and moderate income people... In moving, even tentatively, into this new area of lending, Fannie Mae is taking on significantly more risk, which may not pose any difficulties during flush economic times. But the government-subsidized corporation may run into trouble in an economic downturn, prompting a government rescue similar to that of the savings and loan industry in the 1980s. In 1995, the administration also tinkered with President Jimmy Carter's Community Reinvestment Act of 1977 by regulating and strengthening the anti-redlining procedures. The result was a push by the administration for greater investment, by financial institutions, into riskier loansA 2000 United States Department of the Treasury study of lending trends for 305 cities from 1993 to 1998 showed that $467 billion of mortgage credit poured out of CRA-covered lenders into low and mid level income borrowers and neighbourhoods. Nevertheless, only 25 per cent of all sub-prime lending occurred at CRA-covered institutions, and a full 50 per cent of sub-prime loans originated at institutions exempt from CRA.

Others have pointed out that there were not enough of these loans made to cause a crisis of this magnitude. In an article in Portfolio Magazine, Michael Lewis spoke with one trader who noted that 'There weren't enough Americans with [bad] credit taking out [bad loans] to satisfy investors' appetite for the end product.' Essentially, investment banks and hedge funds used financial innovation to synthesize more loans using derivatives. "They were creating [loans] out of whole cloth. One hundred times over! That's why the losses are so much greater than the loans."

Economist Paul Krugman argued in January 2010 that the simultaneous growth of the residential and commercial real estate pricing bubbles undermines the case made by those who argue that Fannie Mae, Freddie Mac, CRA or predatory lending were primary causes of the crisis. In other words, bubbles in both markets developed even though only the residential market was affected by these potential causes.

REFERENCES

1. www.wikipedia.com

CHAPTER

27

Current Financial Crisis in India

*Dr. S.V. Subba Reddy
**Dr. K. Balasubramanyam

The origin of current crisis traced back to mid 2008 when three things became clear. One, low income or sub-prime US households that had borrowed heavily from banks and finance companies to buy homes were defaulting heavily on their debt obligations. Two, the size of this sub-prime housing loan market was huge at about 1.4 trillion. Three, wall streets financial engineers had packaged these loans to really complicated financial instruments called CDO's (Collateralized Debt Obligations). America and European banks had invested heavily in these products. However, no amount of financial engineering could protect investors from one simple and irrefutable principle—if these housing loans turned 'bad' the instruments that were based on these loans would lose value CDO prices started plummeting as defaults on US home loans rose. Falling prices dented banks investment portfolios and these losses destroyed banks capital. 'Default mortgage loans are the primary reason for the financial crisis sweeping the world'.

* Professor, Incharge Director for M.Com., & MBA, DDE, SYU, Tirupati, Andhra Pradesh
** Academic Consultant, DDE, S.V. University, Tirupati, Andhra Pradesh

As the housing loan crisis intensified, banks grew increasingly suspicious about each other's solvency and ability to honour commitments. The inter-bank market shrank as a result and this began to hurt the flow of funds to the 'real' economy. To cut a long story short today's financial crisis is the culmination of these problems in the global banking system. Inter-bank markets across the world have frozen over. Central bank across the globe had began to revive financial institutions, hit by what former Federal Reserve Governor Alan Greenspan has described as the crisis of the century.

India and Global Financial Crisis

When the financial crisis erupted in a comprehensive manner on wall street, there was some premature traumatism among India policy makers and media persons. It was argued that India would be relatively immune to this crisis, because of the 'strong fundamentals' of the economy and the supposedly well regulated banking system. 'the meltdown in the US has not created any credit crunch in India, but the credit crunch in the US led to panic in India'. Siddharth Ray, Chief economist of the Tata Group avers that, India is bound to be affected by the global.

After a long spell of growth, the Indian economy is experiencing a downturn, industrial growth is faltering, inflation remain to double digit levels, the current account deficit is widening, raising money for new investments through public issues is on hold. Foreign exchange reserve3s are depleting and the rupee is depreciating, the rupee plunged to 50.18 against dollar on November 21, 2009. There are two main factors driving the rupee down.

Firstly, the dollar has been gaining in strength against major currencies. Secondly, there is pressure on the capital account side as the country is witnessing out flows of dollars. If the US stock market continues to remain under pressure will persists on the foreign institutional investors leading to capital outflow and weakening rupee. GDP growth had been lowered from 9 per cent to 705 per cent during 01 of 2008-09. The most immediate effect of this crisis on India has been an outflow of foreign institutional investment from the equity market. Foreign institutional investment pulled out 11.1 billion dollars during the first nine and half months of calendar year 2009.

It is the law of gravity. The falls is always sharper than the rise. The sensex crashed to 300.5 points to 10,527.86 points from is peak level of 21,206 seen in January 10, 2009. The index has plummeted by 50 percentages in just nine months. (*Times of India*, October 10, 2009). Liquidity which was the sole factor that favoured equities on the way up has precisely been the cause of collapse since January,2009. On Friday October 24, 2009, the Sensex closed at 8,701.07 a level last sen on November 24, 2005. On October 27, 2009 the benchmark index of BSE ended the day lower by 1004 points to a three year intra-day low at 7,697.39 points.

RBI's Prescriptions

"We are committed to providing all possible support and assistance to Indian industry and trade to ensure that the Indian economy is least affected by this crisis". (Dr Manmohan Singh, Prime Minister, Hindustan Times, November 12, 2009). Buffeted by an extraordinary global financial shock and many advanced economics close to moving into recession, India's policy makers are grappling with options to deep growth intact while containing prices and infusion liquidity. The sub-prime crisis and the consequent drying up of global liquidity have led to the current financial mess. Sub-prime refers to loan given to a borrower who does not qualify for a regular home loan because of a poor credit record, low income and no job security.

"Indian banks do not have any direct exposure to sub-prime mortgages. The banking sector, through its overseas branches, has some exposure to distressed financial instruments and trapled financial institutions"(D. Subharao, RBI Governer, Times of India, October,12, 2009).

The RBI and government have intensified efforts to improve liquidity condition in the Indian market. Following steps are undertaken by RBI and government to increase liquidity in the market.

On Friday October 10, 2009 when sensex plunged by almost 1000 points to 10,300. RBI swung in to action and announced a one percentage cut in CRR (CRR-proportion of total deposits that bank need to maintain with the central bank). On Monday 7, 2009 RBI had already cut the CRR by 0.5 percentage point. Total CRR cut of 1.5 percentage points applicable from October 11, 2009 and infuse ₹ 60,000 crores in the banking system. RBI also decided to defer the auction of government's bonds of ₹ 10,000 crores under its annual borrowing plan to avoid sucking out liquidity from the system. RBI has also released around ₹ 8,000 crores through unwinding of Market Stabilization Scheme (MSS).

Table 27.1 : Retail Credit Growth

Loans	2008 (upto June)	2009 (upto June)	Growth in percentage
Housing Loans	230,700	259,000	12.27
Personal loans	161,000	193,000	19.88
Auto loans Creditcard	86,000	87,000	1.16
Receivables Consumer	21,000	30,000	42.86
Durables	6,000	4,000	–33.33

Source: Business Standards, October 17,2009, Section II, p 1.

Table 27.2 : RBI Policy Initiatives

Announcement on	Action
October 6, 2009	50 bps CRR cut
October 10, 2009	150 bps CRR cut
October 15, 2009	100 bps CRR cut
October 20, 2009	100 bps repo rate cut
November 1, 2009	100 bps CRR cut
November 1, 2009	50 bps repo rate cut
November 1, 2009	100 bps SLR cut

Source : RBI

As a part of its hectic and continuing to ease the liquidity situation, the RBI on Monday October 20, 2009 cut the repo rate by one percentage point (repo rate – the rate at which banks can borrow short-term funds from RBI). The cost at which banks borrow from RBI will come down so they can lend at lower rates.

On Oct.14, 2009 the RBI announced a special measure for providing money to Mutual Funds by allowing banks to borrow a special 14 days repo auction for a maximum of ₹ 20,000 crores. In a separate notification the RBI relaxed restrictions on bankis for granting loans against. CDs from mutual funds for 15 days. It will not only provide banks with much needed cash for mutual funds facing redemption pressures, but also will be reassuring to investors.

On Oct. 15, 2009 RBI pumped ₹ 40,000 crores in to the banking system to meet its liquidity needs and carry on lending.

Interest rate on foreign currency deposits raised by 0.5 per cent points, it will attract dollar deposits in Indian banks for strengthening the depreciation rupee.

The interest rates on Non-Residents fixed deposits in rupee denominated accounts increased by 0.5 percentage points. It will woo NRI's to park more money in Indian banks and this improved liquidity.

The RBI on Nov. 1, 2009 slashed three key rates to free up cash in banking system and ease the credit crunch. The cut are expected to infuse ₹ 85,000 crores in the banking system. The CRRwas cut by one percent to 5.5 per cent. The repo rate was cut to 0.5 per cent to 7.5 per cent. This should help to ease interest rate by reducing the cost of funds for banks. The statutory liquidity ratio (the percentage of deposits banks have to invest in government securities) was cut by one per cent to 24 per cent. The cuts could help meet industry's credit demands. It also made available of ₹ 80,000 crores to banks for lending.

The RBI also made deposit attractive for NRI's to stabilize the rupee and add cash to the banking system. The central bank is selling US dollars to keep the rupee from falling. The RBI recorded net sales of dollars worth 3.9 billion in the spot market and roughly twice the value (7.6 billion dollars) in forward in September, as per its monthly balefire released on Wednesday Oct. 12, 2009. it has been intervention in the market to stem the falls in the rupee that has unnerved many importers.

In yet another attempt to salvage a sinking stock market, SEBI has made it easier for promotions with over 55 per cent state in companies to increase their holdings through creeping acquisition.

In a move to encourage foreign depositors, the government announced doubling the ceiling on Foreign Institutional Investor (FII) investment in corporate bonds to 6 billon dollars, opening up anew avenue to strengthen resources to sustain growth and investment in the economy.

Indian banks which have been scrambling for dollars to keep their overseas offices afloat, will get a respite. RBI on Friday, November 7, 2009 announced that it would provide foreign exchange liquidity to overseas branches and subsidiaries of local banks through forex swaps. Under this, the bank in need of dollars will do a buy/sell swap with the RBI.

Thus, Since October 6, 2009 RBI has slashed the cash reserve ratio (CRR) by 350 basis points to 5.5 per cent and Repo Rate by 150 bps to 7.5 per cent. On November 1, 2009 it also cut the Statutory Liquidity Ratio (SLR) by 100bps to 24 per cent. Thus, RBI has taken all necessary monetary measures to ease liquidity in to the banking system.

Conclusion

The sub-prime crisis and the consequent drying up of global liquidity has lad to the current financial crisis. RBI has been taken several monetary measures to ease liquidity situation and facilitate the lending exercise. Rupee liquidity of around ₹ 2,25,000 crores has been injected in to the banking system through reduction in the proportion of deposits banks are require to hold as cash reserves, a cut in the amount of deposits banks are required to invest in government bonds and making available liquidity against deposits of government bonds. A further lowering of CRR as well as some reduction in the repo rate will be in order not only to infuse more liquidity but also to lower interest rates to ensure that the growth of the economy is not hampered. The government also followed slew fiscal measures to help industry.

REFERENCES

1. Nimish Shukla 'Sensex Journey' *Times o India,* October 11, 2009.
2. C.P. Chandrashekhar and Jayanti Ghose *'India and the Global Financial Crisis'* Business Line, October, 2009.
3. Rakesh Joshi and Lancelot Joseph, Global Storm Sweep India, *Business India*, Novemeber 2, 2009
4. Rajat Guha '30 FDI Boosting Proposal' *Economic Times,* November 7, 2009
5. Abheek Barua. 'Anatomy of a Crisis', *Times of India,* October 12, 2009.

CHAPTER

28

Impact of Economic Crisis on Housing Finance in India
An Overview

*Dr. S.V. Reddy
**Dr. B. Sakunthala
***Dr. C. Sukumar Reddy

Earthquake squashes, cyclone disasters, volcano smashes, like economy crises cause the closure of many industries in general and bankruptcy of so many banks at particular. The major cause for economic crisis which identified as housing finance i.e. finance to purchase of house, plot or construction of a house etc. Worldwide, Banks and Financial Institutions are in the highly competitive market and they offer and sanction housing loans very generously more than the actual need of an individual. They themselves encourage and even force the individuals to avail the housing finance facility, which is a long term finance. The banks and financial institutions are liberally sanctioned loans to the builders and realtors in India and abroad. The situation is quite calm and happy for a period of five to six years in the later 2001-02. Especially when the software is in boom, the cost of houses, apartments, house

* Reader in Commerce, Principal Investigator, UGC Major Research Project, Visvodaya Govt. Degree College, Venkatagiri-524132, Andhra Pradesh

** Lecturer in Commerce, Govt. Degree College, Karvetinagar, Andhra Pradesh

*** Senior Lecturer in Commerce, S.V.A. Govt. Degree College, Srikalahasthi, Andhra Pradesh

sites rise to a level of un bounded sky. Another important feature for the rise of home loans in India is enjoyment of tax concessions by individuals to a greater extent. In addition, an individual is enjoying own house which is a prestigious and appreciation on one side and on the other side easy finance with low interest rate, less installment, maximum tax concession etc. Inherently, the background for all these effects is a boom in software, realty and stocks.

All of sudden, situation reversed due to recession in USA and abroad. The software collapsed. Many individuals lost their employment. Unemployment rate increased. The loans which are already availed are in dues. They became default. They voluntarily surrender or loose the assets which are mortgaged. The value of the house, plot, flot suddenly has fallen. No body come forward to buy the mortgaged property. Banks and financial institutions are in trouble to recycling their funds. Like tsunami, banks in USA, UK and Europe shutdown their business day by day.

The impact of sub-prime crisis is assuming serious proportions with many investment banks declaring bankruptcy. The collapse of Bear Stearns, Fannie Mae, Freddie Mac, Lehman Brothers Holdings, Washington Mutual, the takeover of Merrill Lynch by Bank of America, ongoing tussle between Citigroup and Wells Fargo to buy Wachovia and such other instances of demise, mergers and acquisitions of large financial institutions have sent fresh shockwaves. The two largest securities firms Morgan Stanley and Goldman Sachs, have been converted into commercial banks to be supervised by the US Federal Reserve. The instances of takeovers, mergers and acquisitions as a part of bailout packages. The impact has also spread to Europe and UK drawing attention of central banks across the world and leading to them infusing ready liquidity in to the cash starved market. The basic idea to promote this chapter is an advertisement which has come across in a T.V. channel stating that SBI and ICICI are going to be auctioned 300 houses on a particular day in and around Hyderabad.

A housing loan which is a fully secured and long term one, is totally mortgaged and the legal complications are also low. Even though, these loans turned as NPAs and caused to serious deficiencies which in turn leads to dissolve a bank. When compared to USA, Indian commercial banks are strong, financially sound and the percentage of NPAs are under control because of the strict monitoring of RBI and most of the banks are nationalized banks. The value of mortgaged property i.e. house/plot slashes down at a greater level makes an individual become defaulter. The borrowers simply forgo the property which they mortgaged due to the variance among borrowed amount and value of the mortgaged property is high. The rivalry group i.e., SBI, ICICI Bank are the major players whose advances are heavy in housing sector. The Indian citizens who worked elsewhere are in search of fresh employment due to crisis and they become defaulters in banks due to termination of employment. RBI as a measure to encourage individuals to avail fresh loans reduces the repo rate at many times and simultaneously commercial banks reduce the rate of interest on housing loans. Even though the percentage of individual borrowers who applied for home loans is very low and the total disbursements are also less during 2007-08.

The employed youth are in dilemma of job retrenchment and they are intense to postpone their needs other than essentials of day to day life. The investments in real estate and securities are almost collapsed during 2005-08. Huge amount of their savings is blocked. They are not in a position to repay their loan installments and to maintain regular life style. In these circumstances, RBI and Govt. of India intervention is essential and they are doing their level best to control the situation. Indian economy position is not so bad when compared to other countries due to mixed economy.

ICICI, HDFC, Citi Bank, LIC HFCL and other Private banks and financial institutions in India offer loans to employed youth especially software professional at their doorsteps for the purchase of house/flat, vehicle etc., They offer loans at cheaper rate of Interest, easy installments with low EMI. Youth being crazy, they avail loans joyfully and enjoy while living in own houses and traveling in own vehicles with lovable family. Days are passing. Loan repayments are regular. Banks are happy by disbursing long term loans i.e. home loans with a term of 20 years. They felt that these loans are fully mortgaged. The original documents are with the banks. Legal complications are also limited. Borrowers are also happy because the loan is disbursed at their doorstep. No waiting, not making any rounds to the bank. EMI through salary deduction. This is the months back story and what is happening today? Crisis in USA and abroad. Software loses its position. Terminations, retrenchments closure, bankruptcy, dissolution, Insolvency petitions, absconding, defaulting, unemployment are the buzzwords we heard elsewhere today. In India, the economic and banking fundamentals are strong, well regulated and hence the impact is low. India could record a robust growth of GDP in the last three years. The GDP increased by 9 per cent in 2005-06, 9.4 per cent in 2006-07 and 9 per cent in 2007-08.

Employment opportunities are limited. Automobiles, Infrastructure (Iron, Steal, Cement) and other industries are in slump. Day by day banks and financial institutions declare bankruptcy, particularly those financial institutions which involved in prime lending operations. World economists, financial advisors cannot help overcome the situation in a day or a week. The situation disturbed many countries economy and caused to severe un-employment and poverty.

Mr. Obama, the President of United States invites the economists in and around America to advise him in connection with US economic crisis and is seeking their valuable suggestions to overcome the problem. The economists and financial analysts expressed that it is a time taking process to revamp the existing crisis situation and it will continue at least for a few years in the downtrend and it will definitely take some years to correct the worse situation. Fall in the stock markets, sudden rise in gold price are common features during the period of economic crisis and the world economy largely depends on US economy. Hence it is essential to recover US economy to its previous position as early as possible to stabilize the world economy. Otherwise the economy of the under-developed countries become worse and it leads to decoitism, internal wars, collapse of governments etc.

The effect of US sub-prime crisis has already started effecting Indian economy. It is the Infosys BPO in Bangalore, India has lost the green point mortgage being the principal clients of Infosys as an immediate consequence of American sub-prime crisis. It is a matter of solace that the sub-prime crisis in USA is so far remained restricted in affecting only one segment of economy that is realty and allied sector. It is now high time to exercise preventive measures in order to ensure transparency and visibility of credit worthiness of credit card holders, car loan, and housing loan holders spread across the country. The bankers and financial market regulators should exercise necessary caution against soft loan holders. More particularly a growing economy like India is more vulnerable to over leveraging. India should take immediate stock of the situation exercise, time honoured preventing control measures.

Conclusion

In conclusion the sub-prime crisis is still very much alive, the dollar is still weak and inflationary pressure exists. The sub-prime stack out will lead to the tightened credit restrictions on all borrowers, which could hurt consumer spending. Credit tightening could also cause further pain in the housing market, dashing hopes of the fresh house loan borrowers.

CHAPTER

29

Global Financial Markets and Economic Crisis
Impact on Indian Economy

*M. Kumar Raju
**A. Reddappa

Introduction

The Indian economy looked to be relatively insulated from the global financial crisis that started in August 2007 when the 'sub-prime mortgage' crisis first surfaced in the US. In fact the RBI was raising interest rates until July 2000 with the view to cooling the growth rate and contains inflationary pressures. But as the financial meltdown, morphed into a global economic downturn with the collapse of Lehman Brothers on 3 September 2000, the impact on the Indian economy was almost immediate. Credit flows suddenly dried-up and, overnight, money market interest rate spiked to above 0 per cent and remained high for the next month. It is, perhaps, judicious to assume that the impacts of the global economic downturn, the first in the center of global capitalism since

* Research Scholar, Department of Economics, Sri Venkateswara University, Tirupati-517502, Andhra Pradesh
** Research Scholar, Department of Economics, Sri Venkateswara University, Tirupati-517502, Andhra Pradesh

the Great Depression, on the Indian economy are still unfolding.

The severity and suddenness of the crisis can be judged from the IMF's forecast for the global economy. For the first time in 60 years, the IMF is now forecasting a global recession with negative growth for world GDP in 2009-10. The IMF has revised its forecasts downwards thrice since July 2000, and it is not yet certain that this will be the last revision.

The WTO has predicted that world trade, which has virtually collapsed in the second half of 2000 is likely to decline by as much as nine per cent in 2009-10. We have already seen exports from world's major exporters, like Germany, Japan and China, plummeting by more than 35 per cent in the last quarter of 2000. The sharp decline in economic activity is despite the large stimulus, estimated at more than US$3 trillion, that OECD economies have put in place. Yet the bad news does not stop. The worst downside scenario could be for the US economy being trapped in a Japan like 'L' shaped recovery for the next few years.

Impact of Global Crisis on Indian Economy

The impact of the global crisis has been transmitted to the Indian economy through three distinct channels, viz., the financial sector, exports and exchange rates. The financial sector including the banking sector, equity markets, external commercial borrowings and remittances has not remained unscathed though fortunately, the Indian banking sector was not overly exposed to the sub-prime crisis. Only one of the larger banks, ICICI, was partly affected but managed to thwart a crisis because of its strong balance sheet and timely action by the government, which virtually guaranteed its deposits. The equity markets have seen a near 60 per cent decline in the index and a wiping off of about US$1.3 trillion in market capitalization since January 2000 when the Sensex had peaked at about 1,000.

The second transmission of the global downturn to the Indian economy has been through the steep decline in demand for India's exports in its major markets. The first sector to be hit was the gems and jewellery which felt the impact in November itself and where more than 300,000 workers have lost their jobs. The negative impact has since covered other export-oriented sectors garments and textiles, leather, handicrafts, and auto components. The one per cent decline in exports in February 2009 is the steepest fall in exports for the last two decades. Therefore, an export slump will bring down GDP growth rate in this year.

The third transmission channel is the exchange rate as the Rupee has come under pressure with the outflow of portfolio investments, higher foreign exchange demand by Indian entrepreneurs seeking to replace external commercial borrowing by domestic financing, and the consequent decline in foreign exchange reserves. This is likely to continue because current account will remain in deficit and the capital account, which has been in deficit in the second and third quarters of 2000-09, will not generate the needed surplus to cover the current account deficit.

The nearly five per cent depreciation in the Rupee's exchange rate has partially nullified the benefits from the decline in global oil and gas prices and increased the cost of commercial borrowings. The weaker Rupee should encourage our exporters and it is possible that with imports declining as sharply as exports, the country's trade deficit may actually improve in the short-run and the external sector balance may remain stable and not pose any major policy issue. Overall, it would be fair to say that the timing of the external shock from the global economic downturn has been rather unfortunate. Coming right on the heels of a policy induced contraction in economic activity, its initial impact, as reflected in the third quarter GDP growth falling to 5.3 per cent and the steep decline in exports, has been perhaps exaggerated.

This negative impact has been, to an extent, ameliorated by the quick policy response both by the RBI and the Central Government. The RBI has infused about US$ 0 billion, as additional liquidity by cutting the CRR, lowering the SLR and unwinding the MSS. The RBI has also signalled its expansionary preference by cutting its repo rate, at which it lends funds to commercial banks from nine to five per cent in less than six months. The reverse-repo rate has also been brought down to 3.5 per cent to discourage banks from parking overnight funds with the RBI. Three fiscal stimuli have been announced between November 2000 to February 2009. These amount to about 1.3 per cent of the GDP.

However, to these stimulus packages we should also add the fiscal outlay of measures announced in the 2000-09 Budget in February 2000. These included some measures that implied a hefty transfer of purchasing power to the farmers and to the rural sector in general. These included, farm loan waivers, funds allocated to the National Rural Employment Guarantee Scheme (NREGS), Bharat Nirman (targeted for improving rural infrastructure), Prime Minister's Rural Road Programme, and a large increase in subsidies on account of fertilizers and electricity supplied to the farmers.

The Economic Advisory Council to the Prime Minister has now also brought down its estimate of 2000-09 GDP growth to 6.5 to seven per cent and not 7.1 per cent as given by CSO in its advanced estimates and used for budget formation by the finance ministry.

The GDP growth is likely to further decline to between 4. to 5.5 per cent in 2009-10. Other agencies like the IMF, the World Bank and the ADB have also estimated Indian GDP growth in 2009-10 at similar levels in their latest forecasts released in March 2009. Thus, Indian economy will come down from the nine per cent trend that it had achieved in the last four years. The growth targets for the 11th Five-Year Plan will also have to be surely lowered.

In India, the impact of the crisis has been deeper than what was estimated by our policy makers although it is less severe than in other emerging market economies. The extent of impact has been restricted due to several reasons such as:

- Indian financial sector particularly our banks have no direct exposure to tainted assets and its off-balance sheet activities have been limited. The credit derivatives market is in an embryonic stage and there are restrictions on investments by residents in such products issued abroad.
- India's growth process has been largely domestic demand driven and its reliance on foreign savings has remained around 1.5 per cent in recent period.
- Rural demand continues to be robust due to mandated agricultural lending and social safety-net programmes.
- India's merchandise exports are around 15 per cent of GDP, which is relatively modest.

Despite these mitigating factors, India too has to weather the negative impact of the crisis due to rising two-way trade in goods and services and financial integration with the rest of the world. Today, India is certainly more integrated into the world economy than ten years ago at the time of the Asian crisis as the ratio of total external transactions (gross current account flows plus gross capital flows) to GDP has increased from 46.8 per cent in 1997-98 to 117.4 per cent in 2007-08. Although Indian banks have very limited exposure to the US mortgage market, directly or through derivatives, and to the failed and stressed financial institutions yet Indian economy is experiencing the knock-on effects of the global crisis, through the monetary, financial and real channels—all of which are coming on top of the already expected cyclical moderation in growth.

I. Stock Market : The economy and the stock market are closely related as the buoyancy of the economy gets reflected in the stock market. Due to the impact of global economic recession, Indian stock market crashed from the high of 20000 to a low of around 8000 points. Corporate performance of most of the companies remained subdued, and the impact of moderation in demand was visible in the substantial deceleration during the current fiscal year. Corporate profitability also exhibited negative growth in the last three successive quarters of the year. Indian stock market has tumbled down mainly because of 'the substitution effect' of:

- Drying up of overseas financing for Indian banks and Indian corporates;
- Constraints in raising funds in a bearish domestic capital market; and
- Decline in the internal accruals of the corporates.

Thus, the combined effect of the reversal of portfolio equity flows, the reduced availability of international capital both debt and equity and the perceived increase in the price of equity with lower equity valuations has led to the bearish influence on stock market.

II. Forex Market : In India, the current economic crisis was largely insulated by the reversal of foreign institutional investment (FII), external commercial borrowings (ECB) and trade credit. Its spillovers became visible in September-October 2008 with overseas investors pulling out a record US$ 13.3 billion and fall in the nominal value of the rupee from ₹ 40.36 per US$ in March 2008 to ₹ 51.23 per US$ in March 2009, reflecting at 21.2 per cent depreciation during the fiscal 2008-09. The annual average exchange rate during 2008-09 worked out to ₹ 45.99 per US dollar compared to ₹ 40.26 per US$ in 2007-08 which is the biggest annual loss for the rupee since 1991 crisis. Moreover, there is reduction in the capital account receipts in 2008-09 with total net capital flows falling from US$ 17.3 billion in April-June 2007 to US$ 13.2 billion in April-June 2008.

Hence, sharp fluctuation in the overnight forex rates and the depreciation of the rupee reflects the combined impact of the global credit crunch and the deliver aging process underway in Indian forex market.

III. Money Market : The money market consists of credit market, debt market and government securities market. All these markets are in some or other way related to the soundness of banking system as they are regulated by the Reserve Bank of India. According to the Report submitted by the Committee for Financial Sector Assessment (CFSA), set up jointly by the Government and the RBI, our financial system is essentially sound and resilient, and that systemic stability is by and large robust and there are no significant vulnerabilities in the banking system. Yet, NPAs of banks may indeed rise due to slowdown as Reserve Bank has pointed out. But given the strength of the banks' balance sheets, that rise is not likely to pose any systemic risks, as it might in many advanced countries.

IV. Slowing GDP : In the past 5 years, the economy has grown at an average rate of 8-9 per cent. Services which contribute more than half of GDP have grown fastest along with manufacturing which has also done well. But this impressive run of GDP ended in the first quarter of 2008 and is gradually reduced. According to the revised estimates released by the CSO (May 29, 2009) for the overall growth of GDP at factor cost at constant prices in 2008-09 was 6.7 per cent as against the 7 per cent projection in the mid-year review of the Economy presented in the Parliament on December 23, 2008. The growth of GDP at factor cost (at constant 1999-2000 prices) at 6.7 per cent in 2008-09 nevertheless represents a deceleration from high growth of 9 per cent and 9.7 per cent in 2007-08 and 2006-07 respectively. The RBI annual policy statement 2009 presented on July 28, 2009 projects GDP growth at 6 per cent in 2009-10.

Table 29.1 : Rate of Growth at Factor Cost at 1999-2000 Prices (per cent)

	2003-04	2004-05	2005-06	2006-07	2007-08	2008-09
Agriculture, forestry and fishing	10.0	0	5.8	4.0	4.9	1.6
Mining & quarrying	3.1	8.2	4.9	8.8	3.3	3.6
Manufacturing	6.6	8.7	9.1	11.8	8.2	2.4
Electricity, gas & water supply	4.8	7.9	5.1	5.3	5.3	3.4
Construction	12.0	16.1	16.2	11.8	10.1	7.2
Trade, hotels & restaurants	10.1	7.7	10.3	10.4	10.1	9.0
Transport, storage & communication	15.3	15.6	14.9	16.3	15.5	9.0
Financing, insurance, real estate & business services	5.6	8.7	11.4	13.8	11.7	7.8
Community, social & personal services	5.4	6.8	7.1	5.7	6.8	13.1
Total GDP at factor cost	**8.5**	**7.5**	**9.5**	**9.7**	**9.0**	**6.7**

Source: Central Statistical Organisation

The slowdown in growth of GDP is more clearly visible from the growth rates over successive quarters of 2008- 09. In the first two quarters of 2008-09, the growth in GDP was 7.8 and 7.7 respectively which fell to 5.8 per cent in the third and fourth quarters of 2008-09. The third quarter witnessed a sharp fall in the growth of manufacturing, construction, trade, hotels and restaurants. The last quarter was an added deterioration in manufacturing due to the deepening impact of the global crisis and a slowdown in domestic demand *(See Table 29.2 of next page)*.

Hence, the slowdown in Indian economy is evident from the low GDP growth with deceleration in the industrial activity, particularly in the manufacturing and infrastructure sectors and moderation in the services sector mainly in the construction, transport and communication, trade, hotels and restaurants.

V. Strain on Balance of Payments : The overall balance of payments (BoP) situation remained resilient in 2008-09 despite signs of strain in the capital and current accounts, due to the global crisis. During the first three quarters of 2008-09 (April-December 2008), the current account deficit (CAD) was US$ 36.5 billion as against US$ 15.5 billion for the corresponding period in 2007-08. The capital account balance declined significantly to US$ 16.09 billion in 2008-09 as compared to US$ 82.68 billion during the corresponding period in 2007-08. As at end-March 2009 the foreign exchange reserves stood at US$ 252 billion.

VI. Reduction in Import-Export : During 2008-09, the growth in exports was robust till August 2008. However, in September 2008, export growth evinced a sharp dip and turned negative in October 2008 and remained negative till the end of the financial year. For the first time in seven years, exports have declined in absolute terms in October 2008.

VII. Reduction in Employment : Employment is worst affected during any financial crisis. So is true with the current

Table 29.2 : Rate of Growth at Factor Cost at 1999-2000 Prices (per cent)

	2007-08				2008-09			
	Q1	Q2	Q3	Q4	Q1	Q2	Q3	Q4
Agriculture, forestry and fishing	4.3	3.9	8.1	2.2	3.0	2.7	-0.8	2.7
Mining & quarrying	0.1	3.8	4.2	4.7	4.6	3.7	4.9	1.6
Manufacturing	10.0	8.2	8.6	6.3	5.5	5.1	0.9	-1.4
Electricity, gas & water supply	6.9	5.9	3.8	4.6	2.7	3.8	3.5	3.6
Construction	11.0	13.4	9.7	6.9	8.4	9.6	4.2	6.8
Trade, hotels, transport & communication	13.1	10.9	11.7	13.8	13.0	12.1	5.9	6.3
Finance, insurance, real estate & business services	12.6	12.4	11.9	10.3	6.9	6.4	8.3	9.5
Community, social & personal services	4.5	7.1	5.5	9.5	8.2	9.0	22.5	12.5
Total GDP	**9.2**	**9.0**	**9.3**	**8.6**	**7.8**	**7.7**	**5.8**	**5.8**

Source: Central Statistical Organisation

global meltdown. This recession has adversely affected the service industry of India mainly the BPO, KPO, IT companies etc. According to a sample survey by the commerce ministry 109,513 people lost their jobs between August and October 2008, in export-related companies in several sectors, primarily textiles, leather, engineering, gems and jewellry, handicraft and food processing. Economic Survey of India gives alarming bell about the on-going effects of the global slowdown on employment and has pressed upon the government the urgency of the major response, especially in the unorganized sector.

VIII. Taxation : The economic slowdown has severely dented the Centre's tax collections with indirect taxes earning the brunt. The tax- GDP ratio registered a steady increase from 8.97 per cent to 12.56 per cent between 2000-01 and 2007-08. But this trend has been reversed as the tax-GDP ratio has fallen to 10.95 per cent during current fiscal year mainly on account of reduction in Customs and Excise Tax due to effect of economic slowdown.

Response to the Crisis

The future trajectory of the economic meltdown is not yet clear. However, the Government and the Reserve Bank responded to the challenge strongly and promptly to infuse liquidity and restore confidence in Indian financial markets. The Government introduced stimulus package while the Reserve Bank shifted its policy stance from monetary tightening in response to the elevated inflationary pressures in the first half of 2008-09 to monetary easing in response to easing inflationary pressures and moderation of growth engendered by the crisis. The fiscal and monetary response to the crisis has been discussed in the following points:

I. Fiscal Response : The Government launched three fiscal stimulus packages between December 2008 and February 2009. These stimulus packages came on top of an already announced expanded safety-net programme for the rural poor, the farm loan waiver package and payout following the Sixth Pay Commission report, all of which added to stimulating demand.

In India monetary transmission has had a differential impact across different segments of the financial market. While the transmission has been faster in the money and bond markets, it has been relatively muted in the credit market on account of several structural rigidities. In order to address these issues, the government has to effectively and carefully take up the following steps :

- Enhance coordination and harmonization of the regulatory apparatus internationally, given the global scope of the recent crises with increased cross border financial integration;
- Introduction of countercyclical prudential regulatory policy;
- Supervision and management of liquidity risk and greater transparency in the financial sector to improve better risk assessment by the customers and investors;
- Improvement in transparency in the structured credit instruments.

The Union Budget for 2009-10, presented against the backdrop of persistent global economic slowdown and the associated dampened domestic demand, has placed the fiscal deficit at 6.8 per cent of GDP in 2009-10 with a view to providing the necessary boost to demand and thereby support a faster recovery.

II. Monetary Response : The RBI has taken several measures aimed at infusing rupee as well as foreign exchange liquidity and to maintain credit flow to productive sectors of the economy such as infusing liquidity through interest rate management, risk management and credit management which is described in detail under the following heads :

1. Interest Rate Management : In order to deal with the liquidity crunch and the virtual freezing of international credit, RBI took steps for monetary expansion which gave a cue to the banks to reduce their deposit and lending rates. The major changes in the interest rate policy of RBI are given below :

- Reduction in the cash reserve ratio (CRR) by 400 basis points from 9.0 per cent in August 2008 to 5 per cent in January 2009;
- Reduction in the repo rate (rate at which RBI lends to the banks) by 425 basis points from 9.0 per cent as on October 19 to 4.75 per cent by July 2009 (the lowest in past 9 years) in order to improve the flow of credit to productive sectors at viable costs so as to sustain the growth momentum;
- In order to make parking of funds with RBI unattractive for banks, the reverse repo rate (RBI's borrowing rate) was reduced by 275 points which currently stands at 3.25 per cent.

*2. **Risk Management :*** There has been a sustained demand from various quarters for exercising regulatory forbearance in regard to extant prudential regulations applicable to the banking sector. As a part of counter-cyclical package, RBI has already made several changes to the current prudential norms for robust risk disclosures, transparency in restructured products and standard assets such as :

- Implementation of Basel II w.e.f. March 2009 by all Scheduled Commercial Banks except RBs which would promote closer cooperation, information sharing and coordination of policies among sector wise regulators, especially in the context of financial conglomerates.
- Reduction in the risk weights for claims on unrated corporate and commercial real estate to 100 per cent;
- Reduction in the provisioning requirement for all standard assets to 0.40 per cent;

- Making the restructured commercial real estate exposures eligible for special treatment if structured before June 30, 2009.

Hence, RBI has ensured perseverance of prudential policies which prevent institutions from excessive risk taking, and financial markets from becoming extremely volatile and turbulent.

3. Credit Management : There was a noticeable decline in the credit demand during 2008-09 which is indicative of slowing economic activity—a major challenge for the banks to ensure healthy flow of credit to the productive sectors of the economy. The reduced funding demand on the banks should enable them to reduce the interest rates on deposit and thereby reduce the overall cost of funds. Although deposit rates are declining and effective lending rates are falling, there is clearly more space to cut rates given declining inflation. In order to facilitate demand for credit in the economy the Reserve Bank has taken certain steps such as :

- Opening a special repo window under the liquidity adjustment facility for banks for on-lending to the non-banking financial companies, housing finance companies and mutual funds;
- Extending a special refinance facility, which banks can access without any collateral;
- Unwinding the Market Stabilization Scheme (MSS) securities, in order to manage liquidity;
- Expanding the refinance facility for exports;
- Expanding the lendable resources available to the Small Industries Development Bank of India, the National Housing Bank and the Export-Import Bank of India.

Future Outlook for India

To sum up we can say that the global financial recession which started off as a sub-prime crisis of USA has brought all nations including India into its fold. The GDP growth rate which was around nine per cent over the last four years has slowed since the last quarter of 2008 owing to deceleration in employment, export-import, tax-GDP ratio, reduction in capital inflows and significant outflows due to economic slowdown.

The demand for bank credit is also slackening despite comfortable liquidity in the system. Higher input costs and dampened demand have dented corporate margins while the uncertainty surrounding the crisis has affected business confidence leading to the crash of Indian stock market and volatility in forex market. Indian financial markets are capable of withstanding the global shock, perhaps somewhat bruised but definitely not battered. India, with its strong internal drivers for growth, may escape the worst consequences of the global financial crisis. In other words, the fundamentals of our economy continue to be strong and robust. The global economic environment continues to remain uncertain, although the rate of contraction in economic activities and the extent of pressures on financial systems eased in the first quarter of 2009-10. Yet, it is not possible to clearly see the path of the crisis and its resolution over the coming months.

In this sense, India is not unique as almost every country, whether or not directly affected, has to manage the current economic crisis under uncertainty. I would like to conclude the chapter in the words of Dr. Rakesh Mohan, former Deputy Governor of RBI :

> *"As the monetary and fiscal stimuli work their way through, and if calm and confidence are restored in the global markets, we can see economic turnaround later this year. Once calm and confidence are restored in the global markets, economic activity in India will recover sharply. Yet there will be a period of painful adjustment which is inevitable."*

Conclusion

The Indian economy has shown considerable resilience in the face of the present global financial crisis. The financial sector has emerged without much damage thanks in part to our strong regulatory framework and in part on account of state ownership of most of the banking sector. While large corporates will no doubt be affected, the worst affected are likely to be the exports and SMEs (small and marginal enterprises) that contribute significantly to employment generation.

RBI's efforts to ease the downward pressure on the rupee (by selling dollars) have added to the domestic liquidity crunch in a scenario where corporates are increasingly turning to the domestic banking sector to make up for the drying up of external sources of finance and the IPO (initial public offering) market. Despite robust growth of 30 per cent in bank credit (year-on-year), corporates are complaining of a credit crunch. The only silver lining is the decline in inflation—latest numbers show inflation at 8.98 per cent for the week ended 1 November 2008. Unfortunately, the scope for fiscal measures that could be targeted at the genuinely needy is limited thanks to the government's large fiscal deficit. The net result is that economic activity is bound to slow down. And though the precise extent of the slowdown is hard to predict, the fact that even the most conservative estimates do not place GDP growth at less than 6 per cent provides some solace.

REFERENCES

1. *Annual Report 2008-09,* Reserve Bank of India
2. *Macroeconomic and Monetary Developments: First Quarter Review 2009-10,* Reserve Bank of India
3. *Bank Quest,* Vol. 80 January- March 2009, IIBF
4. *Economic Survey,* Government of India
5. http://www.economics.harvard.edu/about/views
6. www.finmin.nic.in
7. www.rbi.org.in
8. *Economic Relations* (ICRIER), New Delhi

CHAPTER

30

Impact of Global Crisis on the Indian Economy

*G. Venkatachalam
**Prof. P. Mohan Reddy

Cultivators

The impact of the crisis on agriculture is much more severe than has been recognized. Cultivators in India have already been through more than a decade of agrarian crisis, which persisted even through the period of rising international crop prices. The problems of farming in India are both deep and varied. They include weather problems such as less reliable monsoons, more frequent droughts or floods, soil degeneration, lack of institutional credit and insurance leading to excessive reliance on private moneylenders, problems in accessing reliable and reasonably priced input, difficulties in marketing and high volatility of crop prices.

Except for the first set, these are all related to public policies from the early 1990s onwards, that systematically reduced the protection afforded to farmers and exposed them to import competition and market volatility; allowed private profiteering in agricultural input supply and crop purchases

* Research Scholar, Department of Commerce, S.V. University, Tirupati, Andhra Pradesh
** Department of Commerce, S.V. University, Tirupati, Andhra Pradesh

without adequate regulation; reduced critical forms of public expenditure; tried to cut subsidies by increasing the prices of important inputs like fertilizer and water and electricity rates, ran down or destroyed important public institutions that have direct relevance for farming, including public extension services and marketing arrangements; and did not adequately generate other non-agricultural economic activities.

At the same time that various forms of public protection for cultivation were being reduced, trade liberalization meant that Indian farmers had to operate in a highly uncertain and volatile international environment. They were effectively competing against highly subsidized large producers in the developed countries, whose average level of subsidy amounted to many times the total domestic cost of production for many crops. In addition to increasing the risks of farming, volatile crop prices also generated misleading price signals. Indian farmers tend to respond quickly and extensively to price signals by shifting to more high-priced crops. This caused large and often undesirable shifts in cropping pattern which ultimately rebounded on the farmers themselves.

In dry land areas, traditional staple crops such as millets and sorghum were abandoned in favour of oilseeds such as groundnut which require more irrigation and purchased inputs, and which have also faced major volatility in crop prices. As a result of the shift away from traditional staple grains to cash crops, there was much greater use of a range of purchased inputs, including new varieties of seed and related inputs marketed by major multinational companies. Small cultivators, who took on debt (often from informal credit sources at very high rates of interest) in order to pay for these cash inputs, then found themselves in real difficulty if crops failed or output prices remained low. So the inevitable uncertainties associated with weather fluctuations were compounded by further problems of extremely volatile crop prices, which were no longer inversely related to harvest levels but followed an international pattern. Further, this dramatic volatility of output prices was associated with continuously rising prices of inputs. This was especially marked because of government attempts to reduce fertilizer subsidies, and progressive deregulation of supplies of inputs such as seeds and pesticides. Such exposure to global price volatility was associated with a growing reliance on private debt, because of the lack of extension of institutional credit, coupled with growing inability to meet debt service payments because of the combined volatility of crops and prices. Farmers already had inadequate access to institutional credit, but things got much worse after 1993. Financial liberalization measures caused a significant slowdown in the growth of bank credit, particularly from commercial banks to rural areas, and a relative fall in proportion of bank credit flowing to the priority sectors, especially agriculture. The impact of the slowdown in rural banking fell disproportionately on poor and small borrowers. Volatility of output prices remains a huge problem for farmers. And the central question of the huge burden of farm debt has really not been solved, despite the 'loan waiver' for farmers announced in the 2008-09 Budget. This is because most farmers operate in the informal credit market, and go to private sources who are typically either rural moneylenders or input dealers. Marginal farmers, Global Crisis tenants and women farmers still remain outside the ambit of institutional credit, and most farm debt is informal. The real problems of rural debt cannot be addressed without dealing with cases of both public and private debt and recapitalizing the moneylenders to alleviate the problems of borrowers and keep private rural credit channels flowing.

Meanwhile, crop price volatility has become much worse in the past year, dramatically increasing the difficulties of cash crop producers. Globally, primary commodity prices zoomed upwards in 2007 and the first half of 2008, and then collapsed very rapidly, thereafter. So all the price gains of the period January 2007 to mid-2008 were wiped out by the later fall in prices. Farmers did not benefit from such a short-lived price boom, especially if they produced cash crops. Instead, they now face lower prices of their output even as food prices have continued to increase. This is particularly true for cultivators of cotton and oilseeds, prices of which have crashed compared to a year ago. Cultivators who opted to sow these crops when their prices were at their peak now face a completely different environment with very different configurations of costs and prices that could easily make the cultivation process financially completely unviable.

Migrant Workers

Official sources suggest that there has already been a sharp fall in employment in the export-oriented sectors like textiles and garments and gems and jewellery, and even in industries catering more to the domestic market like metal products, automobiles and construction. Many newly unemployed are migrant workers, often short-term migrants with casual contracts whose very existence tends to be ignored by our official statistics.

The economic boom of the past decade relied heavily on such workers: Not just in the sectors mentioned above but in labour-intensive services, such as cleaning, maintenance, private security, driving and related services. These were not simply informal activities, many of them catered to the requirements of the expanding corporate sector, and in effect subsidized it by providing a cheap and flexible external labour force. Such workers are now forced either to stay in precarious conditions in the urban areas, or go back to their places of origin—villages or smaller towns. They consequently change from becoming providers of remittance incomes to their households, to becoming dependents of these households, even as these households face more fragile material circumstances than before. Many of these migrant workers, for obvious reasons, come from the most depressed and backward regions of the country, where there is currently little potential for productive income generation. These are often also the regions of dry land agriculture, where remittance incomes play a vital role in sheer survival. Unsurprisingly, they are also the regions in which extremist Maoist activity is widely prevalent, because of the anger bred by persistent backwardness and rising inequalities.

Home-based Workers

As opportunities for paid employment have dwindled, even during the boom, home-based subcontracting activities, or work in very small units that do not even constitute manufactories, often on piece-rate-basis and usually very poorly paid and without any known non-wage benefits, substituted to some extent. There are estimated to be more than 15 million women workers in the unorganised sector, and more than half of them are women involved in homebased work for different types of industry, dominantly on a piece-rate basis. This includes zari, charkha or other handloom work; bindi, labels, stitching; food processing; and also potentially hazardous work involving acids and chemicals. Surveys show that most of them are very poorly paid piece rate workers providing specific products or intermediate goods for manufacturing industries such as textiles and garments, engineering and chemical industries, leather and miscellaneous production such as imitation jewellery and petty cosmetic items. Such work typically does not get incorporated in the employment statistics which are based on employers' records. Very recent micro-evidence confirms the poor and sometimes even deteriorating conditions of such work. Even during the boom, there was pressure on piece rate wages because of competition from other and newer centres of such production, both inside the country and outside (such as from China).

Food Security

Much has been made of the slowdown in inflation rates to almost zero, and there are those who have pointed out that this reflects the declining rate of economic growth and could even lead to a deflation that is damaging for growth. But what is often not noted is that even within this overall stagnation in prices, food prices have continued toincrease. Foodgrain prices have gone up the most, by more than 10 per cent in the year April 2008 to March 2009. This cannot be blamed on higher procurement prices alone, since the prices of pulses, which are not covered by public procurement, have also gone up just as much. The prices of fruits and vegetables and eggs, fish and meat have also increased, even if not by as much as for foodgrains. The only food category for which prices have fallen is edible oils, which reflects the decline in oilseed price as world prices have crashed. Other food articles' prices have increased by more than one-fifth in this one year.

This, obviously, affects household budgets, especially among the poor for whom food still accounts for more than half of total household expenditure. Meanwhile, non-food primary product prices have hardly changed. The prices of fibres—mainly cotton, jute and silk—have barely increased at all. Oilseed prices have fallen by more than five per cent. This, immediately, affects all the producers of cash crops, who will be getting the same or less for their products even as they pay significantly more for food. They are also paying more for fertilizer and pesticides, prices of which have increased by more than five per cent. Another major item of essential consumption has also increased in price—that of drugs and medicines, up by 4.5 per cent. This obviously impacts upon the entire population, but especially the bottom half of the population who may find it extremely difficult if not impossible to meet such expenditures in times of stringency. a worrying combination of falling prices faced by agriculturalists who produce cash crops as well as petty producers and others who produce manufactured goods, even as the prices of essential items like food and medicines continue to rise. These groups and their families alone account for the majority of the population in the country. Another little noticed but extremely serious consequence of the downswing is the impact on the finances of state governments, who are responsible for the bulk of the public spending which affects human development, such as basic infrastructure, health, sanitation and education. State governments' tax receipts have fallen and so they are increasingly strapped for cash and unable to meet even essential spending on basic services, not to mention development.

What is to be Done?

Clearly, much more creative and imaginative policy responses are required, in terms of changing directions of investment and consumption in the home market to emphasize wage-led growth, diversifying exports and generally making moves designed to turn economic adversity to advantage. What is immediately required is significantly increased public expenditure, directed towards particular areas—expansion of the employment guarantee scheme within rural areas and extension to urban areas, creative use of NREGS, especially in urban areas, to enable productive use of the tremendous wealth of labour resources available, especially women workers; more resources provided to state governments to enable them to meet basic development and social expenditures; and a package for agriculturalists to protect them from volatile crop prices and to deal with the burden of debt.

REFERENCES

1. *Yojana*, New Delhi
2. www.rbi.org. in
3. Prof. Jayati Ghosh, Jawaharlal Nehru University, New Delhi

CHAPTER

31

Impact of Financial Crisis on Banking Sector

*M. Sudhakar Reddy

Reasons behind the Financial Crisis

The following are the main reasons behind the financial crisis across the World which can be classified on the basis of some parts as follows :

- The Financial Crisis in the world
  - ☛ Began as a crisis in the Sub-prime crisis
  - ☛ Today it is a liquidity crisis (Trust Crisis)
  - ☛ Today the crisis is global. It is not just a problem for the USA.
  - ☛ Fall of Property Ladder as shown in Fig. 31.1 *(See on next page)*
- Reasons for the financial crisis
  - ☛ The bubble in the real estate market
  - ☛ Too many overly complex financial assets (through out the world)

* Senior Lecturer in Commerce, Govt. Degree College, Nagari, Andhra Pradesh

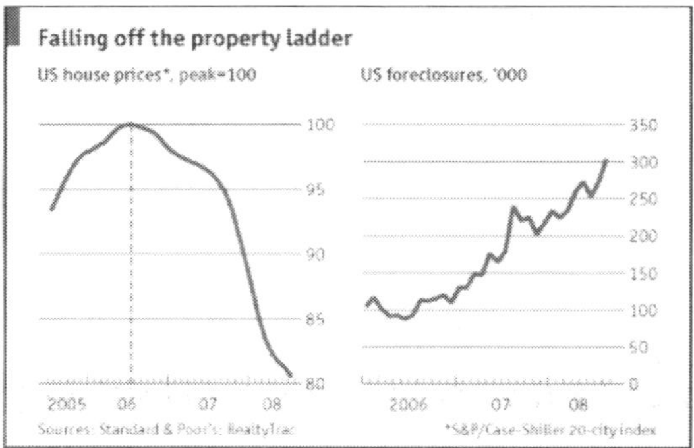

- Financial systems with regulation that is defective or completely absent
- Defective regulation systems in other markets

• Signs of problems in financial markets

- Exists for a long time
- Are reflected in many real markets.
- Are reflected mainly in the 'alternatives Investments' markets
- We did not Connect the Signs
- Government (economists) did not understand the problems.
- No Government Response

The following graphs will show the reasons behind the crisis :

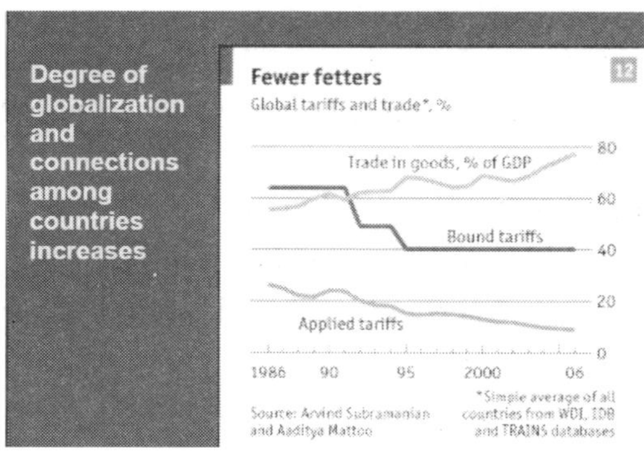

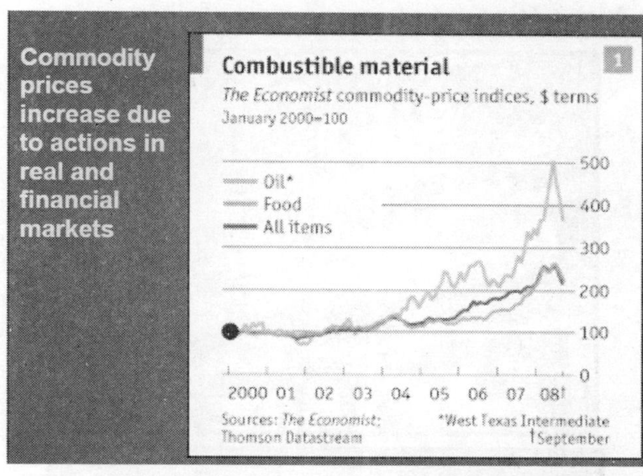

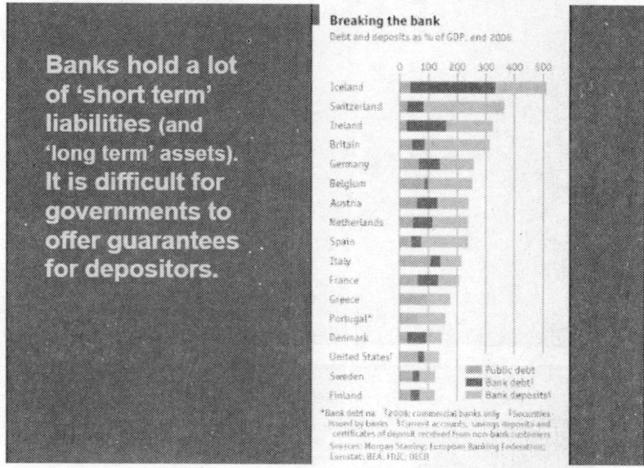

US Mortgage Lending and Sub-prime Crisis

- As we know that the United States of America and other countries across the globe has collapsed in the U.S.Housing Boom, major failure of U.S.Investments Banks further choked the Liquidity of the global credit market.
- The Impact has been deep , dramatic and wide spread.

- Just a few was affected was as follows:

Increasing the trend of delinquency rate

- % of sub-prime loan with adjustable rate mortgages which were *90 days delinquent or in foreclosure proceedings:*

Oct 07	16%
Jan 08	21%
May 08	25%

Sub-prime Losses by Bank *(Since Jan. 07 in US$ bin)*

	Company	Total write downs and credit losses
1.	Wachovia	96.5
2.	Citigroup	68.1
3.	M\errill Lynch	55.0
4.	Washington Mutual	45.6
5.	UBS	44.2
6.	HSBC	33.1
7.	Bank of America	27.4
8.	National City	26.2

...(Contd.)

	Company	Total write downs and credit losses
9.	JP Morgan Chase	20.5
10.	Wells Fargo	17.7
11.	Morgan Stanley	15.7
12.	RBS	15.7
13.	Lehman Brothers	13.8
14.	Credit Suisse	13.4
	Worldwide	**692.5**

Source: Bloomberg

Economic Recession and Outsourcing Issues

1. What is Outsourcing?

   The migration of tasks or functions from internal production to a third party.

2. What is Economic recession?

   Economic Recession means a temporary decline in economic activity or prosperity

3. Some of the outsourcing issues are:

   (*a*) What is to be outsourcing?

   Basically anything Esquire writer testing the limits outsourced reading email, fighting with his wife and reading to his son.

   (*b*) Which IT positions are most popular for outsourcing?

   - trouble ticket/help desk operations
   - hardware and network operations
   - end-user support
   - disaster recovery and power back-ups

   (*c*) By 2010, 30 per cent of Fortune 500 companies will source from three or more countries

(*d*) 60% of world IT outsourcing goes to India.

(*e*) Why organisations outsourcing?Salaries of foreign IT workers are as follows:

Country	Average
USA	$ 75,000
Singapore	$ 33,504
Ireland$_A$	$ 23,000 – $ 34,500
China	$ 8,852
India	$ 5,880 – 15,500
Russa$_A$	$ 5,000 – $ 7,500
Mexico	$ 1400

American Effect

- Americans are losing jobs and not getting them back.
  - ☛ Can't pay for reeducation, mortgage, insurance, retirement.
  - ☛ From 1979 – 1999, through deindustrialization, 37 per cent didn't find new work. 63 per cent showed average 13 per cent drop in salaries.
  - ☛ CEOs and investors make money.
  - ☛ Tax havens
  - ☛ Divide between rich and poor.
- Cycles of offshoring:
  - ☛ Corporations force prices down and more outsourcing.
- What is effect of current recession?

4. Impact of Global Financial Crisis on Different Countries/Economies

Implications for India

- Economic impact
- Social and Development Impact

Annual GDP Growth (%) 1995-2009, Asia versus the G7 Countries

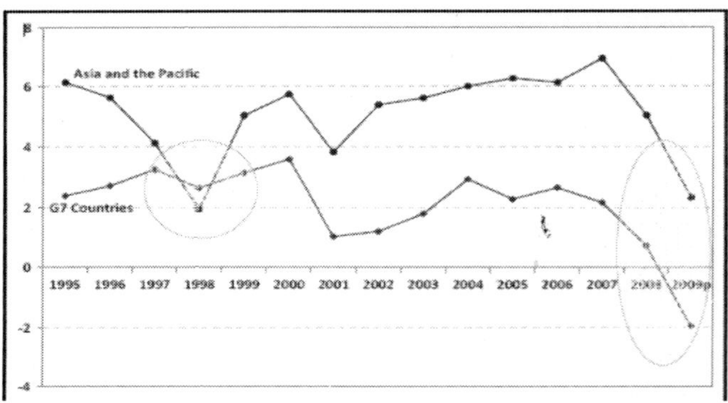

- Rapid growth of speculative lending and deregulation of financial market over the past couple of decades
- Increase in global liquidity and risk appetite e.g. sub-prime lending and mortgage-backed securities
- Comprehensive and global crisis, encompassing the banking sector, securities and currency markets, and institutional and individual investors in most parts of the world
- Impact of the crisis on growth in the United States and its global spillovers to other parts of the world through international trade and financial system.

Impact on Indian Economy

- Growth declined to 7.3 per cent in 2008, down from 9.3 per cent in 2007
- Current Government estimates are for approx 6.5 per cent to 7.5 per cent growth in 2009, but the IMF forecast is for growth to fall to 5.1 per cent
- As economic growth contracts

- ☛ Demand for labour has fallen
- ☛ Rising unemployment and Under employment
- ☛ Downwards pressure on wages

- SME's has been hard hit
- Informal economy has been hit hard
- Reverse migration was found

Impact on Social and Development Sectors

- Impact on employment and Poverty
- Funding for development or development expenditure
- Achievement of the Millennium Development Goals (MDGs)

5. Impact of Financial Crisis on Banking Sector

(*a*) A *banker* or *bank* is a financial institution whose primary activity is to act as a payment agent for customers and to borrow and lend money.

(*b*) conducting current accounts for his customers

(*c*) paying cheques drawn on him, and

(*d*) collecting cheques for his customers.

The money that never was :

- You earn a salary of ₹ 50,000
- Buy a house worth ₹ 20 Lakh

- Assume that you will sell the house at ₹ 40 Lakh and make a 100 per cent profit
- Not able to pay monthly EMI of ₹ 8,500
- Sell the house at a loss
- File for Bankruptcy

"Money is the Creator of Profit and Destroyer of the Same"

Global Economic Slowdown

- *Boon:*
- India's provisional *gem and jewellry exports* increased by 22.27 per cent
- Manufacturing production is expected to increase 1.9 per cent
- Servive sectors grow faster during recession
- *Bane:*
- American International Group (AIG) - $5 Billion loss
- More than 200 troubled banks are likely to be purchased before they reach the point of failure.
- A great hurdle for the IT Industry
- Result of Crashing Oil prices

Solutions

1. The govt has to take necessary steps to solve this problems.
2. Increased subsidies by the Government for promotion of Exports
3. Promotion of Increased Industries in Service Sector
4. Constant check on devaluation of Currency
5. Don't bite off more than you can chew
6. Save at least 5 per cent of the monthly income
7. Wipe out credit debts

Recommendations

(*i*) Agriculture and manufacturing Industries are important for the increase of the National Income.

(*ii*) So,The policy maker of the country may follow the recommendations below for reducing financial crunch.

(*iii*) Domestic liquidity and interest rates.

(*iv*) Permitting higher level FDI (foreign direct investment).

Conclusion

To conclude, lets hope for a stronger India by rectifying all its economic weaknesses through adopting effective plans.

REFERENCES

1. Global Financial Crisis—Impications for Indian Development
2. Tishler Financial Crisis
3. R.B.I Journals
4. National Seminar

CHAPTER

32

Global Financial Crisis
Its Impact on Indian Economy

*C.S. Sukumar Reddy
**Dr. S. Vijayulu Reddy
***M. Sudhakar Reddy

The Indian economy had performed well during the last two decades, resulting in high real GDP growth, besides increase in domestic savings, which is presently at 37 per cent of GDP, and increase in investment and productivity. India's financial sector in the field of institution markets and infrastructure remained moderately strong due to on going reforms from 1990's. The global financial crisis started visibly impacting the Indian economy from September-2008 onwards. Gradually, it spread over all the sectors of the economy. The sub prime lending crisis, which originated in the U.S. has become a financial contagion and has restricted availability of credit in global financial markets. Thousands of borrowers have defaulted and several major sub prime lenders have filed for bankruptcy in the US and in many of the Western and European nations. Initially, companies like Northern Rock in

* Senior Lecturer in Commerce, SVA Govt. Degree College, Srikalahasti, Andhra Pradesh
** Reader in Commerce, Visvodaya Govt. Degree College, Venkatagiri, Andhra Pradesh
*** Senior Lecturer in Commerce, Govt. Degree College, Nagari, Andhra Pradesh

UK and Country-wide Financial who were directly involved in home construction and mortgage lending were affected. But, slowly financial institutions like Bear Stearns which had securitised such mortgages felt the repercussions.

The US financial crisis first spread to other rich countries the UK, Europe and Japan and later to emerging economies including China and India. The impact, of course, has varied from country to country. The Governments have been responding with bailout packages through which more and more liquidity is being made available and interest rates are gradually brought down. Added to the measures taken by the monitory authorities, increasing use is being made of the fiscal stimulus. Countries like Japan, China and India have put up bailout packages to arrest the impact of financial crisis. There is widespread awareness of the impending danger signals and corrective measures are being coordinated world over.

The year 2008 has been of turbulence particularly in the world of financial markets. The year which was also the year of the financial meltdown saw almost all possible worst scenarios in every sector of the economy. From banking, where a record number of banks in the US closed down to un-precedented rise in the price of crud oil (up to $147 per barrel), to a record level of inflation in major economies of the world, and unbearable volatility in stock indices world wide, to name a few. All these factors forced the world economy into the clutches of the severest recession from which we are yet to recover.

Before the global meltdown, India's integration into the world economy was rapid. This has been evidenced by trade merchandise exports and imports increasing from 21.2 per cent in 1997-98 to 34.7 per cent in 2007-08. The ratio of total external transactions to GDP showed a substantial rise of 117.4 per cent in 2007-08 when compared to 46.8 per cent in 1997-98. Corporate external fundings increased the corporates investment in India's GDP by 9 per cent. Further, the capital inflow into India in 2007-08 stood at 9 per cent of GDP. Back home in India we have felt the heat of the financial meltdown where else in the world by way of softening of the earnings of software companies and with double-digit inflation. The stock markets in India also crashed to a record low level and an overall high rate of interest heated the economy. Despite the set backs, the Indian banking sector appears to have escaped the rough weather. Not only have the public sector banks fared well, even private banks have kept their profits intact. This was evident from the financial results of banks in India for FY 2008-09.

Indian banking sector is dominated by the government owned public sector banks which account for 69.9 per cent of aggregate deposits and 72.7 per cent aggregate advances of all scheduled commercial banks as on March-31, 2008. The year 2008 saw several 'run on banks' events in the western countries like the US and UK resulting in collapse of several banks and financial institutions. But due to the Government ownership and public faith that their money is in safe hands, such a situation did not arise in India. The enormous faith of Indian public in public sector banks kept banks afloat in India even during the most turbulent time for the financial world. Thanks to tough stances taken by Reserve Bank of India, despite the global meltdown the banking system stood insulated from the financial crisis. The banking system proved to be sound. This is evident from its comfortable capital adequacy, quality of its assets, profitability and earning capacity. Capital adequacy of banks continuous to remain above the regulatory minimum (9 per cent) and non-performing assets has shown a study decline.

Despite the global financial crisis the emerging Indian economy with stood the crisis reasonably well compared to other advanced and emerging economies because of substantial foreign exchange reserves, a healthy banking sector and robot corporate balance sheets. Besides the RBI has played a very important role by not allowing banks to enter into risky businesses. To further strengthen the Indian economy it is imperative substantial public investment is required. More emphasis must be laid in building the country's infrastructure, public health, roads, sanitation and agriculture. There is need to reshape the economy to meet the challenges from within the world.

Index

A

Active Pharmaceutical Ingredients (APIs), 4
Advani, Ashok H, 65
American International Group, 113
American Medical Association (AMA), 25
Apparel Export Promotion Council (AEPC), 92
Associated Chambers of Commerce and Industry of India (ASSOCHAM), 22
Association of Council (ASCON), 164

B

Babu, M. Syam, 1
Balamuniswamy, D., 174
Balasubramanyam, K., 288
Banerjee, Sujit, 29
Bengal Chemicals and Pharmaceutical Works, 5
Bharati, G. Vijaya, 124
Business Process Outsourcing (BPO), 194

C

Chidambaram, P., 246
China, 192-198
Collateralized Debt Obligations, 146
Committee for Financial Sector Assessment (CFSA), 149
Community Reinvestment Act (CRA), 114
Compound Annual Growth Rate (CAGR), 86
Compounded Annual growth Rate (CAGR), 9
Confederation of Indian Industry (CII), 22
Contract Research and Manufacturing Services (CRAMS), 80
Current financial crisis in India, 288-294
    India and global financial crisis, 289-290
    RBI prescriptions, 290-294

D

Devi, A. Bharathi, 56
Dutch Tulip Mania, 14

E

Economic Survey Report, 264
Effect of global financial collision on Indian banking, 56-64
    best corporate governance practices, 63

best practices, 64
capital adequacy ratio, 59
methodology, 58
non-performing assets, 60-61
off balance sheet items, 61-63
transparency, 64
Embargo Act of 1807, 219
Emerging Market Economies (EMEs), 196
European Central Bank, 19

F

Federal reserve, 118
Federal Reserve Bank, 19
Federation of Indian Export Organization (FIEO), 93
Financial Crisis, 31
Financial globalisation, 141-142
First World Class Treatment, 24
Foreign Direct Investment, 9
Foreign Institutional Investors (FIIs), 57
Foreign investors, 229-232
Forex market, 129-130

G

Ganesamoorthy, L., 82
Generally Accepted Accounting Principles and Standards, 64
Glass-Steagal Act, 115
Global crisis and Indian finance, 226-236
banks, 233-235
financial crises, 227
increase in unemployment, 236
India's exports, 235
Indian stock market, 227-228
real estate, 235
role of foreign investors, 229-232
rupee value, 235-236
Global Economy, 1
Global financial crisis and its impact on Indian corporates, 65-81
effect on sectoral performance, 66
growth sectors, 67
Indian corporates, 67
introduction, 65-66
negative growth, 67-68
recovery, 68-81
Global financial crisis and its impact on Indian economy, 199-217
effects of global meltdown on Indian economy, 209-211
global recessions, 202-204
India and the global economic down turn, 211-213
introduction, 199-202
ongoing global financial crisis, 213-215
raising from the depth of 2007 crisis, 205-207
stabilizing the financial sector, 216
subprime crisis, 204-205
US sneezes, India catches cold, 207-209
Global financial crisis and its impact on the Indian IT sector, 237-244
genesis of global financial crisis, 237-238
impact on Indian IT sector, 238-243
opportunities for India IT sector, 243-244

Global financial crisis and its impact on the Indian real estate sector, 138-144
origins of the global financial crisis, 138-140
is this the 1929 great depression revisited, 140
financial globalisation, 141-142
impact on the Indian real estate sector, 142-144
Global Financial Crisis of 2007, 205
Global financial crisis vs Indian economy, 245-253
best place in outsourcing, 249
comparison of Indian economy with most powerful world economies, 247
global meltdown and its impact on the Indian economy, 249-252
Indian approach in current scenario, 246-247
introduction, 245-246
opportunities for international trade, 249
performance appraisal is gaining ground, 248-249
weaknesses of the economy, 248
Global financial crisis, 31-40, 289-290, 334-337
causes of global financial crisis, 32-35
impact on Indian economy, 36-39
cultivators, 37-38
exchange rates, 37
financial sector, 36
home-based workers, 39
Indian exports, 36-37
migrant employees, 38-39
introduction, 31-32
Global financial markets and economic crisis, 300-315
impact of global crisis on Indian economy, 301-310
introduction, 300-301
response to the crisis, 310-313
Global financial meltdown and its impact on the Indian economy, 88-100
assessment of the impact of the fiscal package, 95-98
effects of economic recession on aggregate demand-aggregate supply curve scenario, 90
impact on Indian economy, 91
packages announced by government of India to lift economy out of recession, 91-95
Global Health Destination, 22
Global meltdown and its impact on Indian economy and the measures taken by Government of India, 101-104
measures taken by the govt. of India, 102-103
second package announced by govt. of India, 103-104
other measures taken by the government, 104
Global recession, 21-30, 124-137
beneficial outcome of global recession, 23-24
competitive advantages of treatment in India, 24

cost effectiveness, 24-26
fiscal responses, 133-134
forex market, 129-130
government efforts towards promoting MT, 29
growth in India, 22-23
impact of the crisis of India, 126-127
impact on the Indian banking system, 128-129
introduction, 124-125
less/no waiting period, 26-27
medical and infrastructure facilities, 28
monetary response, 134-136
money market, 130
qualified professionals, 27-28
reasons of impact crisis in India, 127-128
recession, 125-126
reduction in employment, 133
reduction in import-export, 132
response to the crisis, 133
services offered, 28
slowing GDP, 131-132
stock market, 129
strain on balance of payments, 132
taxation, 133

Global Wage Report 2008-09, 236
Government of India, 5
Great Depression in the 1930s, 1, 54
Great Depression of 1929, 120
Greed, 14-20
Gulf War, 15

H

Hindu, 2008, 153
HIV, 48
Human Resource Development Institute, 28

I

ICICI, 36
IMF, 66
Impact of economic crisis on housing finance in India, 295-299
Impact of financial crisis on banking sector, 323-333
American effect, 329
economic recession and outsourcing issues, 328-329
global economic slowdown, 332
impact of global financial crisis on different counties/ economies, 329-330
impact on Indian economy, 330-331
impact on social and development sectors, 331
reasons behind the financial crisis, 323-325
recommendations, 333
solutions, 332
sub-prime losses by bank, 327-328
US mortgage lending and sub-prime crisis, 325-327
Impact of financial crisis-2009-10, 277-287
causes, 279-281
easy credit conditions, 283
financial crisis of 2007-2010, 278-279

growth of the housing bubble, 281-283
sub-prime lending, 285-287
U.S.currnet account or trade deficit, 283-284
Impact of global crisis on the Indian economy, 316-322
cultivators, 316-319
food security, 320-322
home-based workers, 320
migrant workers, 319-320
what is to be done, 322
Impact of global financial crisis in US, China and India, 192-198
about common people, 193
impact on outsourcing industry, 194-195
impact on Indian economy, 195-196
why this crisis, 193
will China and India maintain their growth levels, 194
Impact of global financial crisis on developing countries, 113-123
causes for financial crisis, 114-115
impact of India, 118-120
Indian economy, 120-121
measures taken by the reserve bank in response to the global financial market developments, 121-122
prelude, 113-114
responses to financial crisis, 117-118
Impact of global financial crisis on Indian economy, 105-112
assessment, 107-109
causes for global financial crisis, 106-107
emerging challenges, 110-111
fiscal impact, 109
impact on the real economy, 110
introduction, 105-106
Impact of global financial recession on Indian banking system, 218-225
background of recession, 219-220
credit cutback, 222-223
exposure of banks, 221
government measures, 223-224
impact on Indian banking sector, 220-221
introduction, 218
mark-to-market losses, 221-222
meaning of recession, 218-219
prudential measures, 224-225
sub-prime lending losses, 222
Impact of global recession on Indian manufacturing sector, 163-173
impact of global recession on
health of service sector employees, 171
Indian car industry, 166-167
Indian textile industry, 168-169
Indian service sector, 169-170
impact of global recession in Indian tourism, 170-171
importance, 163-164
marketing strategies to battle the recession, 172

Impact of international financial crisis, 41-55
Africa and the financial crisis, 47-48
Asia and the financial crisis, 45-47
asset-liability mismatch, 50
contagion, 52
Europe and the financial crisis, 45
fraud, 52
increase borrowing, 53
international financial crisis and wealthy countries, 43
introduction, 41-43
Latin America and the financial crisis, 48
leverage, 49-50
recessionary effects, 52-53
reduce interest rates, 53
reduce taxes, 53-54
regulatory failures, 51
solutions for financial crisis, 53
sources/causes and consequences of financial crises, 49
spend on public works such as infrastructure, 54
strategic complementarities in financial markets, 49
uncertainty and herd behaviour, 50-51
US and the financial crisis, 43-45
Impact of recession on Indian financial system and Indian financial markets, 145-162
introduction, 145-146
meaning of recession, 146-147
methodology, 147
impact of recession on Indian financial system and markets, 148-155
taxation, 156
response to the crisis, 156
results and discussion, 156-160
Impact of recession on Indian financial system and Indian financial markets, 174-191
introduction, 174-175
meaning of recession, 175-176
methodology, 176
Impact of recession on Indian financial system and Indian financial markets, 177-185
response to the crisis, 185-186
results and discussion, 186-189
Impact on and recovery of Indian stock market, 82-87
global financial crisis, 83-84
Indian stock market-growth pattern, 83
introduction, 82
Impact on and recovery of stock market, 84
India financial crisis, 289-290
India in global recession, 270-276
global meltdown in the Indian context, 272-275
India response to recession, 275-276
India, 192-198
India's exports, 235